Leckie
the education publisher
for Scotland

Higher
CHEMISTRY

For SQA 2019 and beyond

D1615097

Student Book

Tom Speirs, Bob Wilson

ISBN 9780008384401

Published by
Leckie & Leckie Ltd
An imprint of HarperCollins Publishers
Westerhill Road, Bishopbriggs, Glasgow, G64 2QT
T: 0844 576 8126   F: 0844 576 8131
leckiescotland@harpercollins.co.uk
www.leckiescotland.co.uk

Publisher: Sarah Mitchell
Project managers: Janice McNeillie and Gillian Bowman

Special thanks to
Sinda López, Louise Robb (proofread)
Jouve (layout and illustration)

Printed in Italy by GRAFICA VENETA S.p.A.

A CIP Catalogue record for this book is available from the British Library.

Acknowledgements

Fig 1.1.5 © dpa picture alliance archive / Alamy, Fig 1.1.6 © Olga Popova / Shutterstock.com, Fig 1.1.7 © Nikolai Galkin / Contributor / Getty, Fig 1.1.8 Public Domain, Fig 1.1.9 Public Domain, Fig 1.1.10 Public Domain, Fig 1.1.12 Public Domain, Fig 1.1.13 Public Domain, Fig 1.1.14 Public Domain, Fig 1.1.19 Licensed under Creative Commons Attribution 3.0 via Wikimedia Common, Achim Hering, Fig 1.1.20 © Clive Streeter / Getty, Fig 1.1.25a © Comstock / Thinkstock, Fig 1.1.25b © Jeffrey Hamilton / Thinkstock, Fig 1.1.27 © Mark Kostich / Thinkstock, Fig 1.1.28 © Jeff J Mitchell / Getty, Fig 1.1.33 © GEOFF TOMPKINSON / SCIENCE PHOTO LIBRARY, Fig 1.1.39 Public Domain, Fig 1.1.40 © JAMES KING-HOLMES / SCIENCE PHOTO LIBRARY, Fig 1.1.42 Licensed under the Creative Commons Attribution-Share Alike 3.0 Unported license, Fig 1.1.52 © J. R. Eyerman / Getty, Fig 1.2.3a © Ingram Publishing / Thinkstock, Fig 1.2.3b © Alexander Raths / Thinkstock, Fig 1.2.5 © Leonid Andronov / Thinkstock.com, Fig 1.2.6 Public Domain, Fig 1.2.24 © Purestock / Thinkstock, Fig 1.2.25 © GeordieBoi / Thinkstock,

Fig 1.2.26 © ArtPix / Alamy, Fig 1.2.33 © Peter Titmuss / Alamy, Fig 1.2.41 © Danny Hooks / Thinkstock, Fig 1.3.1 Licensed under the Creative Commons Attribution-Share Alike 2.5 Generic license, Fig 1.3.2 © CHARLES D. WINTERS / SCIENCE PHOTO LIBRARY, Fig 1.3.9 © IBL / Shutterstock.com

Fig 2.2.10 © MARTYN F. CHILLMAID / SCIENCE PHOTO LIBRARY, Fig 2.2.16 Licensed under the Creative Commons Attribution-Share Alike 3.0 Unported license, Fig 2.3.2 © ANDREW LAMBERT PHOTOGRAPHY / SCIENCE PHOTO LIBRARY, Fig 2.3.7 © Jon Le-Bon / Shutterstock.com, Fig 2.3.13a © Craig Balfour, Fig 2.3.14 Licensed under the Creative Commons Attribution 2.0 Generic license, Fig 2.4.7 © CHRISTINE OLSSON/EPA-EFE / Shutterstock.com, Fig 2.4.18 Public Domain, Fig 2.5.1 © MIKKEL JUUL JENSEN / SCIENCE PHOTO LIBRARY, Fig 2.5.2 © ANDREW LAMBERT PHOTOGRAPHY / SCIENCE PHOTO LIBRARY, Fig 2.5.4 © ANDREW LAMBERT PHOTOGRAPHY / SCIENCE PHOTO LIBRARY, Fig 2.5.5 © ANDREW LAMBERT PHOTOGRAPHY / SCIENCE PHOTO LIBRARY, Fig 2.5.6 © ANDREW LAMBERT PHOTOGRAPHY / SCIENCE PHOTO LIBRARY, Fig 2.5.8 © Henrik Montgomery / AFP / Getty, Fig 2.6.2 Licensed under the Creative Commons Attribution 2.0 Generic license, Fig 2.6.3 © Bob Wilson, Fig 2.6.10 Licensed under the Creative Commons Attribution-Share Alike 3.0 Unported license, Fig 2.7.11 Licensed under the Creative Commons Attribution-Share Alike 3.0 Unported license, Fig 2.7.15 © Everett Collection / Shutterstock.com

Fig 3.1.10 © AFP / Getty, Fig 3.1.18 © David Wall / Alamy, Fig 3.1.24 Public Domain, Fig 3.1.25 Public Domain, Figure 3.2.21© Andrjuss Soldatovs / Thinkstock, Fig 3.2.33 adapted from image © 2013 Yoichi Yamada, RIKEN Center for Sustainable Science, Fig 3.2.34 © M&N / Alamy, Fig 3.3.13 Licensed under the Creative Commons Attribution-Share Alike 3.0 Unported license, Fig 3.4.1 © ANDREW LAMBERT PHOTOGRAPHY / SCIENCE PHOTO LIBRARY, Fig 3.4.6 Licensed under the Creative Commons Attribution-Share Alike 3.0 Unported license, Fig 3.5.1 © JERRY MASON / SCIENCE PHOTO LIBRARY, Fig 3.5.5 © ANDREW LAMBERT PHOTOGRAPHY / SCIENCE PHOTO LIBRARY, Fig 3.5.10 from nasa.gov, Fig 3.5.11 from nasa.gov, Fig 3.5.16 © ANDREW LAMBERT PHOTOGRAPHY / SCIENCE PHOTO LIBRARY

Fig 4.7 © MARTYN F. CHILLMAID / SCIENCE PHOTO LIBRARY, Fig 4.9 © MARTYN F. CHILLMAID / SCIENCE PHOTO LIBRARY

All other images © Shutterstock.com or public domain.

Whilst every effort has been made to trace the copyright holders, in cases where this has been unsuccessful, or if any have inadvertently been overlooked, the Publishers would gladly receive any information enabling them to rectify any error or omission at the first opportunity.

CONTENTS

**Answers for area activities and exam-style questions can be found at
www.collins.co.uk/pages/Scottish-curriculum-free-resources**

Introduction

About this book

This book provides coverage of the content of the Curriculum for Excellence (CfE) Higher chemistry course. The book has been organised to map to the course specification and is packed with examples, explanations, activities and features to deepen your knowledge and understanding of chemistry and show its importance in our everyday life. There are revision questions at the end of the book designed to help you prepare for assessments and the final exam.

Features

YOU SHOULD ALREADY KNOW

Each chapter begins with a list of topics you should already know before you start the chapter. Some of these topics will have been covered at National 4 and National 5, while others will depend on preceding chapters in this book.

You should already know

- All matter is made up of atoms.
- Atoms contain subatomic particles called protons (p), electrons (e⁻) and neutrons (n).

LEARNING INTENTIONS

After the list of things you should be familiar with, there is a list of the topics covered in the chapter which relate directly to the course specification. This tells you what you should be able to do when you have worked your way through the chapter.

Learning intentions

In this chapter you will learn about:

- Factors controlling the rate of reaction and how collision theory can be used to explain their effects: concentration, pressure, temperature, particle size and collision geometry.
- Activation energy and the activated complex.

SQA KEY AREA

Sections that are directly linked to the course specification document published by Scottish Qualification Authority (SQA) are highlighted as 'SQA Key Area'. This identifies the areas covered in the book that could come up in the final examination.

Collision theory

Industry produces a vast range of substances from bulk chemicals such as sodium hydroxide (caustic soda) and ammonia to chemicals made in much smaller quantities such as medicines, chemicals used in the electronics industry and substances of biological origin like vaccines and material for biofuels. Whatever the product, it is important to produce it in the most economical way. This can be achieved through an understanding of the factors that control a chemical reaction. Not only do we need to consider how much of a product a reaction gives and what the energy costs are, we need to know how quickly it can be produced. This is called the rate of the reaction. Rates can vary from incredibly fast, as in the production of gas to inflate an airbag in a car, to very slow, like when paper deteriorates and crumbles.

WORKED EXAMPLE

New topics involving calculations are introduced with at least one worked example, which shows how to go about tackling the questions and activities. Each example breaks the question and solution down into steps, so you can see what calculations are involved, what kind of rearrangements are needed and how to work out the best way of answering the question.

Calculate the mass of silver metal produced when 2·3 g of Cu is added to excess silver(I) nitrate solution.

Worked example: 2

ACTIVITIES

Each chapter features a number of activities, to work on individually, in pairs or small groups. Activities have been carefully designed to test your understanding of the topic and provide experiences to deepen your understanding of the concepts and techniques involved.

GO! Activity 1.2.4

(a) Use the information in table 1.2.1 to draw a spike graph which shows how the boiling points of the alkanes increase with their molecular mass.

(b) Explain why the boiling points of the alkanes increase in this way.

(c) From the graph, estimate the boiling point of octane (C_8H_{18}).

CHEMISTRY IN CONTEXT

Most chapters highlight contemporary applications of chemistry – illustrating the real-world uses of chemistry and how it relates to industrial, commercial and everyday life.

CHEMISTRY IN CONTEXT: HYDROGEN BONDING AND HYDROGEL

Hydrogels are polymers which are hydrophilic, which means they are attracted to water. One common polymer used to make hydrogels is sodium polyacrylate (poly(sodium propionate)). The repeating unit in the polymer is:

HINTS, WORD BANKS AND KEEP UP TO DATE!

Where appropriate, Hint boxes are given in the text to help give extra support. Word banks help to secure the terms and phrases used in the chemistry course to help you to become familiar with them and their usage. Keep up to date! allows you to track developments in chemistry.

> **🔍 Hint**
>
> Ionic compounds and polar molecular compounds generally tend to be soluble in polar solvents like water and insoluble in non-polar solvents like heptane. Non-polar molecular substances tend to be soluble in non-polar solvents and insoluble in polar solvents. Beware, there are exceptions to the solubility rule!

> **📖 Word bank**
>
> • **peptide link**
>
> the amide link formed when the carboxyl group of one amino acid molecule reacts with the amino group of another amino acid molecule

> **KEEP UP TO DATE!**
>
> You can find out how the creation of new elements is developing by looking up 'superheavy elements' or 'making new elements' on the internet.

MAKE THE LINK

Chemistry is not a subject that exists in isolation! Where appropriate, links to other subject areas show the connections that exist between different disciplines. In many cases, the links refer to other aspects of the Higher Chemistry course.

> **Make the Link**
>
> You can calculate the volume of gas produced when an airbag inflates – see page 224.

LEARNING CHECKLIST

Each chapter closes with a summary of learning statements linked to the course specification showing what you should be able to do when you complete the chapter. You can use the Learning checklist to check you have a good understanding of the topics covered in the chapter. Traffic light icons can be used for your own self-assessment.

> ## Learning checklist
>
> In this chapter you have learned:
>
> * Essential oils are concentrated extracts of the volatile, non-water-soluble aroma compounds from plants. ⬭ ⬭ ⬭
>
> * Essential oils are used to give fragrance to perfumes, cosmetic and cleaning products, and are used as flavourings in food. ⬭ ⬭ ⬭

EXAM-STYLE QUESTIONS

Exam-style questions are included at the end of the book. The questions test knowledge and understanding and skills associated with the course.

ANSWERS

Answers for activities and exam-style questions can be found at
https://collins.co.uk/pages/Scottish-curriculum-free-resources

1

Chemical changes and structure

1 Periodicity

an atom has a nucleus surrounded by shells of electrons

the **nucleus** is found at the centre of the **atom** and contains **neutrons** and **protons**

the **electrons** are found in shells around the **nucleus**

Figure 1.1.1

- Atoms are held together in a covalent bond because of the attraction of the nucleus of one atom for the outer electrons of another.
- Dot and cross diagrams can be used to show how atoms share a pair of electrons to form a covalent bond.
- Multiple bonds can be formed between the atoms in some covalent molecules.
- The specific shapes of covalent molecules can be drawn.
- Covalent molecular substances have low melting and boiling points because the forces of attraction between molecules are very weak and not a lot of energy is needed to separate the molecules.
- A covalent network is a giant 3-D structure in which the atoms are covalently bonded to each other.
- Covalent network substances have high melting and boiling points because the atoms are tightly held together by strong covalent bonds and a lot of energy is needed to break the bonds.

(National 5 Chemistry: Chemical changes and structure: Atomic structure and bonding related to properties of materials)

- In metals the outer electrons are delocalised.
- Metallic bonding involves the attraction of metal nuclei for delocalised outer electrons.

(National 5 Chemistry: Chemistry in society: Metals)

Learning intentions

In this chapter you will learn about:
- Bonding and structure in the first 20 elements: metals and non-metals (monatomic, covalent molecular and covalent networks).
- Trends in the periodic table: covalent radius, ionisation energy and electronegativity.

CHEMISTRY IN CONTEXT: MAKING NEW ELEMENTS

The Superheavy Element Factories

All the elements beyond uranium (element 92) in the periodic table have to be made by scientists because they don't exist in large quantities in nature. Many new elements were made by bombarding atoms with neutrons or small atomic nuclei. To make the heaviest (superheavy) elements, however, scientists have had to use a different approach – firing beams of heavy atoms into a disc that holds atoms of another element. The atoms in the beam and target fuse, creating a new atom with a bigger nucleus, perhaps one holding more protons than any other known and therefore creating a new element.

This technique was used to make the four newest elements: nihonium (Nh:113), moscovium (Mc:115), tennessine (Ts:117) and oganesson (Og:118). To create tennessine, for example, scientists combined beams of calcium with a berkelium target. Calcium atoms have 20 protons and berkelium has 97 which, when combined, makes 117 protons, the number found in tennessine's nucleus. It sounds simple, but when tennessine was first made it took 150 days of battering the berkelium and only six atoms were detected. These superheavy elements decay almost instantly which makes it difficult to investigate their properties.

Figure 1.1.2: *The most recent superheavy elements to have been made*

In order to make elements 119 and 120 more of the rare target materials like berkelium, californium and einsteinium have to be made. This is extremely difficult to do and only a few milligrams may be produced at a time. Researchers at the RIKEN Nishina Centre near Tokyo, Japan are using beams of vanadium (element 23) and curium (element 96) as the target material to try to make element 119. Scientists at a new laboratory at the Joint Institute for Nuclear Research (JINR) in Dubna, Russia, known as the Superheavy Element Factory, are planning to fire beams of titanium (element 22) into berkelium (element 97) and californium (element 98) targets to try to make elements 119 and 120.

When elements 119 and 120 are made they will be the first elements in period 8. Computer models predict that the heaviest element it will be possible to make will have up to 126 protons. Any more than that would mean the atomic nucleus would be too unstable to hold together.

Figure 1.1.3: *Element 119 has been given the temporary name ununennium and is also known as eka-francium*

Why is discovering new superheavy elements important?
Scientists are trying to make bigger atoms in the hope these discoveries will give them a better understanding of how nuclei are held together and how they resist the nuclear fission process. The skills gained by conducting these experiments can then be used to solve problems such as an improved understanding of nuclear fission which will help scientists to improve the safety and reliability of nuclear reactors.

How can superheavy elements be used?
As with many scientific discoveries, scientists are not yet sure of the practical applications of superheavy elements. The heavy element americium (first made in 1944) is used in smoke detectors and plutonium (first produced in 1940) is used to make nuclear weapons. Scientists are hopeful that practical applications of superheavy elements also exist and will be developed in the future.

Naming new elements
The International Union of Pure and Applied Chemistry (IUPAC) was formed in 1919 by chemists with the aim of improving communications in the chemical sciences worldwide. IUPAC is responsible for agreeing names for new elements.

> **KEEP UP TO DATE!**
> You can find out how the creation of new elements is developing by looking up 'superheavy elements' or 'making new elements' on the internet.

Figure 1.1.4: *IUPAC concept on blackboard*

Figure 1.1.5: *In 2006, element 111 received its official name, roentgenium (Rg)*

In May 2012 element 114 was named flerovium (Fl). It was named after the Flerov Laboratory of Nuclear Reactions in Russia, a facility where other superheavy elements have been produced. The laboratory is named after Russian physicist Georgy N. Flyorov, who discovered the spontaneous fission of uranium, which led to the USSR's development of an atomic bomb.

Figure 1.1.6: *Element 114 has been named flerovium (Fl), the name of the laboratory which discovered it, which itself was named in honour of the Soviet scientist Georgy N. Flyorov*

Element 116 has been named livermorium (Lv) after the Lawrence Livermore National Laboratory in California, which was involved in the discovery of heavy elements 113 to 118. Another element, lawrencium (atomic number 103), is already named after the lab's founder, Ernest O. Lawrence. In November 2016 the names of elements 113, 115, 117 and 118 were announced. The names of all new elements in general have an ending that reflects their position in the periodic table. This meant names ending in -**ium** for elements 113 and 115, -**ine** for element 117 and -**on** for element 118.

Element 113 was named **nihonium** with the symbol **Nh**. The name was proposed by the RIKEN Nishina Centre for Accelerator-Based Science (Japan). Nihon is one way to say 'Japan' in Japanese, and means 'Land of the Rising Sun'.

Element 115 was named **moscovium** with the symbol **Mc**. Moscovium is in recognition of the Moscow region of Russia, home to the Joint Institute for Nuclear Research, where the discovery experiments were carried out.

Element 117 was named **tennessine** with the symbol **Ts** in recognition of the contribution of the state of Tennessee in the USA to superheavy element research.

Element 118 was named **oganesson** with the symbol **Og** in honour of Professor Yuri Oganessian for his many achievements, including the discovery of superheavy elements.

Figure 1.1.7: Yuri Oganessian was only the second living scientist to have an element named after him, the other being Glenn T. Seaborg (seaborgium)

CHEMISTRY IN CONTEXT: THE DEVELOPMENT OF THE PERIODIC TABLE

The modern periodic table shows the superheavy elements recently created in particle accelerators and nuclear reactors. Scientists working in this area have been referred to as modern-day alchemists. Alchemists were early (medieval) practical chemists who experimented to try to make gold from lead and other metals, not knowing that this was chemically impossible. They are considered to be the first chemists to keep records of their practical work. It is only in the past 200 years that scientists began working more methodically. With better equipment and the invention of electricity, chemists began to discover elements and started trying to organise them.

Significant ideas leading to the modern periodic table

1661
Robert Boyle published a book called The Sceptical Chymist in which he put forward the idea of an element as something which could not be changed into anything simpler. Boyle also encouraged chemists to carry out practical investigations rather than just observe and come up with theories as the ancient Greeks had done. Boyle is best known for Boyle's Law, connecting gas volume and pressure.

Figure 1.1.8: Title page from Robert Boyle's The Sceptical Chymist where he introduced the idea of the practical chemist

1803

John Dalton published his atomic theory which he derived by carrying out experiments. The main points of his theory were:

1. *Elements are made of extremely small particles called atoms.*

2. *Atoms of a given element are identical in size, mass, and chemical properties.*

3. *Atoms cannot be subdivided, created, or destroyed.*

4. *Atoms of different elements combine in simple whole-number ratios to form chemical compounds.*

5. *In chemical reactions, atoms are combined, separated, or rearranged.*

Although some of Dalton's ideas have been found to be incorrect, his idea of elements being composed of atoms of the same kind provided the foundation on which other scientists have built.

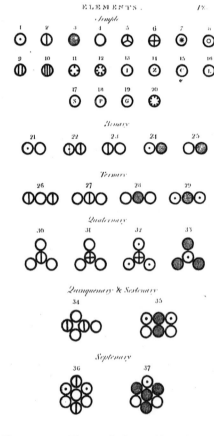

Figure 1.1.9: *The symbols used by John Dalton to represent the elements known at the time*

1829

Johann Döbereiner reported on patterns he had found among the elements known at the time. He noticed that

Figure 1.1.10: *John Dalton*

elements with similar properties could be grouped in threes, or triads, and that there was a pattern in the values of their relative atomic mass (RAM). He noted, for example, that the RAM of the middle element in each triad is about equal to the average of the RAM of the first and third elements. The RAM of sodium (23·0), for example, is the average of the RAM of lithium (6·9) and potassium (39·1). Lithium, sodium and potassium were discovered by Humphry Davy by electrolysing the molten compounds of the metals.

Alkali formers		Salt formers	
Symbol	RAM	Symbol	RAM
Cl	6.9	Cl	35.5
Br	23	Br	79.9
I	39.1	I	126.9

Figure 1.1.11: *Döbereiner recognised the similarities in group 1 metals (alkali formers) and the group 7 halogens (salt formers)*

1864

John Newlands proposed his idea of octaves. Using RAM he found that elements with similar chemical properties were eight positions away from each other. Look at table 1.1.2. If you take lithium as element number 1 and count eight elements you come to sodium. Count another eight and you find potassium. All three elements have similar properties. There were, however, exceptions. Sulfur and iron are eight apart but have completely different properties. One of the issues which Newlands and others didn't realise was that there were elements still to be discovered so gaps should have been left, although he did predict the existence of germanium. For example, the noble gases had not been discovered and would have created an extra group.

Table 1.1.2: *Newlands' periodic table – periods were shown going down the table, with groups going across – the opposite of the modern form of the periodic table*

Figure 1.1.12: *Johann Wolfgang Döbereiner*

	No.		No.		No.		No.		No.		No.		No.		No.
H	1	F	8	Cl	15	Co & Ni	22	Br	29	Pd	36	I	42	Pt & Ir	50
Li	2	Na	9	K	16	Cu	23	Rb	30	Ag	37	Cs	44	Os	51
G	3	Mg	10	Ca	17	Zn	24	Sr	31	Cd	38	Ba & V	45	Hg	52
Bo	4	Al	11	Cr	19	Y	25	Ce & La	33	U	40	Ta	46	Tl	53
C	5	Si	12	Ti	18	In	26	Zr	32	Sn	39	W	47	Pb	54
N	6	P	13	Mn	20	As	27	Di & Mo	34	Sb	41	Nb	48	Bi	55
O	7	S	14	Fe	21	Se	28	Ro & Ru	35	Te	43	Au	49	Th	56

1869

Dmitri Mendeleev published his version of the periodic table based on relative atomic mass and chemical properties. Like Newlands, his original periodic table was laid out with periods going across the way. Menedeleev's brilliant decision was to leave gaps where a pattern didn't seem to work, predicting that the element would be discovered. He realised that similar properties arose every so often, i.e. periodically.

Figure 1.1.13: *The monument dedicated to Dmitri Mendeleev, the 'father of the modern periodic table', in St Petersburg, Russia, showing his original periodic table*

Mendeleev predicted the properties of scandium, gallium and germanium (originally called ekasilicon). He predicted ekasilicon would have chemical properties similar to silicon and tin and that it should be placed between them in the periodic table. Table 1.1.3 shows just how accurate his predictions were.

Table 1.1.3: Mendeleev's predictions of the properties of germanium

	Silicon	Predicted properties for eka-silicon	Actual values for germanium (eka-silicon)	Tin
Atomic mass	28	72	72·59	118
Density/g cm⁻³	2·3	5·5	5·3	7·3
Appearance	grey non-metal	grey metal	grey metal	white metal
Formula of oxide	SiO_2	EkO_2	GeO_2	SnO_2
Formula of chloride	$SiCl_4$	$EkCl_4$	$GeCl_4$	$SnCl_4$
Reaction with acid	none	very slow	slow with concentrated acid	slow

Altogether, Mendeleev predicted properties for ten unknown elements and was later proved correct for eight of them. Because Mendeleev focused on chemical properties and not just relative atomic mass he was not afraid to swap the position of elements, even though the order went against the order based on relative atomic mass – he assumed they had been calculated incorrectly. So, for example, he placed tellurium before iodine despite tellurium having the greater mass.

1913

Henry G.J. Moseley proposed that atomic number, i.e. the number of protons in an atom, should be used to place the elements in the periodic table instead of relative atomic mass. This solved a number of problems with previous attempts at producing an accurate periodic table and confirmed that Mendeleev was right to use chemical properties to put the elements in order. For example, iodine has an atomic number of 53 and tellurium 52 so fits in with Mendeleev's idea of putting elements with similar properties together. Although his reason for doing it was wrong his idea of similar chemical properties was correct.

Figure 1.1.14: *The brilliant English scientist Henry Moseley who was killed at the Battle of Gallipoli on 10 August 1915, at the age of 27*

Key:

| atomic no |
| **symbol** |
| name |
| relative atomic mass |

metal

non-metal

The periodic table

Group	1	2											3	4	5	6	7	0
Period 1	1 **H** hydrogen 1.0																	2 **He** helium 4.0
Period 2	3 **Li** lithium 6.9	4 **Be** beryllium 9.0											5 **B** boron 10.8	6 **C** carbon 12.0	7 **N** nitrogen 14.0	8 **O** oxygen 16.0	9 **F** fluorine 19.0	10 **Ne** neon 20.2
Period 3	11 **Na** sodium 23.0	12 **Mg** magnesium 24.3											13 **Al** aluminium 26.9	14 **Si** silicon 28.1	15 **P** phosphorus 31.0	16 **S** sulfur 32.1	17 **Cl** chlorine 35.5	18 **Ar** argon 39.9
Period 4	19 **K** potassium 39.1	20 **Ca** calcium 40.1	21 **Sc** scandium 45.0	22 **Ti** titanium 47.8	23 **V** vanadium 50.9	24 **Cr** chromium 52.0	25 **Mn** manganese 54.9	26 **Fe** iron 55.9	27 **Co** cobalt 58.9	28 **Ni** nickel 58.7	29 **Cu** copper 63.5	30 **Zn** zinc 65.4	31 **Ga** gallium 69.7	32 **Ge** germanium 72.6	33 **As** arsenic 74.9	34 **Se** selenium 79.0	35 **Br** bromine 79.9	36 **Kr** krypton 83.8
Period 5	37 **Rb** rubidium 85.5	38 **Sr** strontium 87.6	39 **Y** yttrium 88.9	40 **Zr** zirconium 91.2	41 **Nb** niobium 92.9	42 **Mo** molybdenum 95.9	43 **Tc** technetium (98)	44 **Ru** ruthenium 101.1	45 **Rh** rhodium 102.9	46 **Pd** palladium 106.4	47 **Ag** silver 107.9	48 **Cd** cadmium 112.4	49 **In** indium 114.8	50 **Sn** tin 118.7	51 **Sb** antimony 121.8	52 **Te** tellurium 127.6	53 **I** iodine 126.9	54 **Xe** xenon 131.3
Period 6	55 **Cs** caesium 132.9	56 **Ba** barium 137.3	57 **La** lanthanum 138.9	72 **Hf** hafnium 178.5	73 **Ta** tantalum 181.0	74 **W** tungsten 183.9	75 **Re** rhenium 186.2	76 **Os** osmium 190.2	77 **Ir** iridium 192.2	78 **Pt** platinum 195.1	79 **Au** gold 197.0	80 **Hg** mercury 200.6	81 **Tl** thallium 204.4	82 **Pb** lead 207.2	83 **Bi** bismuth 209.0	84 **Po** polonium (209)	85 **At** astatine (210)	86 **Rn** radon (222)
Period 7	87 **Fr** francium (223)	88 **Ra** radium (226)	89 **Ac** actinium (227)	104 **Rf** rutherfordium (261)	105 **Db** dubnium (262)	106 **Sg** seaborgium (263)	107 **Bh** bohrium (264)	108 **Hs** hassium (265)	109 **Mt** meitnerium (266)	110 **Dg** damstadium (269)	111 **Rg** roentgenium (272)	112 **Cn** copernicium (285)	113 **Nh** nihonium (286)	114 **Fl** flerovium (289)	115 **Mc** moscovium (288)	116 **Lv** livermorium (292)	117 **Ts** tennessine (294)	118 **Og** oganesson (294)

Lanthanides:

58 **Ce** cerium 140.1	59 **Pr** praseodymium 140.9	60 **Nd** neodymium 144.2	61 **Pm** promethium (145)	62 **Sm** samarium 150.4	63 **Eu** europium 152.0	64 **Gd** gadolinium 157.3	65 **Tb** terbium 158.9	66 **Dy** dysprosium 162.5	67 **Ho** holmium 164.9	68 **Er** erbium 167.3	69 **Tm** thulium 168.9	70 **Yb** ytterbium 173.0	71 **Lu** lutetium 175.5

Actinides:

90 **Th** thorium 232.0	91 **Pa** protactinium (231)	92 **U** uranium 238.1	93 **Np** neptunium (237)	94 **Pu** plutonium (244)	95 **Am** americium (243)	96 **Cm** curium (247)	97 **Bk** berkelium (247)	98 **Cf** californium (251)	99 **Es** einsteinium (254)	100 **Fm** fermium (253)	101 **Md** mendelevium (256)	102 **No** nobelium (254)	103 **Lr** lawrencium (257)

Figure 1.1.15: *The modern periodic table*

The first 20 elements

The modern periodic table has elements arranged in order of increasing atomic number. It allows chemists to make accurate predictions of physical properties and chemical behaviour for any element based on its position in the periodic table. The similarities between the elements within a group (vertical column) is due to a common number of electrons in the outer energy level (shell). This similarity in the electron arrangement leads to a periodicity (repeating pattern) in the properties of elements, so that the pattern of properties shown by the elements in one period (row) is repeated in the next period. As you move across a period the number of protons in the nucleus of an atom increases as does the number of outer electrons and a move from metallic to non-metallic characteristics.

The first 20 elements can be used to illustrate periodicity. They can be roughly divided into four areas where the bonding and structure within each area is similar – see figure 1.1.15.

individual
covalent molecules

* Carbon can exist as networks and molecules

Figure 1.1.16: *Bonding and structure within the first 20 elements*

Metals

Metals make up over 80% of the periodic table and are found in the centre and to the left-hand side.

Metals have certain properties in common.

- They are good conductors of heat and electricity.
- They tend to be shiny (have metallic lustre).
- They can be shaped (are malleable).
- They can be drawn into wires (are ductile).
- Most have relatively high melting points.

> 📖 **Word bank**
> - **delocalised**
> not confined to a particular atom

These properties of metals can be explained by the bonding within the metals.

In metals the outer electrons of the atoms can move easily from atom to atom. The electrons within the structure are said to be **delocalised**. Metal structures have been described as 'positive ions in a sea of electrons'.

Metals are good electrical conductors. If a voltage is placed across a metal the delocalised electrons will move from the negative terminal towards the positive terminal, i.e. an electrical current will flow through the metal.

Metals have a crystalline structure which can be seen under a powerful microscope.

The positive ions are organised in a regular arrangement. The structure is held together by metallic bonds. These are strong attractive forces between the metal nuclei and the delocalised electrons moving between them. The direction of the bonds is not fixed because the electrons are moving, unlike in covalent substances where the electrons are localised in bonds. This means that the atoms will be able to move in relation to each other and explains why metals can be rolled into thin sheets or drawn into wires.

Kinetic energy is easily transferred from one delocalised electron to another, which explains why metals are such good conductors of heat.

Metallic bonding explains why metals generally have high melting and boiling points. The greater the number of delocalised electrons, the stronger the metallic bond and the more energy is needed to separate the atoms. This is why magnesium has a higher melting point than sodium.

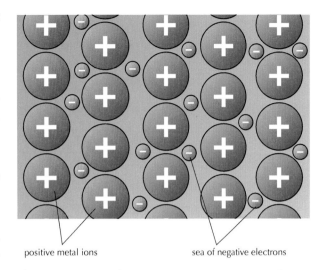

positive metal ions   sea of negative electrons

Figure 1.1.17: *Metals exist as positive ions in a sea of delocalised electrons*

Figure 1.1.18: *Metal crystals on the surface of stainless steel*

Figure 1.1.19: *Titanium was used in the construction of the Guggenheim Museum, Bilbao, because of its resistance to corrosion, lustre, and because it is lightweight but strong*

Activity 1.1.1

1. Copper is one of our most versatile metals. It is a good electrical and heat conductor and can be drawn into wires for use in electrical flexes.

   (a) Describe both the bonding in copper and its structure.

   (b) With reference to the bonding between atoms in copper, explain why copper:

      (i) is a good electrical conductor

      (ii) is a good heat conductor

      (iii) can be drawn into thin wires.

2. Lithium and beryllium are next to each other in the periodic table.

   Explain why beryllium has a much higher melting point than lithium.

CHEMISTRY IN CONTEXT: PALLADIUM

Figure 1.1.20: *Honeycomb structure of catalytic converters coated with palladium*

Figure 1.1.21: *Components inside some computers are linked by connectors plated with palladium because it is an excellent conductor of electricity*

Palladium is one of the platinum group metals and so has similar properties to platinum. Most of the palladium produced in the world comes from the Russian Federation and South Africa.

Softer than platinum, more ductile and less expensive, resistant to oxidation and high temperature corrosion, palladium is useful in eliminating harmful emissions produced by internal combustion engines. The manufacture of catalytic converters is by far the largest use of palladium. Catalytic converters are also the biggest source of recycled palladium.

Palladium has a number of electronic applications. For example, palladium's chemical stability and electrical conductivity make it an effective and durable alternative to gold for plating in electronic components.

Palladium-based alloys are strong and chemically unreactive so are used in dentistry for dental crowns and bridges. Palladium metal is also compatible with human tissue and is used as a radioisotope in medical procedures for the treatment of cancer.

Alone or alloyed with silver or gold, palladium offers some of the same metal working properties as other jewellery metals, and remains tarnish free. It is more precious than silver and whiter than platinum. Earrings made from palladium would only be half the weight of similar earrings made from platinum.

Palladium alloys are actively being researched for applications in fuel cell technology, an area of future use for the metal. The hydrogen fuel cell is the most promising fuel cell being developed. Palladium acts like a sponge and can absorb 800 to 900 times its own volume of hydrogen into its structure at room temperature and atmospheric pressure, which points to it being a useful hydrogen store in the fuel cell.

Figure 1.1.22: *Rings made of 95% palladium*

SQA KEY AREA

Non-metals

The noble gases – monatomic elements

At the far right of the periodic table we find the noble gases in group 0. Both their group name and number indicate a lack of reactivity – they exist as individual atoms. They were at one time called the inert gases but that had to change in the 1960s when a number of noble gas compounds were made. Each noble gas atom has a full outer energy level so does not need to react to achieve this. They are, however, liquefied by lowering the temperature, which indicates there must be some force of attraction between the atoms which is significant at low temperatures but not at room temperature. In fact argon when cooled forms a liquid then a solid. These forces of attraction are known as London dispersion forces. They are caused by the continual movement of electrons in an atom, which causes a temporary uneven distribution of charge at opposite sides of an atom – known as a temporary dipole. This means that one side of the atom is temporarily slightly negative (δ^-) which results in the other side being temporarily slightly positive (δ^+). This in turn induces (causes) a temporary dipole in a neighbouring atom. This results in the δ^- side of one atom attracting the δ^+ side of a neighbouring atom so a force of attraction is formed between them. London dispersion forces are very weak but the more electrons there are in the atom the bigger the London dispersion force.

Although the dipoles are constantly moving they are always present. At room temperature there is enough energy to overcome the London dispersion forces so the elements exist as gases. London dispersion forces are weak, intermolecular forces which exist between all molecular substances, not just between the atoms of noble gas elements.

The lack of reactivity in noble gases gives them a number of uses. When electricity is passed through noble

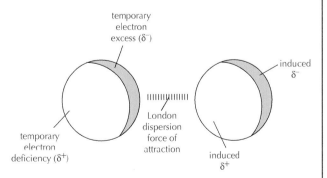

Figure 1.1.23: *The formation of temporary dipoles in an atom results in London dispersion forces forming between neighbouring atoms*

gases they glow. Neon lights are the best known use of noble gases, although the colours obtained are normally due to the gases being mixed with other chemicals.

Figure 1.1.24: *Noble gases glow and give off light when electricity is passed through them*

> **Hint**
>
> The melting and boiling points of the noble gases increase as you go down the group. This is because the number of electrons in the atoms increases, so the strength of the London dispersion forces increases.

Argon mixed with nitrogen is used in traditional filament light bulbs. The very thin metal filament inside the bulb would react with oxygen and burn away if the bulb were filled with air instead of argon. The unreactive argon and nitrogen stop the filament burning away because of their low reactivity. Incandescent bulbs are being phased out in favour of more efficient bulbs like the compact fluorescent lamp (CFL). Instead of a glowing filament, CFLs contain argon and mercury vapour in a spiral-shaped tube. There are concerns that the light produced is not as good as an incandescent bulb and over the fact that the toxic metal mercury is used in CFLs. This has led to environmental issues regarding safe disposal. Light emitting diodes (LEDs) are being developed for use in room lighting. LEDs have many advantages over filament light bulbs including lower energy consumption, longer lifetime, improved physical robustness and smaller size. However, LEDs powerful enough for room lighting are relatively expensive and produce a lot of heat.

Figure 1.1.25: *Traditional filament light bulbs (left) are being replaced by tubular-type compact fluorescent lamps – CFLs (right)*

GO! Activity 1.1.2

1. (a) Describe the forces of attraction which exist between atoms of the noble gases.

   (b) Explain why these forces of attraction are only really significant at low temperatures.

2. (a) Describe the general trend in melting and boiling points as you go down group 0 (the noble gases) in the periodic table.

   (b) Explain the trend observed in **2.** (a)

Figure 1.1.26: *Helium gas cylinders in a laboratory*

CHEMISTRY IN CONTEXT: HIGHLIGHTING HELIUM

You are likely to have seen helium being used in party balloons and airships, like the ones used to give overhead pictures at some sporting events. Helium is much less dense than air, so balloons filled with it rise. Although these are everyday uses of helium they are not the most important uses.

Helium is used as a replacement for nitrogen in the air tanks used by scuba divers. Helium's reduced solubility in the body's cells as compared to nitrogen reduces the risk of decompression sickness, or the bends, a condition which can severely damage the body, possibly leading to death. The reduced amount of dissolved gas in the body reduces the risk of gas bubbles forming in the blood during the decrease in pressure when a diver rises to the surface of the water.

Helium's lack of reactivity means it can also be used as the pressurising agent for liquid fuel rockets.

Helium remains a liquid at temperatures as low as −269°C and consequently is the most effective refrigerant known. It is used to chill the supermagnets used in medical scanners and the Large Hadron Collider, the instrument used to confirm the existence of the Higgs boson.

Helium is used to make the semiconductors found in virtually every electronic device we use and is used during the manufacture of fibre optic cables, essential for high-speed internet, television and telephone connections.

There are growing fears about the availability and waste of helium. It is considered by some scientists and economists to be one of the elements we should be concerned about losing in the twenty-first century. Although helium makes up about 24% of the mass of the universe, it is very rare on Earth, making up only 0·0005% of the atmosphere. By some estimates our helium reserves could run out in 30 to 50 years. Helium's lack of reactivity is one problem – it is not found chemically combined in the Earth's crust or in the atmosphere, and its low density means that atmospheric helium drifts off into the atmosphere and beyond.

Virtually all of our helium comes from the underground decay of radioactive elements such as uranium. Helium is trapped with natural gas in concentrations up to 7% by volume, from which it is extracted commercially by low-temperature fractional distillation. The USA has 80% of the world's reserves and has been selling cheap helium since 1998 but can't keep up with world demand. New helium plants have opened in Qatar and Russia to try to ease the shortage. Some experts forecast consumption of helium to continue growing on a global scale and estimate that by 2030 consumption of helium could reach 238–312 million cm^3 while production will be lagging behind at 213–238 million cm^3. This means that the world could be facing a helium shortage. Not only will helium production need to be increased considerably in order to meet the shortage, we will have to take more care in how we use it.

Figure 1.1.27: *Helium is used as a coolant for magnets in MRI machines*

GO! Nobel Prize winners

Professor Peter Higgs and François Englert were awarded the Nobel Prize in Physics in 2013. Professor Higgs had jointly predicted the existence of the Higgs boson in the 1960s while working at the University of Edinburgh. In 2012, the boson was detected in the Large Hadron Collider particle accelerator which was built underground near Geneva in Switzerland.

Figure 1.1.28: *Professor Peter Higgs giving a press conference at the University of Edinburgh*

Covalent molecular elements

Apart from the noble gases (group 0), the bonding between atoms in non-metals is covalent. In a covalent bond the atoms are held together by the attraction of the positive nucleus of one atom for the outer electrons of another atom which results in a shared pair of electrons. The mutual attraction of the nuclei for the shared pair of electrons is the covalent bond.

Hydrogen, nitrogen, oxygen and the halogens (group 7) all exist as diatomic molecules, i.e. two atoms covalently bonded. Most are gases at room temperature but are easily liquified at low temperatures. Bromine is a liquid and iodine a solid at room temperature. This indicates that there are forces of attraction between the molecules. London dispersion forces attract the molecules to each other but in some of the molecules these forces are so small that there is enough energy at room temperature to overcome these weak forces of attraction and separate the molecules from each other. This is why most of the diatomic molecules are gases. Bromine and iodine are bigger molecules and have more electrons than the smaller gas molecules so the London dispersion forces are much stronger

shared pair
of electrons

Figure 1.1.29: *A covalent bond is formed between the atoms of two non-metals by the attraction of the nucleus of one atom for the electrons of another*

between their molecules and it takes more energy to separate their molecules. This explains why they exist as a liquid and solid at room temperature. It is important to realise that when a molecular substance melts or boils it is the weak London dispersion forces between molecules (intermolecular forces) which are broken and not the strong covalent bonds holding the atoms together in the molecule.

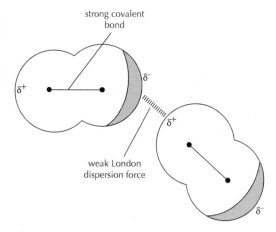

Figure 1.1.30: *Strong covalent bonds hold the atoms in molecules together but weak London dispersion forces act between molecules*

Activity 1.1.3

1. (a) Describe the trend in melting and boiling points as you go down group 7 (the halogens).

   (b) Explain the trend observed in 1. (a)

2. Discuss the intermolecular forces and internal bonding present in iodine.

Phosphorus and sulfur exist as solids with low melting and boiling points. Phosphorus exists as P_4 molecules and sulfur as S_8 molecules. The atoms which make up the molecules are held together by covalent bonds and the molecules are held together by London dispersion forces. Because of the size of the molecules (P_4 and S_8), there are more electrons than there are in smaller molecules so the London forces are stronger and at room temperature there is not enough energy to break the forces and separate the molecules, so the elements are solid.

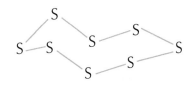

P_4: mp = 44°C
    bp = 280°C

S_8: mp = 115°C
    bp = 445°C

Figure 1.1.31: S_8 molecules need more energy to overcome the London dispersion forces holding the molecules together so have higher melting and boiling points than P_4 molecules

Carbon had for a long time been thought only to exist in the form of graphite and diamond, which are covalent networks (see page 24). In the 1980s, however, a molecular form of carbon was made. The first molecule of carbon had 60 carbon atoms (C_{60}) and was named Buckminsterfullerene (often shortened to buckyball or fullerene), named after the American architect who designed a geodesic dome for the 1967 World Fair in Montreal, which was made up of a series of geometric shapes. Buckminsterfullerene is made up of a series of carbons arranged in hexagons and pentagons joined in a ball shape, as shown in figure 1.1.32. Since then a number of bigger fullerene molecules have been made. You can find out more about fullerenes and their uses in the Chemistry in Context section on page 22.

Like all covalent molecular elements the molecules in Buckminsterfullerene are held together by

Figure 1.1.32: Models of Buckminsterfullerene (C_{60}) – the hexagon and pentagon shapes are clearly seen in the football

GO! Activity 1.1.4

C_{70} molecules have also been discovered in nature. Predict how the temperature at which C_{70} sublimes would compare to C_{60} and explain your reasoning.

London dispersion forces. Because the molecules are so big a lot of energy is needed to separate them. Buckminsterfullerene sublimes (changes from solid to gas) at around 600°C.

GO! Nobel Prize winners

Richard E. Smalley, Robert F. Curl, Jr., and Harold W. Kroto were awarded the Nobel Prize in Chemistry in 1996 for discovering fullerenes.

Figure 1.1.33: *Sir Harry Kroto was awarded the Nobel Prize in Chemistry in 1996 for his work on fullerenes*

CHEMISTRY IN CONTEXT: FULLERENES

Buckminsterfullerene (C_{60}) is one member of a family of fullerenes, pure carbon molecules which exist as a cage of carbon atoms. These cages can be closed (buckyballs: see figure 1.1.32) or stretched into rods and cones, known as buckytubes or nanotubes, and shown in figure 1.1.34.

Figure 1.1.34: *A fullerene nanotube; considered by some scientists to be the building block of the twenty-first century*

Fullerenes were discovered in 1985, in soot produced by vaporising graphite with a laser. In 1992, fullerenes were found to occur naturally in certain kinds of rock. Fullerenes are highly stable chemically and have a variety of unusual properties. Chemists have been able to add branches of other molecules to them and place atoms inside them. Fullerenes can be made to be magnetic, act as superconductors, absorb light and act as a lubricant.

When fullerenes were first made, C_{60} molecules were the most abundant, followed by C_{70}. Fullerenes with 72, 76, 84 and even up to 100 carbon atoms are commonly obtained. The structure of the C_{60} molecule contains 12 pentagons made up of carbons joined with 20 hexagons. It is the pentagon shapes which allow the bending of the molecule to form the ball shape.

Fullerenes have been found in nature and in outer space. According to astronomer Letizia Stanghellini, 'It's possible that buckyballs from outer space provided seeds for life on Earth.'

Nanotubes are cylindrical fullerenes. These tubes of carbon are usually only a few nanometres wide ($1nm = 10^{-9}m = 1$ billionth of a metre), but can be several millimetres in length. They often have closed ends, but can be open-ended as well. Their unique molecular structure results in extraordinary properties, including high strength, electrical and heat conductivity, high ductility, and relative chemical inactivity because it has no exposed atoms that can be easily replaced.

Because of the nanotube's structure it could be used to transport a drug in the body. The drug could be placed inside the nanotube and not released until it reaches the part of the body where it is needed and so reduces the risk of damaging other areas of the body.

Another proposed use of carbon nanotubes is in paper batteries, developed in 2007 by researchers at Rensselaer Polytechnic Institute. A paper battery is an ultra-thin electric battery formed by combining carbon nanotubes with a sheet of cellulose (the main constituent of paper). It incorporates nanoscale structures to act as high surface-area electrodes to improve the conduction of electricity.

Paper batteries are thin, flexible and environment-friendly, and have the potential to be used in a wide range of products. They work in a similar way to conventional chemical batteries with the important difference that they are non-corrosive and are so flexible they can be made into unusual shapes. There are many uses for this new technology, including in health care. They can power tiny medical diagnostic equipment and even drug delivery through skin patches.

The paper-like quality of the battery combined with the structure of the nanotubes embedded within gives them their light weight, making them attractive for portable electronics, aircraft, automobiles, and toys (such as model aircraft). Their ability to use electrolytes in blood makes them potentially useful for medical devices such as pacemakers. The medical uses are particularly attractive because paper batteries do not contain any toxic materials and can be biodegradable.

However, commercial applications may be a fair way off, because nanotubes are still relatively expensive to make. Currently they are making batteries several centimetres in size. In order to be commercially useful, they would have to be newspaper size; a size which, taken all together, could be powerful enough to power a car. Although research in this area is very promising it is predicted that commercial use of paper batteries is many years away.

KEEP UP TO DATE!
You can find out how the development of paper batteries for commercial use is progressing by looking up 'paper batteries' on the internet.

Covalent network elements

Some non-metal elements have extremely high melting and boiling points which indicates that there must be forces other than London dispersion forces holding their structures together. This can be seen in the elements carbon, silicon and boron.

Diamond and graphite – covalent carbon networks

Until molecules of buckminsterfullerene (C_{60}) were discovered in the 1980s it was thought that carbon only existed as giant covalent networks in the form of diamond and graphite. Diamond and graphite are formed naturally in the Earth's crust by the combined action of heat and pressure deep under the Earth's crust. In diamond each carbon atom is covalently bonded to four other carbon atoms in a tetrahedral arrangement. All the outer electrons in the atom of each carbon are used to make single covalent bonds with neighbouring atoms, which results in a giant covalent network – there are no individual molecules in a network. In order to separate the atoms in a covalent network strong covalent bonds have to be broken, which requires a lot of energy. This explains why elements with covalent network structures have high melting and boiling points. Diamond and graphite are unusual in that rather than melt when heated to very high temperatures they sublime. Sublimation is the transition of a substance directly from the solid to the gas phase without passing through an intermediate liquid phase.

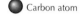
Carbon atom

There are no unbonded (delocalised) electrons in the diamond structure so diamond is a non-conductor of electricity. It is, however, an excellent conductor of heat at room temperature. Diamond is also the hardest substance known and the least compressible, due to its internal structure and the fact that its atoms are more closely packed than atoms in any other material. In its pure form diamond is transparent and highly valued as a jewel.

Diamond's extreme properties make it very useful. Its hardness makes it useful as an abrasive and as a cutting tool in industry and surgery. Because of its excellent heat conduction it is used to cool electronic components rapidly.

Figure 1.1.35: *All the carbon atoms in diamond are covalently bonded resulting in a giant covalent network. In its purest form, diamond is highly prized as a jewel*

The other form of carbon, graphite, is an opaque dark grey-black brittle material which feels slippery to the touch and conducts electricity. When ground down, mixed with clay and compressed it is used as the 'lead' in a pencil. Its properties are very different to diamond and this is because of the way the carbon atoms are arranged as shown in figure 1.1.35. Graphite is considered to have a covalent network structure and like diamond it takes a lot of energy to break the strong covalent bonds between the atoms.

A close look at its structure shows that any one carbon atom is bonded to only three other carbon atoms unlike diamond where it is four. The diagram shows that the atoms form hexagonal plates held together by weak London dispersion forces. The layers are able to slide over each other which explains why graphite can be used in pencils.

With only three of each carbon atom's outer electrons used in bonding, the fourth electron in graphite is delocalised – it can move through the structure in a similar way to the delocalised electrons in metals. This explains why graphite is a good conductor of electricity. Graphite is used to make electrodes for use in electrolysis. You may have broken a graphite rod when carrying out electrolysis in the class – this is because graphite is very brittle! It is particularly useful for electrolysis at high temperatures because it will not melt. Graphite is commonly used as an electrode in lithium-ion batteries, which are assuming ever greater importance as electric powered vehicles are being developed.

Top view of one layer of graphite – like a honeycomb

weak London dispersion forces between layers

layer of graphite

delocalised electrons free to move

Figure 1.1.36: *The internal structure of graphite showing carbons joined in hexagonal plates arranged in layers held together by weak London dispersion forces*

Figure 1.1.37: *Graphite is shiny and slippery and can be used as the 'lead' in pencils*

When ground to a fine powder graphite can be used as a lubricant for delicate mechanisms. It has the ability to absorb fast-moving neutrons, so can be used in nuclear reactors to control the speed of the nuclear fission reaction. A pebble-bed reactor (PBR) is a small, modular nuclear reactor in which the uranium fuel is imbedded in graphite balls the size of tennis balls. The first prototype is operating in China and the country is thought to have plans to build 30 PBRs.

Industrial grade diamonds can be made from graphite and carbon-containing compounds like coal. The extreme conditions under which diamonds are formed in nature have to be replicated – temperature around 2000°C and a pressure of 100000 atmospheres are needed. These extreme conditions are necessary because of the huge activation energy needed to break the bonds between the carbon atoms in graphite so that they can then recombine to give the network structure of a diamond. The quality of industrial diamonds is steadily improving and may soon be as good as the quality of natural diamonds.

Figure 1.1.38: *A graphite pebble used to control the nuclear fission reactions in a pebble-bed reactor*

GO! Activity 1.1.5

1. The table details some of the properties of graphite and diamond.

Graphite	Diamond
(a) extremely high sublimation point	extremely high sublimation point
(b) electrical conductor	electrical insulator
(c) easily split into layers (brittle)	hardest substance known

Explain the properties described in (a), (b) and (c) for both graphite and diamond.

2. Graphite is used in many types of batteries and in electrolysis, particularly at high temperatures.

   (a) What property of graphite makes it useful in batteries and electrolysis?

   (b) What property of graphite makes it useful at high temperature?

3. Pebble-bed reactors are being developed in some countries.

   (a) Very high temperatures are reached in a reactor. Helium is used to cool the reactor down. Give two reasons for using helium.

   (b) Some scientists have safety concerns about using graphite in a reactor. Suggest what one of their concerns might be.

CHEMISTRY IN CONTEXT: GRAPHENE

Figure 1.1.39: *Layers of graphene one atom thick can be laid down on materials like flexible plastic*

Nanotechnology can be described as the three-dimensional structural control of materials and devices at the atomic scale. Graphene is a one atom thick, transparent, conductive sheet of carbon atoms arranged in hexagonal rings or a honeycomb pattern. Scientists at the University of Manchester won the Nobel Prize in Physics in 2010 for isolating graphene. Graphene's structure gives it unique optical, heat, mechanical and electrical properties. It is stronger and more flexible then steel, conducts heat 10 times faster than copper and can carry 1000 times the density of electrical current of copper wire. Graphene is stronger than diamond, yet is flexible and can be stretched by a quarter of its length. It is a remarkable material with many exciting potential applications.

In 2012, the UK government, realising the potential of graphene, allocated 50 million pounds to graphene research. The European Commission chose graphene as Europe's first 10-year, one billion Euro Future Emerging Technology flagship in 2013, with the aim of taking graphene development out of the laboratory and into society.

There are high hopes for using graphene in the electronics industry, perhaps one day replacing silicon. It also has potential for use in the energy field in the form of advanced, lightweight batteries.

Flexible electronic screens may be the first commercial use of graphene, one idea being e-paper (electronic paper) which is designed to have the appearance of ordinary paper. Fuel cells commonly use platinum as a catalyst for the reactions taking place to produce electricity. Applying a layer of platinum two atoms thick onto a layer of graphene one atom thick saves a lot of money. The platinum bonds strongly to the graphene surface so has a longer life than when the platinum is bonded to another metal surface. This method also maximises the surface area of the platinum available for reactants to attach to.

Graphene is so thin that graphene paint could possibly act as a rust protector or an electronic ink. A small amount of graphene mixed into plastics makes them conduct electricity. Graphene-enhanced heat conducting epoxy paste adhesives aimed at use in the space and defense industries have been produced.

Graphene's purity and large surface area could make it suitable for medical uses too, from aiding drug delivery to building new human tissue. However, some experts say that the cost and technical difficulties involved mean this will not happen before 2030.

It is the same with most of the proposed uses of graphene – it has to make financial sense to make it worth switching from existing materials to graphene. One key indicator of the potential success of any new product is how many patents (right to use) a country and companies take out. At the start of 2017 there were more than 50 000 patents on graphene, with more than half held by China. The South Korean company Samsung holds more than 600 patents – they seem convinced that this miracle material will be a success.

Nobel Prize winners

In 2010 Andre Geim and Konstantin Novoselov of the University of Manchester were awarded the Nobel Prize in Chemistry for their work on graphene.

Figure 1.1.40: *Professor Andre Geim with a model of graphene*

'No one can accurately predict what the future holds for us but with so many potential technologies that have already been suggested for graphene, even statistically the chances are sky high that graphene will bring around some really important future technologies.'

– Prof. Sir Andre Geim, Group Flagship Chairman, University of Manchester (from Wordpress.com)

KEEP UP TO DATE!
You can find out how the development of graphene-based materials for commercial use is progressing by looking up 'uses of graphene' on the internet.

Silicon

Silicon is in group 4 of the periodic table and has properties similar to diamond – it has a very high melting point, is very hard and in the pure state is a poor conductor of electricity. It would be reasonable to predict that the silicon atom forms four covalent bonds with four other silicon atoms and forms a covalent network, similar to diamond.

Figure 1.1.41: *The internal structure of silicon is similar to diamond*

Figure 1.1.42: *Single-crystal silicon, which is cut into thin wafers and used in the electronics industry*

Silicon is the second most abundant element found on Earth, mainly found in compounds as silicates and silica (silicon dioxide – SiO_2), common sand. Its main use as an element is as a semiconductor in the electronics industry where an ultrapure crystal form is grown and cut into wafer thin discs. A semiconductor is a material which has electrical conductivity to a degree between that of a metal (such as copper) and that of an insulator (such as glass). Semiconductors are the foundation of modern electronics, including transistors, solar cells and light-emitting diodes (LEDs).

CHEMISTRY IN CONTEXT: SILICON AS A SEMICONDUCTOR

Silicon, like diamond, does not conduct electricity because it doesn't have delocalised electrons. That can be changed by a process called doping. In doping, a small amount of an impurity (the dopant) is mixed into the silicon crystal. There are two types of doping – n-type and p-type. n-type impurities are either phosphorus or arsenic. When included into the crystal structure of silicon they provide delocalised electrons so the doped silicon conducts electricity. In p-type doping, boron atoms can be used as the dopant. When mixed into the silicon network, they form holes in the lattice where a silicon electron has nothing to bond to. Holes can move around the network and act as charge carriers, so p-type silicon is an electrical conductor. Although doped silicon can conduct, it is not as good as a metal, hence the name semiconductor.

Figure 1.1.43: *The structure of n-type silicon*

Figure 1.1.44: *The structure of p-type silicon*

A solar cell converts light energy into electrical energy – you may have a calculator which gets its electricity from a solar cell. One type of solar cell consists of two joined layers of silicon, one layer n-type and the other p-type. When n-type and p-type silicon are connected, electrons flow from the n-type to the p-type. When sunlight hits the p-type layer electrons move from the p-type to the n-type layer. The electrons return to the p-type layer via an external circuit and in doing so make an electric current.

Figure 1.1.45: *A solar cell uses silicon to convert light energy into electrical energy*

Figure 1.1.46: *Solar cells are being used on houses to make electricity from sunlight*

SQA KEY AREA

Boron

Boron is similar to carbon in its ability to form stable covalent networks. Boron is a very hard, black material with a high melting point of above 2000 °C. It exists in the Earth's crust mainly as the minerals borax and kernite. Obtaining very pure boron from its minerals is an extremely difficult process as it tends to leave boron with impurities such as carbon.

Major industrial-scale uses of boron compounds are in sodium perborate bleaches and in fibreglass insulation. Boron polymers play specialised roles as high-strength, lightweight structural materials. Boron compounds are used in silica-based glasses and ceramics to give them resistance to heat.

SQA KEY AREA

Trends in the periodic table

Examining the periodic table shows that the properties exhibited by elements are often repeated at regular intervals, i.e. there is periodicity. This can be seen in the size of atoms, measured as covalent radii (also known as atomic radii), the energy needed to remove an electron from an atom (ionisation energy) and the attraction an atom involved in a bond has for the electrons of the bond, known as electronegativity.

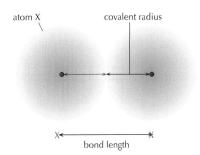

Figure 1.1.47: *The covalent radius is half the distance between the nuclei of two atoms joined by a single covalent bond*

Covalent radius

The size of an isolated atom cannot be measured as it is not possible to know where the boundary of the atom is because of the electrons constantly moving. Instead, the covalent radius is taken as half the distance between the nuclei of two atoms joined by a single covalent bond, as shown in figure 1.1.47.

1 H 30																		2 He
3 Li 152	4 Be 111											5 B 88	6 C 77	7 N 70	8 O 66	9 F 64	10 Ne
11 Na 186	12 Mg 160											13 Al 143	14 Si 117	15 P 110	16 S 104	17 Cl 99	18 Ar
19 K 231	20 Ca 197	21 Sc 160	22 Ti 146	23 V 131	24 Cr 125	25 Mn 129	26 Fe 126	27 Co 126	28 Ni 124	29 Cu 128	30 Zn 133	31 Ga 122	32 Ge 122	33 As 121	34 Se 117	35 Br 114	36 Kr
37 Rb 244	38 Sr 215	39 Y 180	40 Zr 157	41 Nb 143	42 Mo 136	43 Tc 136	44 Ru 133	45 Rh 134	46 Pd 138	47 Ag 144	48 Cd 149	49 In 168	50 Sn 140	51 Sb 141	52 Te 137	53 I 133	54 Xe
55 Cs 262	56 Ba 217	57 La 188	72 Hf 157	73 Ta 143	74 W 137	75 Re 137	76 Os 134	77 Ir 135	78 Pt 138	79 Au 144	80 Hg 155	81 Tl 171	82 Pb 175	83 Bi 146	84 Po 140	85 At 140	86 Rn
(87) Fr 270	88 Ra 220	89 Ac 200															

Figure 1.1.48: *Covalent radii of the elements, measured in picometres (10^{-12}m)*

Change in covalent radius down a group

Figure 1.1.49 shows that as you go down a group the covalent radius, i.e. the size of the atom, increases. This corresponds to an increase in atomic number, i.e. the number of protons in the nucleus. At the same time the number of electrons in each atom increases. It might be expected that with an increase in nuclear charge there would be a greater attraction for the electrons and so the covalent radius would be smaller. However, as the atomic number increases down a group the number of electron shells occupied increases and the inner electron shells screen the outermost electrons from the full pull of the positive nucleus. This means the outer electrons can move further from the nucleus.

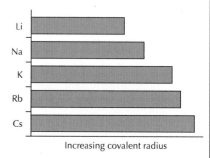

Figure 1.1.49: *Covalent radii increase down a group*

Change in covalent radius across a period

Figure 1.1.50 shows that as you go across a period the covalent radius decreases. Moving across a period, the atomic number increases by one each time so the number of protons in the nucleus increases by one. At the same time each atom gains an electron but in the same shell so there is no increased screening effect from inner shells of electrons. As a result, as the atomic number increases across a period the electrons in the outer shell are more strongly attracted to the nucleus and so the covalent radius decreases.

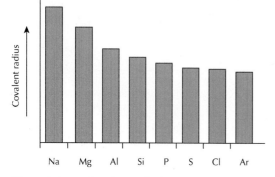

Figure 1.1.50: *Covalent radii decrease across a period*

Summary:

Going down a group:
- the number of screening shells of electrons increases
- the attraction between the atom's nucleus and its outermost electrons decreases
- the covalent radius increases.

Going across a period:
- the number of screening shells of electrons is the same
- the attraction of the nucleus for the outermost electrons gets stronger
- the covalent radius decreases.

Knowledge of the size of atoms has practical applications. For example when designing new medicines the covalent radius of an element is often considered in deciding the size and shape of the molecule.

GO! Activity 1.1.6

1. (a) Explain what covalent radius is.
   (b) Describe the trend in covalent radius as you go across period 3 of the periodic table.
   (c) Explain the pattern observed in 1(b).
   (d) Describe the trend in covalent radius as you go down group 6 of the periodic table.
   (e) Explain the pattern observed in 1(d).

2. Many periodic tables either do not show covalent radii for the noble gases or have estimated values rather than measured values. Explain why this is. (Hint: Look at your answer to **1.** (a).)

Ionisation energy

The first ionisation energy is the energy required to remove an electron from every atom in a mole of atoms in the gaseous state. Ionisation energy is measured in kJ mol^{-1}. The first ionisation energy of any element can be represented in an equation as:

$E(g) \rightarrow E^+(g) + e^-$ where E is any element and (g) indicates it is gaseous.

For example, the first ionisation energy for sodium would be written as:

$Na(g) \rightarrow Na^+(g) + e^-$

Table 1.1.4 shows the first ionisation energies (in kJ mol^{-1}) for some elements in periods 2 to 5.

Table 1.1.4: *The first ionisation energies (in kJ mol⁻¹) for some elements in periods 2 to 5*

Li	Be	B	C	N	O	F	Ne
526	905	807	1090	1410	1320	1690	2090
Na	Mg	Al	Si	P	S	Cl	Ar
502	744	584	792	1020	1010	1260	1530
K	Ca	Ga	Ge	As	Se	Br	Kr
425	596	577	762	953	941	1150	1350
Rb	Sr	In	Sn	Sb	Te	I	Xe
409	556	556	715	816	870	1020	1170

decrease down group

——— overall increase along period ⟶

As you go down a group in the periodic table the first ionisation energy generally decreases. This indicates that it becomes easier to remove an electron from an atom. As you go down a group the covalent radius of the atoms increases, i.e. the atoms get bigger. This means that the outer electrons are further away from the pull of the nucleus. In addition, the number of filled electron energy levels increases and they screen the outer electrons from the pulling effect of the nucleus. A combination of both effects makes it easier to remove an outer electron from an atom as you go down a group.

As you go across a period in the periodic table the first ionisation energy generally increases. This indicates that as you go across a period it gets harder to remove an electron from an atom. Across a period electrons are being added to the same energy level and at the same time protons are being added to the nucleus. As the nuclear charge increases the electrons are held more tightly and so it becomes harder to remove an outer electron from an atom.

It is possible to remove two or more electrons from an atom. The second ionisation energy is the amount of energy required to remove a second mole of electrons. This can be represented as:

$$E^+(g) \rightarrow E^{2+}(g) + e^-$$

Using magnesium as an example:

First ionisation energy

$$Mg(g) \rightarrow Mg^+(g) + e^- \qquad \Delta H = +744 \text{ kJ mol}^{-1}$$

Second ionisation energy

$$Mg^+(g) \rightarrow Mg^{2+}(g) + e^- \qquad \Delta H = +1460 \text{ kJ mol}^{-1}$$

Second ionisation energies are always higher than first because while electrons are being removed the number of protons in the nucleus remains the same so the pull on the remaining electrons is increased.

The total amount of energy required to remove two moles of electrons from a mole of magnesium atoms is the first ionisation energy and second ionisation energy added together, i.e. +2204 kJ mol^{-1}. It is theoretically possible to remove a third electron from an atom of magnesium but energetically this is not possible during a chemical reaction. Magnesium has the electronic arrangement 2,8,2. In other words, an atom of magnesium has two outer electrons which are relatively easy to remove. To remove a third electron requires going into an energy level closer to the nucleus so there is less shielding and the nucleus has a strong attraction for the electron. This explains why magnesium easily forms Mg^{2+} ions when it reacts, e.g. magnesium oxide ($Mg^{2+}O^{2-}$).

GO! Activity 1.1.7

1. The graph shows the first ionisation energies for the first 20 elements.

Use the graph to answer the following questions:
  (a) Describe the general trend in first ionisation energy as you go down group 1 in the periodic table.
  (b) Explain the trend you described in part (a).
  (c) Describe the general trend in first ionisation energy as you go across period 3 in the periodic table, from sodium to argon.
  (d) Explain the trend you described in part (c).
  (e) Explain why the first ionisation energies for the noble gases (group 0) are much higher than the other elements.

2. The table shows ionisation energy values (in kJ mol^{-1}) for an aluminium atom forming ions:

first	second	third	fourth
584	1830	2760	11600

  (a) Write equations to represent the first, second and third ionisation energies of aluminium.
  (b) Explain why there is an increase in the ionisation energy from 1st to 4th.
  (c) Explain why there is such a large difference between the 3rd and 4th ionisation energy values.
  (d) Calculate the total energy required for a mole of gaseous aluminium atoms to form a mole of aluminium 3+ ions.

Electronegativity

Electronegativity is the attraction an atom involved in a bond has for the electrons of the bond. A scale was devised by one of the twentieth century's most famous scientists, Linus Pauling. He assigned numbers to elements depending on how electronegative an element was. Fluorine, the most electronegative element, was assigned a value of 4·0 and francium, the least electronegative, a value of 0·8. The difference in electronegativity values of atoms bonded together gives a good indication of the type of bonding which mainly exists between the atoms. This is dealt with in more detail in Chapter 1.2.

Figure 1.1.51: *Periodic table showing the trends in electronegativity*

Figure 1.1.51 shows that electronegativity:

- decreases down a group
- increases across a period.

Although the nuclear charge on an atom increases down a group the atoms get bigger and the outer electrons are further from the attraction of the nucleus. In addition the number of shells of electrons increases down a group so the screening effect of the inner electrons on the bonding electrons increases.

Across a period, the nuclear charge on an atom increases and the atoms get smaller. The attraction of the nucleus for the bonding electrons increases. As electrons are added across the period they go into the same shell so there is no increase in the screening effect of the inner electrons.

GO! Nobel Prize winners

Linus Pauling received the Nobel Prize in Chemistry in 1954 for his work on chemical bonding – his book *The Nature of the Chemical Bond* has had a great influence on chemists. He was also awarded the Nobel Peace Prize in 1962 for his work as a peace activist.

Figure 1.1.52: *Linus Pauling*

Hint

You don't need to memorise covalent radii, ionisation energies or electronegativity values – they are listed in the SQA data booklet.

GO! Activity 1.1.8

(a) Explain the meaning of the term electronegativity.

(b) Describe the trend in electronegativity as you go across period 2 of the periodic table.

(c) Explain the pattern you observed in (b).

(d) Describe the trend in electronegativity as you go down group 7 of the periodic table.

(e) Explain the pattern you observed in (d).

Learning checklist

In this chapter you have learned:

* In the periodic table elements are arranged in order of increasing atomic number. ⬭ ⬭ ⬭

* Groups are vertical columns in the periodic table containing elements with similar chemical properties because they have the same number of electrons in the outer shell (energy level). ⬭ ⬭ ⬭

* Periods are rows of elements arranged in increasing atomic number and show a change from metallic to non-metallic character. ⬭ ⬭ ⬭

* The first 20 elements in the periodic table are categorised according to their bonding and structure: ⬭ ⬭ ⬭

  * metallic (Li, Be, Na, Mg, Al, K, Ca) ⬭ ⬭ ⬭

  * monatomic (He, Ne, Ar) ⬭ ⬭ ⬭

  * covalent molecular (H_2, N_2, O_2, F_2, Cl_2, P_4, S_8 and C (fullerenes)) ⬭ ⬭ ⬭

  * covalent network (B, C (diamond and graphite), Si). ⬭ ⬭ ⬭

Metals
* Metal nuclei (positive ions) are arranged in a crystal structure held together by metallic bonds. ⬭ ⬭ ⬭

* Metals conduct electricity because the delocalised electrons can move through the structure. ⬭ ⬭ ⬭

* Metals are malleable and ductile because the direction of the bonds in a metal are not fixed so can move in relation to each other. ⬭ ⬭ ⬭

- Metals are good heat conductors because the delocalised electrons can transfer energy.
- Metals have high melting and boiling points because metallic bonding is very strong.

Non-metals – monatomic
- The noble gases are monatomic elements with weak London dispersion forces between the atoms.
- London dispersion forces are weak forces of attraction between atoms and molecules when temporary dipoles are formed within atoms or molecules.

Covalent molecular
- Hydrogen, nitrogen, oxygen and the halogens exist as individual diatomic molecules with London dispersion forces between the molecules (intermolecular) and strong covalent bonds between the atoms in a molecule.
- Sulfur and phosphorus are small individual molecules with strong London dispersion forces between molecules so are solids at room temperature.
- Carbon can exist as large individual covalent molecules (fullerenes).
- Fullerene molecules can be ball or tube shaped and have relatively high melting points because of the large London dispersion forces between molecules.

Covalent network
- Carbon can exist as large covalent networks (diamond and graphite).
- The carbon atoms in diamond are bonded to four other carbons in a strong 3D network which makes it very hard.
- The network structure of diamond results in diamond having a very high melting point.
- Diamond is a non-conductor of electricity because it has no delocalised electrons.
- Graphite forms a network in which each carbon is only bonded to three other carbons, which results in graphite having delocalised electrons so it conducts electricity.
- The carbon atoms in graphite form hexagonal plates which are held together by London dispersion forces.

- The layers in graphite can be easily separated, which means graphite is not as hard as diamond.
- Boron and silicon exist as covalent networks and have properties associated with covalent networks, e.g. very high melting and boiling points.

Trends in the periodic table
- The covalent radius is a measure of the size of an atom.
- The covalent radius increases down a group as the number of occupied electron shells increases. Although the number of protons increases the electron shells screen the outer electrons from the pull of the nucleus.
- The covalent radius decreases going across a period. The number of protons in the nucleus increases and there is no increased screening effect as electrons are added to the same electron shell.
- The first ionisation energy is the energy required to remove one mole of electrons from one mole of gaseous atoms.
- First ionisation energy decreases down a group as the outer electrons get further from the nucleus and are screened from the pull of the nucleus by the shells of inner electrons.
- First ionisation energy generally increases across a period as the outer electrons are held more tightly by the nucleus as electrons are added to the same energy level and the charge on the nucleus increases.
- Second and subsequent ionisation energies refer to the energies required to remove further moles of electrons.
- Electronegativity is a measure of the attraction an atom has for the electrons of the bond.
- Electronegativity decreases down a group as atoms get bigger and the attraction of the nucleus for bonding electrons decreases. Although the nuclear charge increases the bonding electrons are further from the nucleus. The number of screening shells of electrons also increases.
- Electronegativity increases across a period as the atoms get smaller and the attraction of the nucleus for bonding electrons increases. The nuclear charge increases and the number of screening shells of electrons stays the same.

2 Structure and bonding

You should already know

- Covalent bonds are formed when atoms of non-metal elements join by sharing electrons.
- Covalent compounds which exist as molecules have low melting and boiling points so can exist as gas, liquid or solid at room temperature and pressure.
- Covalent compounds do not conduct electricity in any state.
- Ionic compounds form when metal atoms transfer electrons to non-metal atoms resulting in positive metal ions and negative non-metal ions.
- The attraction of positive and negative ions is called an ionic bond.
- Ionic compounds are solids at room temperature and conduct electricity only when molten or dissolved in water (solution).

(National 4 Chemistry: Chemical changes and structure: Atomic structure and bonding related to properties of materials)

- How to draw the specific shapes of covalent molecules.
- Covalent molecular substances have low melting and boiling points because the forces of attraction between molecules are very weak and not a lot of energy is needed to separate the molecules.
- A covalent network is a giant 3-D structure in which the atoms are covalently bonded to each other.
- Covalent network substances have high melting and boiling points because the atoms are tightly held together by strong covalent bonds and a lot of energy is needed to break the bonds.
- Ionic substances exist as lattices in which electrostatic attractions hold the oppositely charged ions in a 3D structure.
- Ionic compounds have high melting and boiling points because it takes a lot of energy to break the ionic bonds.
- Solid ionic compounds do not conduct electricity because the ions cannot move.
- Ionic substances can conduct electricity when melted or in solution because the ions are free to move.
- When ionic compounds dissolve in water the electrostatic attraction between ions is replaced by attractive forces between the ions and water molecules.

- Many ionic compounds are highly coloured compared to covalent substances.

(*National 5 Chemistry: Chemical changes and structure: Atomic structure and bonding related to properties of materials*)

Learning intentions

In this chapter you will learn about:
- Bonding in compounds: covalent, polar covalent and ionic.
- The bonding continuum.
- Intermolecular forces: London dispersion forces, permanent dipole – permanent dipole interactions and hydrogen bonding.
- Viscosity, solubility and miscibility.

CHEMISTRY IN CONTEXT: MAKING MOLECULES

Making artificial molecules

Molecules form well known shapes, depending on the number of non-bonded electrons in the outer energy levels of the atoms involved in the compound (Figure 1.2.1).

A team of scientists at New York University, led by David Pine, has developed a technique to make imitation atoms which can be joined to make copy molecules without the need for bonding electrons to be present. These imitation atoms are made up of microscopic polystyrene spheres which can be made to join to give a molecule with the same shape as real molecules but more than 2000 times bigger than real molecules. Scientists forced the spheres to join together to form clusters of between two and seven spheres. They filled the gaps between the spheres with liquid styrene which swelled and solidified into balls of various sizes each with 'bumpy hills'. DNA was added to the bumpy hills to create 'sticky areas' where other microspheres coated in complementary DNA could join onto the fake atom. This is shown diagrammatically for balls with four microspheres acting like a carbon atom and forming an artificial methane type structure (Figure 1.2.2).

carbon dioxide – linear

water – angular

ammonia – trigonal pyramidal

methane – tetrahedral

Figure 1.2.1: *Covalent molecules can form a variety of shapes*

microscopic polystyrene spheres cluster together

filler added leaving sticky 'bumpy hills' exposed (fake carbon atom)

'hydrogen' microspheres stick to the 'hills'

fake methane molecule with tetrahedral shape

Figure 1.2.2: *Artificial molecules can be made to mimic real molecules*

Like many new discoveries and ideas, at first there appeared to be few practical applications of fake molecules, but as technology develops, uses arise. Pine and his team think that artificial carbon atoms can be joined to make a semiconductor for light. Electrical semiconductors are well known and they think that it should be possible to control light in a similar way. They think that crystals made out of artificial carbons could be better than real atoms at transferring light because the size of the synthetic atoms matches the wavelength of light. These 'photonic crystals' could be useful in ultra-fast optical computers and optical communication.

Making new molecules

A knowledge of the 3-D structure of chemicals and how a molecule's shape affects its biological activity is essential in the manufacture of new drugs. Drugs work on complex chemical receptor sites around the body, a bit like a key fitting a lock. Scientists use X-ray crystallography to work out the structure and shape of receptor molecules. They can design a drug which fits into the site. Computer simulations play a big part in the research because 3-D molecular shapes can easily be visualised on screen. The active part of a drug is known as the pharmacophore. Computer databases contain the shapes of thousands of compounds and they can be matched with the pharmacaphore of the drug. Computers will not replace laboratory research but they do cut down the cost and time to find appropriate compounds to investigate further.

Figure 1.2.3: *The use of computer technology has transformed the manufacture of new drugs*

GO! Nobel Prize winners

In 2013, three US scientists, Martin Karplus, Michael Levitt and Arieh Warshel, won the Nobel Prize in Chemistry for pioneering work on computer programs that simulate complex chemical processes and which have revolutionised research in areas including drugs and solar energy.

The Royal Swedish Academy of Sciences said their work had effectively taken chemistry into cyberspace. Long gone were the days of modelling reactions using plastic balls and sticks.

'Today the computer is just as important a tool for chemists as the test tube,' the academy said in a statement. 'Computer models mirroring real life have become crucial for most advances made in chemistry today.'

CHEMISTRY IN CONTEXT: X-RAY CRYSTALLOGRAPHY

X-ray crystallography is a method used for working out the atomic and molecular structure of a crystal in which the atoms cause a beam of X-rays to scatter (diffract) into many specific directions. By measuring the angles and intensities of these scattered beams, scientists can produce a 3-D picture of the density of electrons within the crystal. From this electron density, positions of the atoms in the crystal can be worked out as well as their chemical bonds.

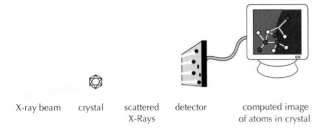

X-ray beam   crystal   scattered   detector   computed image
X-Rays   of atoms in crystal

Figure 1.2.4: *The structure of compounds can be worked out by the way their crystals scatter X-rays*

In 1912 the German scientist Max von Laue first suggested atoms in crystals might scatter X-rays because the wavelength of X-rays is about the same as the distance between the nuclei of the atoms in a crystal. The English scientists William and Lawrence Bragg (father and son) worked out the mathematical calculations to match patterns to 3-D positions. They were awarded the Nobel Prize in Physics in 1915. In 1945 Dorothy Hodgkin used X-ray crystallography to work out the structure of penicillin, and by 1956 she had unravelled the complicated structure of vitamin B_{12} – a molecule with more than 90 atoms. Once the structure was known, chemists could make the vitamin and use it to treat some medical conditions. By 1969 Hodgkin had worked out the structure of insulin, a complex molecule with over 800 atoms. Insulin is a protein essential to the body for the absorption of glucose from the blood. Some people with diabetes have to inject insulin into their body.

Since many materials can form crystals, X-ray crystallography has been fundamental in the development of many scientific areas. In its first decades of use, this method was used to work out the size of atoms and the lengths and types of chemical bonds. It was also used to work out the atomic-scale differences among various materials, especially minerals and alloys. The method also revealed the structure and function of many biological molecules, including vitamins, drugs, proteins and nucleic acids such as DNA. X-ray crystallography is still the main method for working out the atomic structure of new materials. X-ray crystallography of structures can also account for unusual electronic or elastic properties of a material, shed light on chemical interactions and processes, or serve as the basis for designing drugs to treat diseases. X-ray crystallography was used to confirm the structure of buckminsterfullerene (C_{60}) and has been used to work out the structures of over 1000 proteins.

Figure 1.2.5: *The structure of insulin was discovered using X-ray crystallography*

GO! Nobel Prize winners

William and Lawrence Bragg were awarded the Nobel Prize in Physics in 1915 for their pioneering work on X-ray crystallography. Dorothy Hodgkin was awarded the Nobel Prize in Chemistry in 1964 for her work on discovering the structure of vitamin B_{12} using X-ray crystallography – so far she is the only female British scientist to have been awarded a Nobel Prize.

Figure 1.2.6: *Dorothy Hodgkin pioneered the use of X-ray crystallography*

Figure 1.2.7: *The structure of the protein gliadin, present in wheat and several other cereals, is essential for giving bread the ability to rise properly during baking. X-ray crystallography was used to help determine its structure.*

Types of chemical bond

Covalent bonding – pure and polar

Covalent bonds are formed when non-metal atoms share pairs of electrons. The positive nuclei of the atoms are held together by their common attraction for the shared pair of electrons. When two atoms of the same non-metal element bond, the bonding electrons are shared equally. This is because the atoms have the same attraction for the bonding electrons – both atoms have the same electronegativity value. This is known as pure covalent bonding. Pure covalent bonds can also be formed in compounds. Nitrogen and chlorine have the same elecronegativity value (3·0) so both atoms have the same attraction for the bonding electrons, and the covalent bond can be described as pure.

$H \overset{\times}{\underset{\bullet}{}} H$ $\delta^+ H \overset{\times}{\underset{\bullet}{-}} Cl^{\delta^-}$ $N \overset{\times}{\underset{\bullet}{}} Cl$

pure	polar	pure covalent
covalent	covalent	bond
bond	bond	(compound)
(element)	(compound)	

$\times$ **and** $\bullet$ **= bonding electrons**

Figure 1.2.8: *Equal sharing of bonding electrons in pure covalent bonding and unequal sharing of electrons in polar covalent bonding*

Most covalent compounds are formed between elements with different electronegativity values. This means that one atom has a greater attraction for the bonding electrons than the other. The atom with the greater attraction for the bonding electrons will have a slightly negative charge ($\delta-$), leaving the other atom with a slightly positive charge ($\delta+$). A permanent dipole is formed. Bonding in which there is a permanent dipole is known as polar covalent bonding (polar bonding).

Not all polar bonds have the same strength. The difference in electronegativity values gives a measure of how polar a bond is. Fluorine is the most electronegative element with a value of 4·0. When bonded with hydrogen with a value of 2·1 the bond formed is extremely polar covalent – the difference in electronegativity is 1·9.

A difference of 2·0 and above generally indicates that the bonding is more ionic than covalent and is usually referred to as ionic. Carbon and hydrogen have a small difference in electronegativities, so the C–H bond is generally regarded as being non-polar.

Ionic bonding

An ionic bond is an electrostatic attraction between positive and negative ions. The most common ionic compounds are formed between metals and non-metals – sodium chloride is one of the best known. A look at their respective electronegativity values shows there is a difference of 2·0, which indicates it is just ionic. Caesium fluoride on the other hand has a difference in electronegativity of 3·2, which indicates it is extremely ionic – it is considered to be the most ionic compound. Differences in electronegativity values greater than 2 indicate that the electron movement from the atom of the element with the lower electronegativity value to the atom of the element with the greater electronegativity is complete, resulting in the formation of ions.

Electron density maps obtained from X-ray crystallography of compounds show that in ionic compounds there is no shared electron density between positive and negative ions whereas the map for a molecule with pure covalent bonding shows electron density shared between the two nuclei.

Figure 1.2.9: *The electron density map for sodium chloride (left) shows no shared electron density whereas shared electron density is clearly seen in fluorine (right)*

Ionic compounds exist as giant lattices in which the oppositely charged ions attract each other. The electrostatic attraction between the positive ions and the negative ions is not in any particular direction as is the case with covalent bonds. This means that each positive ion attracts neighbouring negative ions and negative ions attract neighbouring positive ions. Eventually a giant structure of repeating units is produced which stretch in all directions. The repeating unit in an ionic lattice is often referred to as a unit cell. Ionic formulae give the simplest ratio of each type of ion in an ionic compound eg

> **GO! Activity 1.2.1**
> (a) Identify the type of bonding which exists between the atoms in the following substances:
> (i) bromine (Br_2)
> (ii) hydrogen iodide (HI)
> (iii) water (H_2O)
> (b) Draw the molecules in (a) which have polar covalent bonds and add the δ^- and δ^+ symbols.

> **🔍 Hint**
> Beware of assuming that all metal and non-metal compounds are ionic. For example, tin(IV) chloride shows a lot of covalent character, which is indicated by the difference in electronegativity values of the two elements, which is 1·2.

sodium chloride: Na^+Cl^-. Ionic compounds are solids which have very high melting and boiling points because it takes a lot of energy to break the strong electrostatic attractions between the ions. They are non-conductors of electricity in the solid state because the ions are not free to move and carry the charge. When melted or dissolved in water the lattice structure is broken down and the ions are free to move and act as charge carriers.

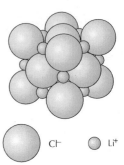

Figure 1.2.10: *The unit cell of sodium chloride*

GO! Activity 1.2.2

1. Some commercially available table salt is a mixture of sodium chloride and potassium chloride rather than pure sodium chloride. The manufacturers claim that the mixture has the same taste as pure sodium chloride but it is less damaging for people with high blood pressure. Discuss the similarities between sodium chloride and potassium chloride. Include bonding, structure, melting and boiling points and solubility.

2. Look at Figure 1.2.11. Suggest why caesium chloride has a different lattice structure to sodium chloride.

3. Sketch a simple electron density map for potassium chloride.

The bonding continuum

Labelling a compound as ionic, pure covalent or polar covalent is a convenient way of indicating bonding but it is not necessarily the most accurate way. As discussed in ionic bonding, some compounds appear more ionic than others and some show some covalent characteristics. Polar covalent compounds also show different degrees of polarity. The idea of a bonding continuum gives a more realistic indication of the bonding in a compound. The bonding continuum has ionic bonding at one end and pure covalent at the other end, with polar covalent in between. To say that bonding is on a continuum means that the type of bonding changes gradually as the difference in electronegativity between atoms increases. There is no sharp distinction between covalent and ionic bonds. Although looking at the differences in electronegativity is a useful indicator of bonding, it has to be taken alongside the physical properties of the compound to be absolutely sure of the type of bonding present.

Figure 1.2.11: *The structures of the ionic lattices formed by some group 1 chlorides*

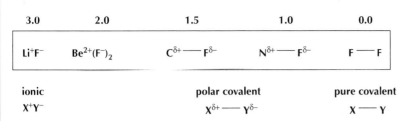

Figure 1.2.12: *The bonding continuum – the numbers are the difference in electronegativity between the bonded atoms*

Activity 1.2.3

1. Discuss this question with a partner then complete the bonding continuum summary below.

2. (a) Using the electronegativity values on page 34 work out the type of bonding which predominates in each of the following compounds:

   (i) rubidium chloride (RbCl) (ii) tin(iv) iodide (SnI_4) (iii) phosphine (PH_3).
   (b) Explain your answer in each case.

Intermolecular forces

Many covalent molecular substances exist as liquids and low melting and boiling point solids at room temperature and most of those which exist as gases can be liquefied by lowering the temperature. This indicates that there are forces of attraction between molecules which hold them together. The intermolecular forces acting between molecules are known as van der Waals' forces. There are several different types of van der Waals' force such as London dispersion forces, permanent dipole–permanent dipole interactions, including hydrogen bonding.

London dispersion forces

London dispersion forces occur between molecules and are explained in detail in Chapter 1.1. They are caused by the continual movement of electrons which causes a temporary uneven distribution of charge at opposite sides of a molecule – known as a temporary dipole. This means that one side of the molecule is temporarily slightly negative (δ^-) which results in the other side being temporarily slightly positive (δ^+). This in turn induces (causes) a temporary dipole in a neighbouring molecule. This results in the δ^- side of one molecule attracting the δ^+ side of a neighbouring molecule so a force of attraction is formed between them. London dispersion forces are very weak but the more electrons there are in the molecule, the bigger the London dispersion force.

London dispersion forces are the only significant forces between non-polar molecules. Hydrocarbons are good examples of compounds which have molecules held together by London dispersion forces only. The boiling points of some liquid hydrocarbons are shown in table 1.2.1. As the molecular mass increases the number of electrons in the molecules also increases so the London dispersion forces get stronger and more energy is needed to separate the molecules, so the boiling point increases.

Table 1.2.1

Homologous series	Boiling point (°C)
alkanes	
pentane	36
hexane	69
heptane	98
cycloalkanes	
cyclobutane	12
cyclopentane	49
cyclohexane	81
alkenes	
pent-1-ene	30
hex-1-ene	63
hept-1-ene	94

GO! Activity 1.2.4

(a) Use the information in table 1.2.1 to draw a spike graph which shows how the boiling points of the alkanes increase with their molecular mass.

(b) Explain why the boiling points of the alkanes increase in this way.

(c) From the graph, estimate the boiling point of octane (C_8H_{18}).

Permanent dipole–permanent dipole interactions

Permanent dipole–permanent dipole interactions occur between polar molecules. It might at first seem obvious that if a molecule contains polar bonds then the molecule itself will be polar, but this is not necessarily the case. A molecule needs to have a slightly negative side (δ^-) and a slightly positive side (δ^+) to be overall polar and this depends on the atoms in the molecule and the shape of the molecule. This means that a molecule can contain polar bonds but the molecule need not necessarily be polar. Figure 1.2.13 shows examples of polar and non-polar molecules.

Polar molecules

$\delta+$H─┼─Cl$\delta-$

$\delta+$ side of | $\delta-$ side of
molecule | molecule

(hydrogen chloride)

$\delta-$ side of molecule

O $\delta-$

H   H
$\delta+$ $\delta+$

$\delta+$ side of molecule

(water)

$\delta-$ side of molecule

N $\delta-$

H | H
$\delta+$ H $\delta+$
    $\delta+$

$\delta+$ side of molecule

(ammonia)

Non-polar molecules

$\delta-$O═C$\delta+$═O$\delta-$

(carbon dioxide)

Cl $\delta-$
|
C $\delta+$
Cl | Cl
$\delta-$ Cl $\delta-$
  $\delta-$

(tetrachloromethane)

Figure 1.2.13: *Polar molecules have a slightly negative ($\delta-$) side and a slightly positive ($\delta+$) side. Non-polar molecules are symmetrical so they have no slightly negative ($\delta-$) or slightly positive ($\delta+$) side*

It can clearly be seen in figure 1.2.13 that the polar molecules do not have their bonds symmetrically arranged, which results in them having a slightly negative side ($\delta-$) and a slightly positive side ($\delta+$). These molecules have a permanent dipole where electrons are pulled towards one side of the molecule. The non-polar molecules in figure 1.2.13 are symmetrical and there is no permanent dipole, i.e. there is no slightly negative ($\delta-$) side or slightly positive side ($\delta+$). The polarity of the bonds in a non-polar molecule cancel each other out because of the symmetrical shape.

It isn't possible to tell by looking at two liquids if they are polar or not but a simple experiment can be carried out to tell them apart, as shown in figure 1.2.14.

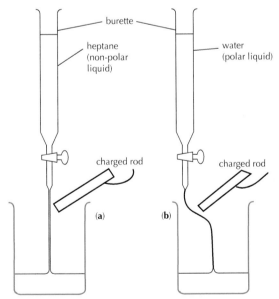

Figure 1.2.14: *Polar substances are attracted to a charged plastic rod (b) but non-polar substances are not (a)*

Figure 1.2.15: *The diagram shows that phosphorous(III) chloride molecules are polar*

Phosphorus trichloride (PCl_3) is a liquid at room temperature with a low boiling point. Phosphorus trichloride has molecules which have a permanent dipole. Its shape is similar to ammonia. Since one end of the molecule is slightly negative it can form an attraction with the slightly positive end of a neighbouring molecule. Although these forces of attraction are stronger than London dispersion forces they are still relatively weak which explains why although phosphorus trichloride is a liquid at room temperature due to the permanent dipole attractions, it still has a low boiling point.

intermolecular force

Figure 1.2.16: *Permanent dipole-permanent dipole attractions between phosphorus(III) chloride molecules*

The effect of the difference in strength between permanent dipole attractions and London dispersion forces can be shown by comparing the melting points of iodine monochloride (ICl: mp = +27°C) and bromine (Br$_2$: mp = −7°C). They both have 70 electrons in their molecules so should have the same strength of London dispersion forces. We would expect them to have similar melting points, which they don't. This difference is due to the difference in the forces of attraction between their molecules. Iodine monochloride has polar molecules so there are permanent dipole–permanent dipole interactions between molecules whereas bromine is non-polar so bromine has only London dispersion forces between the molecules. It takes more energy to separate molecules with permanent dipole interactions than molecules which only have London dispersion forces between molecules.

Br —— Br ------ Br —— Br

Br —— Br

London dispersion force

mp = −7°c

I$^{\delta+}$ —— Cl$^{\delta-}$ ------ I$^{\delta+}$ —— Cl$^{\delta-}$

I$^{\delta+}$ —— Cl$^{\delta-}$

permanent dipole interaction

mp = 27°c

Figure 1.2.17: *Iodine monochloride has permanent dipole–permanent dipole interactions between molecules which are much stronger than London dispersion forces*

Although permanent dipole–permanent dipole interactions are stronger than London dispersion forces, both attractions exist between polar molecules. London dispersion forces can be significant in big molecules. Figure 1.2.18 shows the permanent dipole–permanent dipole interactions and London dispersion forces between molecules of 1-chlorooctane. The London dispersion forces occur between the large alkyl groups and the permanent dipole–permanent dipole interactions are seen at the polar end of the molecules.

London dispersion forces

permanent dipole–permanent dipole attraction

Figure 1.2.18: *Both London dispersion forces and permanent dipole–permanent dipole interactions are effective between 1-chlorooctane molecules*

🔵 Activity 1.2.5

1. The shapes of chloromethane, trichloromethane and tetrachloromethane are shown.

chloromethane   trichloromethane   tetrachloromethane

For each substance, state whether the molecules are polar or non-polar and explain each of your answers.

2. Silicon(IV) chloride and boron trichloride both have polar bonding within their molecules. The molecules themselves however are non-polar.

Draw a possible shape for each of the molecules and explain your choice.

3. The structural formulae for propanone and butane are shown.

propanone : bp = 56°C

butane : bp = 0°C

Explain why propanone has a much higher boiling point than butane even though they have a similar number of electrons.

Hydrogen bonding

When hydrogen is bonded to the highly electronegative elements fluorine, oxygen and nitrogen it results in the electrons in the bond being more strongly attracted away from the hydrogen atom than would be the case if other non-metal atoms were attached to the hydrogen. The hydrogen atom is so small that the partial positive charge on the atom is unusually high and the bond is highly polar. This results in a very strong permanent dipole–permanent dipole interaction between molecules called a hydrogen bond. Hydrogen bonds are the strongest of the van der Waals' forces and they cause some unusual and unexpected properties in compounds in which the hydrogen bonds are present.

Hydrogen fluoride (HF), water (H_2O) and ammonia (NH_3) are compounds with hydrogen bonds between their molecules. Figure 1.2.19 shows the trend in the boiling points of the group 6 hydrides.

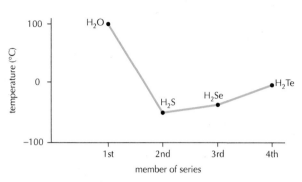

Figure 1.2.19: *Boiling points of the group 6 hydrides*

All but water show the expected gradual increase in boiling point. As you go down group 6 the number of electrons in the atoms of each element increases so there are stronger forces of attraction between molecules so more energy is needed to separate the molecules. Water might be expected to have a boiling point well below zero but it has a boiling point of 100°C. The unexpected boiling point is due to the presence of strong hydrogen bonding. More energy is needed to separate the molecules than would be needed if there were only normal permanent dipole–permanent dipole interactions and London dispersion forces between molecules.

A similar pattern is seen when the boiling points of the hydrides of groups 5 and 7 are added to figure 1.2.19 (figure 1.2.21). Ammonia and hydrogen fluoride both have higher boiling points than expected because of hydrogen bonding between the molecules. Also shown in figure 1.2.21 are the boiling points of the group 4 hydrides. They follow the expected pattern – as the molecules get bigger their boiling points increase. This is because there is no hydrogen bonding between any of the molecules. They are non-polar molecules so have only weak London dispersion forces between the molecules. As the molecules get bigger, the number of electrons increases and so the London dispersion forces increase and it takes more energy to separate the molecules.

Figure 1.2.20: *Hydrogen bonding in water*

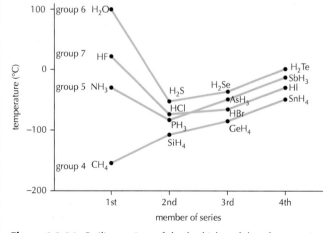

Figure 1.2.21: *Boiling points of the hydrides of the elements in groups 4 to 7*

(continued)

Trends in melting points of the group 4 to 7 hydrides (figure 1.2.22) follow a similar pattern to boiling points and can be explained in the same way:

- Groups 7, 6 and 5 hydrides: HF, H_2O and NH_3 have higher melting points than the other hydrides in their periodic group because they have hydrogen bonding between their molecules. The molecules of the other hydrides in the groups are held together by permanent dipole–permanent dipole interactions and London dispersion forces which are not as strong as hydrogen bonds so require less energy to separate them.

- Group 4 hydrides: the molecules are non-polar and are held together by weak London dispersion forces which do not need much energy to separate them.

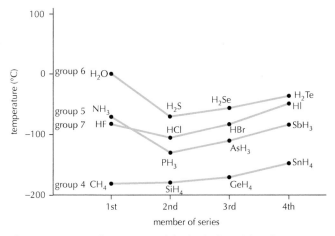

Figure 1.2.22: *Melting points of the hydrides of the elements in groups 4 to 7*

Water exhibits some unusual properties due to hydrogen bonding. All liquids contract on cooling – their density increases. Water is unusual in that when it is cooled and reaches 4°C it begins to expand again. At its freezing point it is less dense than liquid water – this explains why ice cubes and icebergs float on water. It also explains why water pipes can burst in winter. When the water freezes and expands the force causes pipes to crack. This expansion of water is due to the ordering of the molecules into an open structure, with an increased number of hydrogen bonds, which is less dense than the arrangement of the molecules in liquid water.

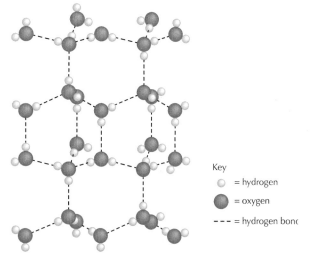

Key
○ = hydrogen
● = oxygen
--- = hydrogen bond

Figure 1.2.23: *The open arrangement of the water molecules in ice creates more hydrogen bonds and results in ice being less dense than water*

Figure 1.2.24: *Ice is less dense than water so floats in water*

CHEMISTRY IN CONTEXT: SURFACE TENSION

Hydrogen bonding also explains why water forms droplets and insects can run along the surface of water. Water has a very high surface tension as the water molecules are held together by strong hydrogen bonding.

Figure 1.2.25: *Water forms droplets because of hydrogen bonding between the water molecules*

Figure 1.2.26: *The surface tension in water is due to hydrogen bonding between water molecules*

GO! Activity 1.2.6

1. Look at the boiling points of the group 4 and group 5 hydrides. Explain why the boiling point of methane (CH$_4$) follows the same pattern as the other group 4 hydrides but the boiling point of ammonia (NH$_3$) does not follow the same pattern as the rest of the group 5 hydrides.

2. A student put a plastic bottle full of water in the freezer and left it overnight. The next morning the water was frozen but the bottle was found to have cracked.
   (a) Explain what has happened to the water molecules to cause this to happen.
   (b) Suggest what the student could have done to avoid the bottle cracking but still have frozen water in the morning.

3. Use the word bank to help you complete the summary on intermolecular forces of attraction.

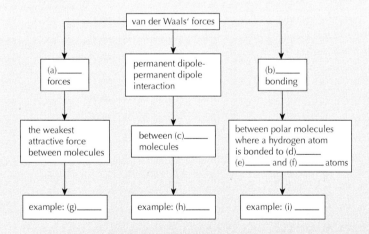

📖 Word bank

bromine, fluorine, hydrogen, hydrogen chloride, London dispersion, nitrogen, oxygen, polar, water

CHEMISTRY IN CONTEXT: HYDROGEN BONDING AND HYDROGEL

Hydrogels are polymers which are hydrophilic, which means they are attracted to water. One common polymer used to make hydrogels is sodium polyacrylate (poly(sodium propenoate)). The repeating unit in the polymer is:

If all of the Na^+ ions are removed the negative charges on the oxide ions repel each other and the polymer chains uncoil. Water molecules are attracted to the negative charges and hydrogen bonds form.

Figure 1.2.27: *Hydrogen bonding enables hydrogel to absorb water*

The hydrogel can absorb hundreds of times its own weight in water which makes hydrogel suitable for use in disposable nappies. Hydrogels are also used in the manufacture of soft contact lenses, wound dressings and drug delivery systems. Scientists in Australia have developed a stronger hydrogel material which could eventually be used for spinal cord replacements and as a synthetic human cartilage. Scientists at the National University of Singapore have developed a superhydrogel which can absorb water in the atmosphere

KEEP UP TO DATE!
You can keep up to date with the development and uses of hydrogels by looking up 'uses of hydrogels' or 'development of hydrogels at Singapore university' on the internet.

which has evaporated from the sea. This provides a source of fresh water from sea water. Sunlight can then be used to evaporate the water from the gel. The hydrogel can then be reused.

Viscosity, solubility and miscibility

Viscosity

The type of bonding present between molecules affects the viscosity (thickness) of a liquid. This can be demonstrated in the simple experiment shown in figure 1.2.28. The steel balls are released at the same time.

substance:	water	ethanol	diethyl ether
structure:	$\overset{\delta-}{O}$ $\underset{\delta+}{H}$ $\underset{\delta+}{H}$	$\overset{\delta-}{O}$ $\underset{\delta+}{H}$ C_2H_5	O C_2H_5 C_2H_5
molecular mass:	18	46	74
number of electrons:	10	26	42

Figure 1.2.28: *The presence of hydrogen bonding increases the viscosity of a liquid so a steel ball falls at different speeds depending on viscosity*

We might expect the liquid with the biggest molecules (diethyl ether) to be the most viscous – the more electrons the bigger the London dispersion forces. However, it is the least viscous of the liquids. Ethanol is more viscous than diethyl ether because it has hydrogen bonding between molecules but it is less viscous than water. This is because water has more highly polar -OH groups than ethanol, which allows more strong hydrogen bonds to form between water molecules than between ethanol molecules.

GO! Activity 1.2.7

1. The experiment in figure 1.2.28 was repeated using glycerol (molecular mass = 92):

$$H_2C - O^{\delta-} - H^{\delta+}$$
$$HC - O^{\delta-} - H^{\delta+}$$
$$H_2C - O^{\delta-} - H^{\delta+}$$

   (a) Predict how the time taken for the steel ball to reach the bottom of the cylinder would compare to other liquids used in the experiment.
   (b) Explain your answer to (a).

2. A bottle of ethanol left in a freezer at −18°C for several hours was found to be more viscous than when it was at room temperature.
   Explain this observation.

Solubility

Water is often referred to as the universal solvent which gives an indication of the fact that water will dissolve many compounds. Water's ability to dissolve a wide range of substances is due to the high polarity of the bonds within water. Water is particularly efficient at dissolving polar and ionic substances.

Hydrogen chloride (HCl) is an example of a polar covalent compound which dissolves easily in water to form hydrochloric acid:

$$HCl(g) \;+\; H_2O(\ell) \;\rightarrow\; H^+(aq) \;+\; Cl^-(aq)$$

The (aq) symbol is used to indicate that the ions are hydrated in solution – the polar covalent bond between the hydrogen and the chlorine breaks and the resulting ions are attracted to water molecules.

Figure 1.2.29: *Hydrogen chloride dissolves readily in water to form hydrochloric acid*

Sugars like glucose are soluble in water because they can form hydrogen bonds with water molecules. Glucose molecules have five hydroxyl groups each of which can form hydrogen bonds, as shown in figure 1.2.30 (only three hydroxyl groups are shown forming hydrogen bonds to make the diagram clearer):

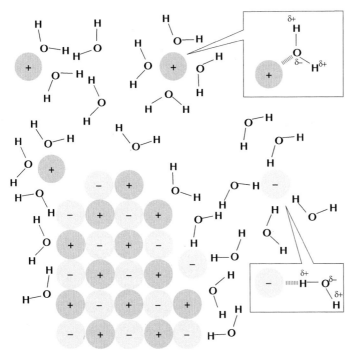

Figure 1.2.30: *Hydrogen bonding between glucose and water molecules*

Ionic substances dissolve in a similar way to polar substances, bearing in mind that the ions already exist in the lattice. The water molecules interact with the ions in the lattice, break the electrostatic attraction between the ions and the ions go into solution. A force of attraction is created between the ions and the polar water molecules – the ions are hydrated with water molecules. This is shown diagrammatically for an ionic solid in figure 1.2.31.

Figure 1.2.31: *The ions in an ionic solid become hydrated when it dissolves*

Non-polar substances like wax cannot form strong intermolecular forces of attraction with water so are not dispersed throughout the water like soluble polar covalent and ionic substances. Fats and oils are also non-polar so do not dissolve in water. However, there are non-polar solvents which can dissolve non-polar substances like fat by forming London dispersion forces between the molecules. One of these is tetrachloromethane (CCl_4) which used to be used as a solvent in dry cleaning – so called because it doesn't involve water. Soil sticks to clothes and skin because of natural oils from the skin. The non-polar solvents can dissolve the oil and the soil is released. The action of tetrachloromethane on fat is shown diagrammatically in figure 1.2.32.

SQA KEY AREA

= fat particle

= tetrachloromethane

> **Hint**
>
> Ionic compounds and polar molecular compounds generally tend to be soluble in polar solvents like water and insoluble in non-polar solvents like heptane. Non-polar molecular substances tend to be soluble in non-polar solvents and insoluble in polar solvents. Beware, there are exceptions to the solubility rule!

Figure 1.2.32: *Non-polar solvents can dissolve non-polar solids like fat*

Figure 1.2.33: *New cooking techniques have been developed as chefs better understand the chemistry and physics behind cooking techniques*

Figure 1.2.34: *Asparagus being cooked in water loses flavour as flavour molecules dissolve into the water*

CHEMISTRY IN CONTEXT: HOW COOKING AFFECTS FLAVOUR

Flavour molecules and solubility

Chefs such as Heston Blumenthal, using an understanding of the science of cooking, began exploring different food combinations and ways of retaining and enhancing the flavour of foods. They also began increasing the theatre of the dining experience. This can be seen in television shows such as The Great British Menu.

Cooking vegetables – the influence of functional groups

When you cook green vegetables their cellulose walls break down, softening the vegetable. However, flavour as well as vitamins may be lost during the cooking process. Some flavour molecules are soluble in water, others in oil. This depends on the structure of the molecules.

Asparagus is traditionally steamed or cooked in water. However, the flavour molecules in asparagus are soluble in water. Heston Blumenthal realised cooking asparagus in the traditional method robbed it of flavour. In the case of asparagus, he realised a better flavour could be achieved by tossing the spears in butter or oil.

For other green vegetables, such as broccoli and green beans, the reverse was true. Their flavour molecules were soluble in oil rather than in water. These vegetables are best cooked using water.

The solubility of flavour compounds depends on the structures of the flavour molecules.

The vanilloids, vanillin, zingerone, eugenol and capsaicin, are flavour compounds whose molecules share a structural similarity.

They all contain a carbon ring with a methoxy- and a hydroxy- group attached to the ring. They differ in the other groups attached to the ring (X) (see figure 1.2.36).

Figure 1.2.35: Some flavour molecules have the structure shown, where X can vary

vanillin: found in vanilla pods

zingerone: found in ginger root

eugenol: found in cloves

capsaicin: one of the molecules which gives chilli its hot taste

Figure 1.2.36: Vanilloids all have a structural similarity

Vanillin and zingerone both have the hydroxyl group on the ring, and a side chain containing a carbonyl group. These groups can form hydrogen bonds to water molecules. Vanillin and zingerone are water soluble flavour molecules.

Eugenol and capsaicin also have the hydroxyl group. However, the presence of hydrocarbon chains as part of their structure makes them more soluble in oils.

They can travel through cell walls into body cells where they can have differing effects.

Eugenol has a numbing effect if rubbed on our gums, and is used as an analgesic by dentists. Oil of cloves, which contains eugenol, is still used as a remedy to soothe toothache. A solution containing only 10 parts per million of capsaicin will have a burning effect if placed on our tongues. Rubbing your face after cutting a chilli can cause considerable pain as capsaicin dissolves in oils on our skins and is quickly absorbed.

CHEMISTRY IN CONTEXT: DRY-CLEANING SOLVENTS

Tetrachloromethane is envionmentally unfriendly, contributing to the depletion of the ozone layer. It is a carcinogen and also a toxic substance linked to liver damage, so it is no longer used in dry cleaning. Perchloroethene (tetrachloroethene), also known as perc, is perhaps the most used solvent in the UK for dry-cleaning. It has excellent cleaning power and is stable, non-flammable and gentle on most garments. However, like most solvents of this kind, human exposure should be kept to a minimum.

Figure 1.2.37: *Perc is the most widely used solvent for dry-cleaning in the UK*

At one time the machines used in dry-cleaning were vented; their fumes and drying exhausts were released into the atmosphere, the same as modern tumble-dryer exhausts. This not only contributed to environmental contamination but also much reusable perc was lost to the atmosphere. Much stricter controls on solvent emissions have ensured that all dry-cleaning machines in the developed world are now fully enclosed, and no solvent fumes are released into the atmosphere. In enclosed machines, solvent recovered during the drying process can be reused to clean further loads. The majority of modern enclosed machines also incorporate a computer-controlled drying sensor, which automatically senses when all traces of perc have been removed. This system ensures that only the smallest amount of perc fumes will be released when opening the door at the end of the cycle.

Figure 1.2.38: *A dry-cleaning advert from the 1950s*

The dry-cleaning industry is in the process of replacing perc with other chemicals. Siloxane is an odourless, colourless, non-oily liquid used as a carrier for detergents during dry-cleaning. It is becoming increasingly popular because it is promoted as a 'green' solvent. Siloxane does not interact with the textiles and helps to maintain their colour and quality. The detergents carried by the solvent release the soiling and allow the solvent to carry it away.

The use of liquid carbon dioxide as an environmentally safe cleaning agent has been developed as an alternative to the traditional solvents. A detergent is added to increase the cleaning ability of the liquid CO_2 allowing it to remove dirt from the garments. After the cleaning cycle, the dry-cleaning machine pulls the mixture of liquid CO_2 and detergent away from the clothes and then cleans and re-uses the chemicals.

This process does not require heating the garments, and therefore is gentle on the fabric. However, there is some resistance to change from the dry-cleaning industry, mainly because of the cost of converting the machinery.

GO! Activity 1.2.8

1. Using + to represent a positive ion and – to represent a negative ion, sketch a diagram to show how three water molecules arrange themselves around the ions when they hydrate them.

2. Perc is the most widely used dry-cleaning solvent. Its structure is shown:

$$\begin{array}{c} \text{Cl} \\ \diagdown \\ \text{C}=\text{C} \\ \diagup \diagup \\ \text{Cl} \text{Cl} \end{array}$$

(a) What type of bonding exists between carbon and chlorine atoms in perc? (You may wish to look at the electronegativity values on page 34.)

(b) What type of intermolecular force exists between perc molecules?

(c) With the help of the diagrams below, explain how perc is able to dissolve fat.

= 'perc' molecule

= fat molecule

(d) Explain why water cannot dissolve fat molecules.

(e) By considering the polarity of the carbon dioxide molecule, suggest why carbon dioxide could be used in dry-cleaning instead of perc.

Miscibility

Miscibility is the property of liquids to mix in all proportions, forming a solution. Water and ethanol, for example, are miscible and this forms the basis for alcoholic drinks. The water and ethanol molecules are both polar and they can hydrogen bond with each other which allows them to mix completely.

Figure 1.2.39: *Water and ethanol are miscible because hydrogen bonds form between the water and ethanol molecules*

Figure 1.2.40: *The alcohol in whisky is mixed with water before it is bottled. The ice in the glass will gradually melt and also mix with the alcohol.*

Oil and water are two well-known liquids which are immiscible – they form two separate layers when mixed. Oil is non-polar so does not form forces of attraction with the polar water molecules so they separate when shaken together. You are likely to have added bromine solution (bromine dissolved in water) to hexane in the laboratory to see if the hexane decolourises the bromine. You should have noticed that the hexane forms a separate layer on top of the water and the mixture has to be shaken to get the hexane in contact with the bromine. Hexane, like oil, is non-polar so does not form hydrogen bonds with water. Also, the non-polar bromine moves from the water layer into the non-polar hexane layer as it is more soluble in hexane.

Figure 1.2.41: *Oil is immiscible with water so floats on top of the water causing widespread environmental problems*

GO! Activity 1.2.9

The structure of propanone is shown:

$$H_3C$$
$$C = O$$
$$H_3C \quad \delta^+ \quad \delta^-$$

Suggest, with the aid of a diagram, why propanone is miscible with water.

CHEMISTRY IN CONTEXT: PROTEINS IN FABRICS

Proteins are a good example of how the various types of bonding and interactions can exist together. Figure 1.2.42 shows how four types of interaction between the various side chains of the different amino acids, including hydrogen bonding, hold the protein molecule in a particular shape.

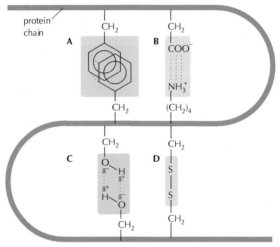

Figure 1.2.42: *There are four types of interactions which hold the protein molecule in a specific shape: A: London dispersion forces between non-polar groups; B: ionic bonds between COO^- and NH_3^+ ions; C: hydrogen bonding between polar groups such as $-O^{\delta-} - H^{\delta+}$; D: covalent bond formed between two sulphur atoms*

Learning checklist

In this chapter you have learned:

- In a covalent bond atoms share pairs of electrons. The nuclei of the atoms are held together by their mutual attraction for the shared electrons.

- In pure covalent bonding the shared pair of electrons are shared equally by the atoms in the molecule.

- In polar covalent bonding there is unequal sharing of the bonded electrons which results in one atom having a slightly negative charge (δ^-) and the other having a slightly positive charge (δ^+). This creates a permanent dipole.

- Ionic bonds are the electrostatic attraction between positive and negative ions.

- Ionic compounds form lattice structures of oppositely charged ions.

- Ionic formulae give the simplest ratio of each type of ion in the substance.

- Electronegativity is a numerical measurement on a scale of 0 – 4 (high) of an element's ability to attract bonding electrons.

- The difference in electronegativity between the atoms in a compound gives an indication of the type of bonding present.

- The type of bonding changes gradually as the difference in electronegativity between atoms increases – this is known as the bonding continuum.

- The bonding continuum has ionic at one end and pure covalent at the other and polar covalent between the two extremes.

- Compounds formed between metals and non-metals are not always ionic.

- Physical properties of substances need to be considered when deducing bonding type.

- Intermolecular forces act between molecules and are known as van der Waals' forces.

- London dispersion forces, permanent dipole–permanent dipole interactions including hydrogen bonding are all types of van der Waals' forces.

- London dispersion forces are weak attractions between temporary dipoles in all molecules and are particularly significant between non-polar molecules.

- The more electrons there are in an atom or molecule the stronger the London dispersion forces.

- Permanent dipole–permanent dipole interactions are attractions between polar molecules which have permanent dipoles.

- A molecule will only be polar if one side of the molecule is slightly negative (δ^-) and the other side slightly positive (δ^+).

- Permanent dipole–permanent dipole interactions are stronger than London dispersion forces for molecules with similar numbers of electrons, which results in higher melting points and boiling points in the substance with permanent dipole–permanent dipole interactions.

- Hydrogen bonds form between highly polar molecules which have hydrogen bonded to the highly electronegative elements fluorine, oxygen or nitrogen.

- A hydrogen bond is stronger than other forms of permanent dipole–permanent dipole interactions but weaker than covalent bonds.

- Hydrogen bonding gives compounds unusually high melting and boiling points because they are the strongest van der Waals' force so need more energy to separate the molecules, e.g. water.

- When water is cooled to 4ºC and below it expands and decreases in density because the water molecules form a more open structure with increased hydrogen bonding.

- Compounds with molecules which have hydrogen bonding between them are more viscous than compounds with molecules with other intermolecular forces.

- The polar nature of water makes it a good solvent for ionic compounds and polar covalent molecular compounds.

- Non-polar solvents can dissolve non-polar substances.

- The molecules of polar covalent liquids which are miscible with water form hydrogen bonds with water molecules.

- To predict the solubility of a compound the key features to be considered are the possibility of hydrogen bonds being formed and whether the shape of the molecule makes it polar.

3 Oxidising and reducing agents

You should already know

- Extraction of a metal from its ore is called reduction.
- Reduction of ores involves metal ions gaining electrons.
- Oxidation is the opposite of reduction and involves the loss of electrons by an atom or ion.
- Reduction and oxidation always take place together. The combined reaction is called a redox reaction.
- Reducing agents help reduction to take place by providing electrons.
- Ion-electron equations can be written to describe the processes of reduction and oxidation.
- Redox equations can be formed by combining the ion-electron equations for reduction and oxidation.

(National 5 Chemistry: Chemistry in society: Metals)

Learning intentions

- In this chapter you will learn about:
- Elements, molecules, group ions and compounds as oxidising and reducing agents.
- Uses of oxidising agents.
- Ion-electron equations for reduction and oxidation and redox equations.
- The electrochemical series.

Oxidation and reduction

Many chemical reactions involve electrons being lost by one 'particle' and gained by another. The 'particle' can be an atom, molecule or ion. These types of reaction are known as redox reactions. The particles losing electrons are said to be oxidised. The particle gaining electrons is said to be reduced. Ion-electron equations can be written for oxidation and reduction and they can be added to form the redox reaction. In a redox reaction reduction and oxidation take place at the same time.

🔍 Hint

Memory aid for what happens to the electrons:

Oxidation	Reduction
Is	Is
Loss	Gain

In the thermite reaction aluminium reacts with iron(III) oxide, and molten iron and aluminium oxide are produced in a very exothermic reaction. The liquid iron can be run off to repair cracks in the likes of railway lines. The iron(III) ion is reduced to iron and the aluminium atom is oxidised to aluminium(III) ion:

$$Fe^{3+}(s) + 3e^- \rightarrow Fe(\ell) \qquad \text{reduction}$$

$$Al(s) \rightarrow Al^{3+}(s) + 3e^- \qquad \text{oxidation}$$

$$Fe^{3+}(s) + Al(s) \rightarrow Fe(\ell) + Al^{3+}(s) \qquad \text{redox}$$

Figure 1.3.1: *The thermite reaction is an extremely exothermic reaction where aluminium reduces iron oxide to iron*

Elements as oxidising and reducing agents

In the thermite reaction the iron(III) ions are reduced by gaining electrons from the aluminium atoms. The aluminium atoms are acting as **reducing agents**. The aluminium atoms are oxidised and lose electrons to the iron(III) ions. The iron(III) ions are acting as **oxidising agents**.

> ### 🔍 Hint
>
> Reducing agents lose electrons in a reaction and are themselves oxidised. Oxidising agents gain electrons in a reaction and are themselves reduced.

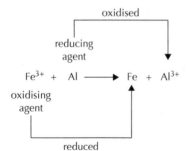

Many metals have one, two or three electrons in their outer energy levels which are available to be transferred to other particles. Metals therefore act as reducing agents.

Worked example

When zinc is added to copper(II) sulfate solution the copper(II) ions are displaced from solution by the zinc and copper metal, and zinc ions are formed. The sulfate ions do not take part in the reaction and are called spectator ions.

$Cu^{2+}(aq) + 2e^- \rightarrow Cu(s)$	reduction
$Zn(s) \rightarrow Zn^{2+}(aq) + 2e$	oxidation
$Cu^{2+}(aq) + Zn(s) \rightarrow Cu(s) + Zn^{2+}(aq)$	redox

The copper(II) ions are being reduced by the zinc atoms which are acting as reducing agents. The zinc atoms are being oxidised by the copper(II) ions which are acting as oxidising agents.

Figure 1.3.2: *Zinc displaces blue copper(II) ions from solution. The zinc atoms act as reducing agents*

Oxidising agents must be able to accept electrons easily. Many non-metal elements have electron arrangements that are only one, two or three electrons short of the electron arrangement of a noble gas. This means that the atoms of these non-metals can gain electrons to make a stable octet of electrons. Non-metal elements therefore act as oxidising agents.

Worked example

When green chlorine gas is bubbled through colourless potassium bromide solution, the solution turns orange. The bromide ions are displaced from solution and form bromine molecules. The chlorine molecules are reduced to chloride ions. The potassium ions do not take part in the reaction – they are spectator ions.

$2Br^-(aq) \rightarrow Br_2(aq) + 2e^-$	oxidation
$Cl_2(g) + 2e^- \rightarrow 2Cl^-(aq)$	reduction
$Cl_2(g) + 2Br^-(aq) \rightarrow 2Cl^-(aq) + Br_2(aq)$	redox

The chlorine molecules are acting as oxidising agents and are themselves reduced to chloride ions. The bromide ions are acting as reducing agents and are themselves oxidised to bromine molecules.

Electronegativity values (page 34) can be used to estimate if an element is likely to be an oxidising or reducing agent. Electronegativity is a measure of the attraction the atoms of an element have for bonding electrons. The higher the value, the greater the attraction for electrons so fluorine, with a value of 4·0, will be a strong oxidising agent. The group 7 elements (halogens) are all strong oxidising agents.

The lower the electronegativity value the more likely the element is to be a reducing agent. The group 1 metals (alkali metals) have low electronegativity values and are strong reducing agents.

Table 1.3.1: *Electronegativity values for the group 1 and group 7 elements*

Strong reducing agents	Strong oxidizing agents
Group 1	Group 7
Li 1·0	F 4·0
Na 0·9	Cl 3·0
K 0·8	Br 2·8
Cs 0·8	I 2·5
Fr 0·8	At 2·1

● GO! Activity 1.3.1

For each of the redox reactions described below:

(i) write down the ion-electron equations for the reduction and oxidation processes taking place (label each equation as reduction/oxidation).

(ii) balance the ion-electron equations and combine them to form the overall redox equation.

(iii) identify the oxidising and reducing agents.

(a) Zinc metal reacting with silver nitrate solution to form silver metal and zinc nitrate solution.

$$Zn(s) + 2AgNO_3(aq) \rightarrow 2Ag(s) + Zn(NO_3)_2(aq)$$

(b) Bromine solution reacting with potassium iodide (KI(aq)) solution to form iodine and potassium bromide solution.

$$Br_2(aq) + 2KI(aq) \rightarrow I_2(aq) + 2KBr(aq)$$

(c) Chromium metal reacting with tin(II) sulfate solution to form chromium(III) sulfate solution and tin.

$$2Cr(s) + 3SnSO_4(aq) \rightarrow Cr_2(SO_4)_3(aq) + 3Sn(s)$$

CHEMISTRY IN CONTEXT: MANUFACTURE OF BROMINE

Compounds of bromine are mainly used for flame-proofing, as pesticides and in the manufacture of dyes. Bromide salts are found in sea water but in such small concentrations as to not be economically viable. Some inland seas, such as the Dead Sea, contain bromine at a concentration over 100 times higher than in normal sea water.

The bromine plant at the Dead Sea, together with a plant manufacturing bromine compounds, have made Israel one of the biggest producers of bromine in the world.

Chlorine is used to displace the bromide ions from solution. Chlorine gas is bubbled through acidified sea water and the bromine formed is removed as a gas from the water by blowing air through it:

Figure 1.3.3: *Bottle of liquid bromine*

$$Cl_2(g) + 2Br^-(aq) \rightarrow Br_2(aq) + 2Cl^-(aq)$$

The chlorine is acting as an oxidising agent.

The bromine vapour is difficult to handle and so is converted back into bromide ions by reacting with sulfur dioxide and water:

$$Br_2(g) + SO_2(g) + H_2O(\ell) \rightarrow H_2SO_4(aq) + 2HBr(aq)$$

This results in a much more concentrated solution of bromide ions from which it is easier to produce high-purity bromine. Chlorine is again passed through the solution and bromine vapour is produced which is then purified by distillation.

Figure 1.3.4: *The salt concentration in the Dead Sea is so high that the water is dense enough for people to easily float on its surface*

Compounds, group ions and molecules as oxidising and reducing agents

The industrial extraction of iron from iron oxide is carried out in a blast furnace (see page 252). The iron ions are reduced by carbon monoxide molecules, which are acting as **reducing agents**:

$$Fe_2O_3(s) + 3CO(g) \rightarrow 2Fe(\ell) + 3CO_2(g)$$

Hydrogen peroxide (H_2O_2) is one of the most powerful **oxidising agents** known.

Examples of hydrogen peroxide acting as an oxidising agent:

1. In acidic solutions Fe^{2+} is oxidised to Fe^{3+}:

$2Fe^{2+}(aq) \rightarrow 2Fe^{3+}(aq) + 2e^-$	oxidation
$H_2O_2(\ell) + 2H^+(aq) + 2e^- \rightarrow 2H_2O(\ell)$	reduction
$2Fe^{2+}(aq) + H_2O_2(\ell) + 2H^+(aq) \rightarrow 2Fe^{3+}(aq) + 2H_2O(\ell)$	redox

2. Again, in acidic solutions, the sulfite ion is oxidised to the sulfate ion:

$SO_3^{2-}(aq) + H_2O(\ell) \rightarrow SO_4^{2-}(aq) + 2H^+(aq) + 2e^-$	oxidation
$H_2O_2(\ell) + 2H^+(aq) + 2e^- \rightarrow 2H_2O(\ell)$	reduction
$SO_3^{2-}(aq) + H_2O_2(\ell) \rightarrow SO_4^{2-}(aq) + H_2O(\ell)$	redox

Working out ion-electron equations

The reduction equations in examples 1 and 2 and the oxidation equation in example 2 are more complex than previous examples encountered. These more complicated ion-electron equations involve hydrogen ions and water molecules and can be worked out as follows:

1. Write down the main reactant(s) and product(s) for the reduction/oxidation and make sure there is the same number of each element (not oxygen) on each side of the equation.

2. Add water to one side to balance the oxygen.

3. Add $H^+(aq)$ to the other side to balance the hydrogen atoms.

4. Add electrons to the same side as the $H^+(aq)$ ions so that both sides of the equation have the same charge.

> **Hint**
>
> Although you have to know how to write ion-electron equations many of them are listed in the electrochemical series in the SQA data booklet.

Applying these rules to example 2:

(a) Reduction:

1. There are two hydrogens on each side so there is no need to balance.
$$H_2O_2(\ell) \rightarrow H_2O(\ell)$$

2. The oxygen atoms are not balanced. Add one water molecule to the right–hand side:
$$H_2O_2(\ell) \rightarrow 2H_2O(\ell)$$

3. Add two $H^+(aq)$ ions to the left hand side to balance the hydrogen atoms.
$$H_2O_2(\ell) + 2H^+(aq) \rightarrow 2H_2O(\ell)$$

4. Add two electrons to the left–hand side to balance the 2+ charge so that there is zero charge on both sides of the equation:
$$H_2O_2(\ell) + 2H^+(aq) + 2e^- \rightarrow 2H_2O(\ell)$$

(b) Oxidation:

1. There is one sulfur on each side so there is no need to balance.
$$SO_3^{2-}(aq) \rightarrow SO_4^{2-}(aq)$$

2. The oxygens are not balanced so add one water to the left–hand side
$$SO_3^{2-}(aq) + H_2O(\ell) \rightarrow SO_4^{2-}(aq)$$

3. Add $2H^+(aq)$ to the right–hand side to balance the hydrogen atoms.
$$SO_3^{2-}(aq) + H_2O(\ell) \rightarrow SO_4^{2-}(aq) + 2H^+(aq)$$

4. Add two electrons to the right–hand side to balance the 2+ charge.
$$SO_3^{2-}(aq) + H_2O(\ell) \rightarrow SO_4^{2-}(aq) + 2H^+(aq) + 2e^-$$

The SO_3^{2-} ion is an example of a group ion acting as a reducing agent. The permanganate ion (MnO_4^-) and dichromate ion ($Cr_2O_7^{2-}$) are examples of group ions which act as strong oxidising agents when in an acidic solution.

Acidified potassium permanganate (potassium manganate(VII)) solution reacting with iron(II) sulfate.

Worked example: 1

acidified MnO_4^- (aq)

$Mn^{2+}(aq) + Fe^{3+}(eq)$

$Fe^{2+}(aq)$

Figure 1.3.5: *Acidified pemanganate acting as an oxidising agent*

The iron(II) ions are reduced to iron(III) ions.

$Fe^{2+}(aq) \rightarrow Fe^{3+}(aq) + e^-$ oxidation

The permanganate ions act as oxidising agents and are reduced to manganese(II) ions.

$MnO_4^-(aq) \rightarrow Mn^{2+}(aq)$ reduction

The ion-electron equation for the reduction reaction can be worked out using the balancing rules:

1. There is one Mn ion on each side so there is no need to balance.

$$MnO_4^-(aq) \rightarrow Mn^{2+}(aq)$$

2. The oxygens are not balanced so four H_2O need to be added to the right–hand side

$$MnO_4^-(aq) \rightarrow Mn^{2+}(aq) + 4H_2O(\ell)$$

3. Add eight $H^+(aq)$ to the left–hand side to balance the hydrogen atoms.

$$MnO_4^-(aq) + 8H^+(aq) \rightarrow Mn^{2+}(aq) + 4H_2O(\ell)$$

4. There is a total of 7+ charge on the left–hand side and 2+ on the right–hand side. Add five electrons to the left–hand side to balance the 2+ charge on the right.

$$MnO_4^-(aq) + 8H^+(aq) + 5e^- \rightarrow Mn^{2+}(aq) + 4H_2O(\ell)$$

The two ion-electron equations can be combined to give the redox equation. The number of electrons in each ion-electron equation must be the same, so the oxidation equation must be multiplied by 5:

$5Fe^{2+}(aq) \rightarrow 5Fe^{3+}(aq) + 5e^-$ oxidation

$MnO_4^-(aq) + 8H^+(aq) + 5e^- \rightarrow Mn^{2+}(aq) + 4H_2O(\ell)$
reduction

$$MnO_4^-(aq) + 8H^+(aq) + 5Fe^{2+}(aq) \rightarrow Mn^{2+}(aq) + 5Fe^{3+}(aq) + 4H_2O(\ell) \quad \text{redox}$$

Note: The potassium and sulfate ions do not take part in the reaction – they are spectator ions.

Worked example: 2

Acidified potassium dichromate reacting with tin(II) chloride.

The tin(II) ions are oxidised to tin(IV) ions.

$$Sn^{2+}(aq) \rightarrow Sn^{4+}(aq) + 2e^- \quad \text{oxidation}$$

The dichromate ions act as oxidising agents and are reduced to chromium(III) ions.

$$Cr_2O_7^{2-}(aq) \rightarrow Cr^{3+}(aq) \quad \text{reduction}$$

The ion-electron equation for the reduction reaction can be worked out using the balancing rules.

1. There are two Cr ions on the left–hand side so two Cr ions are needed on the right hand side.

$$Cr_2O_7^{2-}(aq) \rightarrow 2Cr^{3+}(aq)$$

2. The oxygens are not balanced so seven H_2O need to be added to the right–hand side

$$Cr_2O_7^{2-}(aq) \rightarrow 2Cr^{3+}(aq) + 7H_2O(\ell)$$

3. Add $14H^+(aq)$ to the left–hand side to balance the hydrogen atoms.

$$Cr_2O_7^{2-}(aq) + 14H^+(aq) \rightarrow 2Cr^{3+}(aq) + 7H_2O(\ell)$$

4. There is a total of 12+ charge on the left–hand side and 6+ on the right–hand side. Add six electrons to the left–hand side to balance the 6+ charge on the right.

$$Cr_2O_7^{2-}(aq) + 14H^+(aq) + 6e^- \rightarrow 2Cr^{3+}(aq) + 7H_2O(\ell)$$

The two ion-electron equations can be combined to give the redox equation. The number of electrons in each ion-electron equation must be the same, so the oxidation equation must be multiplied by 3:

$$3Sn^{2+}(aq) \rightarrow 3Sn^{4+}(aq) + 6e^- \quad \text{oxidation}$$

$$Cr_2O_7^{2-}(aq) + 14H^+(aq) + 6e^- \rightarrow 2Cr^{3+}(aq) + 7H_2O(\ell) \quad \text{reduction}$$

$$3Sn^{2+}(aq) + Cr_2O_7^{2-}(aq) + 14H^+(aq) \rightarrow 3Sn^{4+}(aq) + 2Cr^{3+}(aq) + 7H_2O(\ell) \quad \text{redox}$$

Potassium dichromate can be used as an oxidising agent to oxidise alcohols (see page 142).

GO! **Activity 1.3.2**

1. When copper is added to nitric acid with a certain concentration, nitrogen monoxide and copper(II) nitrate are formed. Part of the equation for the reaction is shown below:

    $$Cu(s) + NO_3^-(aq) \rightarrow Cu^{2+}(aq) + NO(g)$$

    (a) Write the ion-electron equation for the oxidation reaction.
    (b) Write the ion-electron equation for the reduction reaction.
    (c) Combine the oxidation and reduction equations to give the balanced redox equation.
    (d) Identify the oxidising and reducing agents in the reaction.

2. Thiosulfate ions ($S_2O_3^{2-}$) can decolourise iodine molecules:

    $$2S_2O_3^{2-}(aq) + I_2(aq) \rightarrow S_4O_6^{2-}(aq) + 2I^-(aq)$$

    (a) Write the ion-electron equation for the oxidation reaction.
    (b) Write the ion-electron equation for the reduction reaction.
    (c) Identify the oxidising and reducing agents in the reaction.

3. In each of the following examples complete the ion-electron equations and state whether it is oxidation or reduction.

    (a) $ClO_3^-(aq) \rightarrow Cl_2(g)$
    (b) $ClO^-(aq) \rightarrow Cl^-(aq)$
    (c) $V^{3+}(aq) \rightarrow VO_3^-(aq)$
    (d) $FeO_4^{2-}(aq) \rightarrow Fe^{3+}(aq)$

Using oxidising agents

Hydrogen peroxide is an extremely strong oxidising agent and acts as a very effective 'bleach' as it is able to break down coloured compounds. It is used to bleach wool, cotton and paper as well as lighten hair and even whiten teeth.

High concentration hydrogen peroxide, when mixed with a fuel, acts as an oxidising agent. This combination has been used in a type of jet pack used to propel individuals through the air. Peroxide was thought to have been used as an oxidising agent in the bombs used in the 7 July 2005 London bombings.

The strong oxidising power of **potassium permanganate** makes it useful in a number of areas, particularly as an antiseptic. Dilute solutions are used to treat mild skin conditions and fungal infections of the hands and feet and can also cause some viruses to become inactive. Potassium permanganate is used in the water treatment industry to remove iron and hydrogen sulfide (rotten egg smell). It can be used in fish farms to kill parasites which infect the fish. Some florists use potassium permanganate for extending the life of fresh-

Figure 1.3.6: *The European Union chemical hazard symbol for oxidising agents*

Figure 1.3.7: *Hydrogen peroxide acts as an oxidising agent which removes colour when it is used to bleach hair*

cut flowers. It is also added for its disinfectant properties, as they help to control algae spread in the water.

Potassium permanganate reacts with ethene, which makes it useful for removing ethene produced by ripening fruit when it is being transported – when used in this way it is referred to as a 'gas scrubber'.

Potassium permanganate/ethane-1,2-diol–filled 'ping–pong balls' are used in some countries like Australia to help fight bush fires. One firefighting technique involves deliberately burning an area in front of an advancing bush fire in a controlled way, which effectively creates a barrier between the fire and the surrounding area. The ping–pong balls can be dropped from a helicopter in the desired area. The potassium permanganate is such a strong oxidising agent it causes the ethane-1,2-diol to ignite. This in turn causes any flammable debris around it to burn so that when the bush fire reaches the area there is nothing left to burn.

Figure 1.3.8: *Controlled fires created using potassium permanganate/glycerol ping-pong balls dropped from helicopters to create 'backfires'*

The electrochemical series

The electrochemical series (table 1.3.2) lists various substances in order of how well they act as reducing/oxidising agents. The ion-electron equations are written as reductions but the $\rightleftharpoons$ symbol indicates that they are reversible, so the oxidation ion-electron equation is the reverse of the reduction. The strongest reducing agents are the elements at the top right of the series and the strongest oxidising agents are the substances at the bottom left of the series. This is in line with some of the deductions made about elements and their electronegativity values – group 1 elements are strong reducing agents (top right in the electrochemical series) and group 7 elements are strong oxidising agents (bottom left in the electrochemical series).

Notice also that the strong oxidising agents $MnO_4^-(aq)$ and $Cr_2O_7^{2-}(aq)$ detailed above appear at the bottom left of the electrochemical series and the ion-electron equation is given for each. The sulfite ion ($SO_3^{2-}(aq)$), which can be oxidised by hydrogen peroxide, appears on the right–hand side of the table, so to get the oxidation equation the reduction equation is reversed.

The electrochemical series can be used to predict whether a redox reaction will occur. Just looking at the substance involved alone gives no indication as to whether it will react. The general rule is that if an oxidising agent is below the reducing agent in the electrochemical series then a reaction will occur.

 Hint

The electrochemical series is in the SQA data booklet so you don't need to memorise it.

Table 1.3.2: *The electrochemical series*

Reaction		Strong reducing agents
$Li^+(aq) + e^-$	$\rightleftharpoons$	$Li(s)$
$Cs^+(aq) + e^-$	$\rightleftharpoons$	$Cs(s)$
$K^+(aq) + e^-$	$\rightleftharpoons$	$K(s)$
$Ca^{2+}(aq) + 2e^-$	$\rightleftharpoons$	$Ca(s)$
$Na^+(aq) + e^-$	$\rightleftharpoons$	$Na(s)$
$Mg^{2+}(aq) + 2e^-$	$\rightleftharpoons$	$Mg(s)$
$Al^{3+}(aq) + 3e^-$	$\rightleftharpoons$	$Al(s)$
$Zn^{2+}(aq) + 2e^-$	$\rightleftharpoons$	$Zn(s)$
$Cr^{3+}(aq) + 3e^-$	$\rightleftharpoons$	$Cr(s)$
$Fe^{2+}(aq) + 2e^-$	$\rightleftharpoons$	$Fe(s)$
$Ni^{2+}(aq) + 2e^-$	$\rightleftharpoons$	$Ni(s)$
$Pb^{2+}(aq) + 2e^-$	$\rightleftharpoons$	$Pb(s)$
$2H^+(aq) + 2e^-$	$\rightleftharpoons$	$H_2(g)$
$Sn^{4+}(aq) + 2e^-$	$\rightleftharpoons$	$Sn^{2+}(aq)$
$Cu^{2+}(aq) + 2e^-$	$\rightleftharpoons$	$Cu(s)$
$O_2(g) + 2H_2O(\ell) + 4e^-$	$\rightleftharpoons$	$4OH^-(aq)$
$I_2(s) + 2e^-$	$\rightleftharpoons$	$2I^-(aq)$
$Fe^{3+}(aq) + e^-$	$\rightleftharpoons$	$Fe^{2+}(aq)$
$Ag^+(aq) + e^-$	$\rightleftharpoons$	$Ag(s)$
$Br_2(\ell) + 2e^-$	$\rightleftharpoons$	$2Br^-(aq)$
$O_2(g) + 4H^+(aq) + 4e^-$	$\rightleftharpoons$	$2H_2O(\ell)$
$Cr_2O_7^{2-}(aq) + 14H^+(aq) + 6e^-$	$\rightleftharpoons$	$2Cr^{3+}(aq) + 7H_2O(\ell)$
$Cl_2(g) + 2e^-$	$\rightleftharpoons$	$2Cl^-(aq)$
$MnO_4^-(aq) + 8H^+(aq) + 5e^-$	$\rightleftharpoons$	$Mn^{2+}(aq) + 4H_2O(\ell)$
$F_2(g) + 2e^-$	$\rightleftharpoons$	$2F^-(aq)$
Strong oxidising agents		

Worked example: 1

Nobel Prize winners

Figure 1.3.9: *Akira Yoshino, John B. Goodenough and M. Stanley Whittingham after their Nobel lectures*

John B. Goodenough, M. Stanley Whittingham and Akira Yoshino were jointly awarded the 2019 Nobel Prize for the development of lithium-ion (Li-ion) batteries. This lightweight, rechargeable and powerful battery has been developed over many years and is now used in everything from mobile phones and laptops to electric vehicles. It can also store significant amounts of energy from solar and wind power, making possible a fossil-free society. Lithium-ion batteries are based on lithium ions moving backwards and forwards between electrodes. As in all electrochemical cells, oxidation and reduction reactions take place at the electrodes.

Will chlorine react with potassium bromide solution?

From the electrochemical series we see that chlorine is bottom left so is a strong oxidising agent (easily reduced) and bromide ions are above chlorine on the right–hand side, so the reaction will occur.

We can also get the ion-electron equations from the electrochemical series.

The chlorine is reduced so the equation is written as it is in the electrochemical series:

$$Cl_2(g) + 2e^- \rightarrow 2Cl^-(aq)$$

The bromide ions are on the right–hand side so the equation must be reversed:

$$2Br^-(aq) \rightarrow Br_2(aq) + 2e^-$$

Note that the potassium ion (K^+) is top left in the electrochemical series so would not be able to act as a reducing agent – it is a spectator ion.

Worked example: 2

Will iron(II) sulfate solution react with potassium dichromate solution?

From the electrochemical series we see that Fe^{2+} is bottom right so is a reducing agent and $Cr_2O_7^{2-}$ ions are on the bottom left so are oxidising agents, so the reaction will occur.

The reduction equation is written as it is in the electrochemical series:

$$Cr_2O_7^{2-}(aq) + 14H^+(aq) + 6e^- \rightarrow 2Cr^{3+}(aq) + 7H_2O(\ell)$$
$$\text{reduction}$$

The Fe^{2+} ions are on the right–hand side so the equation must be reversed:

$$Fe^{2+}(aq) \rightarrow Fe^{3+}(aq) + e^- \quad \text{oxidation}$$

Worked example: 3

Will a solution of iron(III) ions react with a solution of bromide ions?

The electrochemical series shows that although Fe^{3+} ions are oxidising agents and Br^- ions are reducing agents, Fe^{3+} ions are above the Br^- ions so reaction will not take place.

Will MnO_4^{2-} ions react with iodine (I_2) solution?   **Worked example: 4**

Both are on the left–hand side of the electrochemical series so are oxidising agents so reaction will not take place.

GO! Activity 1.3.3

(a) Use the electrochemical series to predict whether the following reactions will take place:

   (i) $Br_2(aq) + SO_3^{2-}(aq) \rightarrow 2Br^-(aq) + SO_4^{2-}(aq)$
   (ii) $2Ag(s) + Cu^{2+}(aq) \rightarrow 2Ag^+(aq) + Cu(s)$
   (iii) $Cr_2O_7^{2-}(aq) + Fe^{2+}(aq) \rightarrow 2Cr^{3+}(aq) + Fe^{3+}(aq)$
   (iv) $MnO_4^-(aq) + 2Br^-(aq) \rightarrow Mn^{2+}(aq) + Br_2(aq)$
   (v) $Cl_2(g) + I_2(aq) \rightarrow 2Cl^-(aq) + 2I^-(aq)$

(b) For the reactions in (a) which do take place, use the electrochemical series to write oxidation and reduction ion-electron equations.

(c) Combine the ion-electron equations in (b) to form redox equations.

(d) Identify the oxidising and reducing agents in each reaction.

Learning checklist

In this chapter you have learned:

- Reduction is a gain of electrons by a reactant in any reaction. ⬭ ⬭ ⬭

- Oxidation is a loss of electrons by a reactant in any reaction. ⬭ ⬭ ⬭

- In a redox reaction, reduction and oxidation take place at the same time. ⬭ ⬭ ⬭

- An oxidising agent is a substance which accepts electrons. ⬭ ⬭ ⬭

- A reducing agent is a substance which donates electrons. ⬭ ⬭ ⬭

- Oxidising agents are reduced. ⬭ ⬭ ⬭

- Reducing agents are oxidised. ⬭ ⬭ ⬭

- Elements can act as reducing and oxidising agents. ⬭ ⬭ ⬭

- Elements with low electronegativity values, like the group 1 metals, are strong reducing agents. ⬭ ⬭ ⬭

- Elements with high electronegativity values, like the group 7 elements, are strong oxidising agents.

- How to write reduction and oxidation ion-electron equations involving elements.

- Compounds, group ions and molecules can act as oxidising and reducing agents.

- How to write reduction and oxidation ion-electron equations involving compounds, group ions and molecules.

- Given a group ion, work out the balanced ion-electron equation.

- How to balance reduction and oxidation ion-electron equations and combine them to form the redox equation.

- Recognise oxidising and reducing agents in a redox equation.

- Carbon monoxide is a compound which acts as a reducing agent.

- Hydrogen peroxide, acidified permanganate and acidified dichromate solutions are strong oxidising agents.

- The oxidising property of hydrogen peroxide makes it useful as a bleach to remove colour from materials.

- The oxidising property of the permanganate ion makes it effective in killing fungi and bacteria and can inactivate viruses.

- The electrochemical series lists substances in order of how well they act as reducing/oxidising agents.

- Strong reducing agents are found at the top right of the electrochemical series.

- Strong oxidising agents are found at the bottom left of the electrochemical series.

- Ion-electron equations in the electrochemical series are written as reductions but can be reversed to obtain the oxidation equation.

- The positions of substances in the electrochemical series can be used to predict whether a redox reaction will take place.

- If an oxidising agent is below the reducing agent in the electrochemical series then a reaction will occur.

2

Nature's chemistry

1 Systematic carbon chemistry, alcohols and carboxylic acids

You should already know

- For straight-chain alcohols with up to eight carbons in the chain:
  - The effect of increasing size of alcohols on melting points and boiling points.
  - Saturated straight-chain alcohols contain the hydroxyl functional group and can be represented by the general formula $C_nH_{2n+1}OH$.
  - The molecular formulae for the alcohols and how to represent them as structural formulae.
- For straight-chain carboxylic acids with up to eight carbons in the chain:
  - The effect of increasing size of straight-chain carboxylic acids on melting points, boiling points and solubility in water.
  - Saturated straight-chain carboxylic acids contain the carboxyl functional group and can be represented by the general formula $C_nH_{2n+1}COOH$.
  - The molecular formulae for the alcohols and how to represent them as structural formulae.

(National 5 Chemistry: Nature's chemistry: Everyday consumer products)

Learning intentions

In this chapter you will learn about:

- The systematic nature of carbon chemistry.
- Systematic naming of straight-chain and branched alcohols from their structural formula.
- Drawing structural formulae for straight-chain and branched alcohols.
- Classifying alcohols due to the position of the hydroxyl group.
- Alcohols with more than one hydroxyl group.
- Properties of alcohols relating to structure.
- Systematic naming of straight-chain and branched carboxylic acids.
- Drawing structural formulae for straight-chain and branched carboxylic acids.
- Reaction of carboxylic acids with bases.

Systematic carbon chemistry

The study of the formulae and properties of carbon compounds shows that many of the compounds are related. Compounds can be grouped together thanks to these relationships. An understanding of patterns of formulae and properties gained in relation to one group of compounds can then be applied in relation to other groups of compounds and can aid understanding of these new compounds.

Carbon chemistry is described as **systematic** because of the patterns and order observed when studying the properties and formulae of related compounds.

Some revision of the terms and chemistry covered in relation to these groups of compounds in National 5 will help in understanding the chemistry that will be covered in Higher.

In National 5 some of these patterns were studied in relation to four different groups of carbon compounds: alkanes, alkenes, alcohols and carboxylic acids. Each group contains compounds that are related in terms of formulae and properties. A group of compounds related in this way is referred to as **homologous series**.

> ### 📖 Word bank
>
> • **homologous series**
>
> a family of carbon compounds that have similar chemical properties and show a gradual change in physical properties (e.g. boiling point) and can be represented by the same general formula

Alkanes and alkenes

Alkanes and alkenes are two homologous series of hydrocarbon compounds, i.e. compounds that only contain carbon and hydrogen atoms.

Alkanes

The alkanes, with the exception of methane which has only one carbon atom, are hydrocarbon molecules in which the carbon atoms are connected by single carbon-to-carbon bonds.

The formula for a carbon compound can be given as a molecular formula, a shortened structural formula or as a full structural formula.

Propane, the third member of the group, has molecular formula C_3H_8. This formula does not show, however, that the carbons are connected by single carbon-to-carbon bonds. A full structural formula shows the bonds between atoms, while a shortened structural formula does not.

full structural formula

$CH_3CH_2CH_3$ ← shortened structural formula

Alkane molecules which can be straight-chain or branched are referred to as **saturated**.

Alkenes

The alkenes are hydrocarbon molecules in which the two of the carbon atoms are connected by a double carbon-to-carbon bond. See, for example, the full structural formula for propene.

propene

SQA KEY AREA

Compounds that contain at least one double carbon-to-carbon bond are described as **unsaturated**.

It is possible to distinguish between saturated and unsaturated compounds using bromine solution. Unsaturated compounds will quickly decolourise bromine solution.

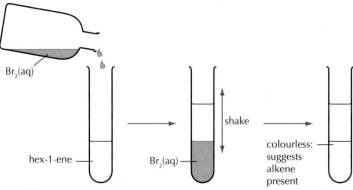

This reaction is an example of an **addition reaction**. In an addition reaction a double bond is broken, allowing two molecules to join together to form a single product molecule.

Figure 2.1.1: *Bromine solution is immediately decolourised when shaken with hex-1-ene*

hex-1-ene (colourless)   bromine solution (orange)   1,2-dibromohexane (colourless)

Isomers

Isomers are compounds which have the same molecular formula but different structural formulae.

Isomers can belong to the same homologous series or to different homologous series entirely.

Generally, if isomers belong to the same homologous series they will have slightly different physical properties.

Propan-1-ol and propan-2-ol have molecular formula C_3H_8O and are isomers. They have differences in their chemical and physical properties.

propan-1-ol
m.p. -124°C b.p. 97°C

propan-2-ol
m.p. -88°C b.p. 82°C

Propene and cyclopropane both have the molecular formula C_3H_6 but very different structures. One is unsaturated and would quickly decolourise bromine solution. The other is saturated and would not have this effect.

propene   cyclopropane

Propene and cyclopropane illustrate the point that isomers need not belong to the same homologous series.

Explaining differences in physical properties between carbon compounds

Trends in a homologous series – physical properties of alkanes

Physical properties refer to properties such as melting and boiling points, volatility (how easily they change from liquid to vapour) and density. The trend in boiling points of the first six alkanes is shown in table 2.1.1.

Table 2.1.1: *The shortened structural formulae and boiling points of the first six straight-chain alkanes*

Alkane	Shortened structural formula	Boiling point (°C)
methane	CH_4	−164
ethane	CH_3CH_3	−89
propane	$CH_3CH_2CH_3$	−42
butane	$CH_3(CH_2)_2CH_3$	−1
pentane	$CH_3(CH_2)_3CH_3$	36
hexane	$CH_3(CH_2)_4CH_3$	69

The increase in the boiling points of the alkanes is due to the increasing strengths of intermolecular forces. As the size of the molecules increases, the number of electrons increases creating more and stronger London dispersion forces between alkane molecules. This in turn means more energy is required to separate molecules and hence the trend in increasing boiling points as molecular size in the alkane homologous series increases.

The effect of different intermolecular forces

The type and relative strengths of intermolecular forces between molecules can also be used to explain the differences in properties such as boiling points, volatility and solubility.

ethane	methylamine	methanol	fluoromethane
b.p. −89°C	b.p. 49°C	b.p. 65°C	b.p. −79°C

Each of the molecules represented contains 18 electrons. However, the boiling points of the compounds are very different. The boiling points of methylamine and methanol are much higher than those of fluoromethane and ethane. This is because methylamine and methanol have hydrogen bonding between molecules. Fluoromethane is a polar molecule and there will be permanent dipole–permanent dipole interactions between molecules. In ethane only London dispersion forces can exist between molecules.

The ability to form hydrogen bonds to water molecules can also be used to explain the solubility of methylamine and methanol in water.

Figure 2.1.2: *Hydrogen bonds between methylamine molecules and a water molecule*

Alcohols

Naming straight-chain alcohols

All alcohols contain the hydroxyl (-OH) functional group.

—O—H
hydroxyl group

Straight-chain alcohols are named according to the number of carbons in the chain and the position of the carbon atom that the hydroxyl group is attached to in the chain.

The structure below represents pentan-2-ol.

> ### 🔍 Hint
> Carbon chains are numbered from the end nearer the carbon that a functional group is attached to.

The alcohol molecule contains five carbons and is saturated, so the first part of the name is pentan-.

The hydroxyl group is attached to the second carbon in the chain therefore -2-.

All alcohols have the ending –ol.

The name of the alcohol is therefore pentan-2-ol.

Naming branched alcohols

1. Name the longest carbon chain that contains the carbon to which the hydroxyl group is attached.
2. Number the chain from the end that the hydroxyl group is nearer to and split name with number of carbon which has hydroxyl group.
3. Name any branches (side chains). Branches are ordered alphabetically.

        e.g. CH_3 — methyl; C_2H_5 — ethyl; etc.

4. Indicate the position of the branches on the main chain.

Worked example

4	-ethyl	-3-	methyl	hexan-2-ol

Systematic name would be

1 and 2: Six carbons with hydroxyl on carbon 2.
3: Two branches
4: Branches on 3rd and 4th carbon

Drawing branched alcohols

Worked example

2-ethyl-4-methylpentan-1-ol

1. **pentan-1-ol** indicates five carbons in the longest straight chain, with the —OH group on carbon 1 Carbons are numbered so that the —OH group has the lowest number.
2. **4-methyl** indicates a —CH_3 group on the fourth carbon.
3. **2-ethyl** indicates a —C_2H_5 group on the second carbon.

Molecular formula: $C_8H_{18}O$

GO! Activity 2.1.1

1. Name the compounds with the following structural formulae:

(i)
```
    H   H   H   H   H   H
    |   |   |   |   |   |
H — C — C — C — C — C — C — H
    |   |   |   |   |   |
    H   |   H   |   O   H
      H—C—H H—C—H |
        |     |   H
        H     H
```

(ii)
```
                          H
                          |
                        H—C—H
          H             |
          |      H  H—C—H  H
      H—C—H H    |   |    |
        |   |    |   |    |
    H — C — C — C — C — C — H
        |   |    |   |    |
      H—C—H H H—C—H O   H
        |     |    |    H
        H     H    H
```

2. Draw full structural formulae for the following compounds:

   (i)   2,3-dimethylhexan-2-ol

   (ii) 2,5-dimethyl-4-propyloctan-3-ol

Primary, secondary and tertiary alcohols

Alcohols can be classified as **primary**, **secondary** or **tertiary** alcohols depending on the structure of the molecules and the position of the hydroxyl group in the molecule.

In **primary** alcohols the carbon that the hydroxyl group is attached to is attached to one other carbon in the chain. Methanol is the exception as it has only one carbon atom.

Butan-1-ol is an example of a primary alcohol.

```
    H   H   H   H
    |   |   |   |
H — C — C — C — C — O — H
    |   |   |   |
    H   H   H   H
```
butan-1-ol

In **secondary** alcohols the carbon that the hydroxyl group is attached to is attached to two other carbon atoms.

Butan-2-ol is an example of a secondary alcohol.

```
    H   H   H   H
    |   |   |   |
H — C — C — C — C — H
    |   |   |   |
    H   H   O   H
            |
            H
```
butan-2-ol

In **tertiary** alcohols the carbon atom that the hydroxyl group is attached to is attached to three other carbons.

2-Methylpropan-2-ol is an example of a tertiary alcohol.

2-methylpropan-2-ol

Diols and triols

Alcohols with **two hydroxyl groups** are referred to as **diols**.

Alcohols with **three hydroxyl groups** are referred to as **triols**.

The simplest diol is ethane-1,2-diol.

The simplest triol is propane-1,2,3-triol.

Propane-1,2,3-triol is also known as glycerol, the alcohol part of fats and oils (see page 111).

GO! Activity 2.1.2

1. There are eight isomeric alcohols with molecular formula $C_5H_{12}O$.
   (a) Draw structures for the isomers and name them.
   (b) Classify the isomers as primary, secondary or tertiary alcohols.

2. Draw a full-structural formula for the following compounds and state whether the alcohol is primary, secondary or tertiary.
   (i) 3-methylpentan-2-ol
   (ii) 2,3-dimethylhexan-3-ol

3. State whether each structural formula represents a primary, secondary or tertiary alcohol and name the alcohol.

   (i)

   (ii)

   (iii) $CH_3CH_2CH(CH_3)CH_2CH(OH)CH_3$

   (iv) $CH_3CH_2C(C_2H_5)(OH)CH_2CH_3$

4. Draw a structural formula for butan-2,3-diol.

Properties of alcohols relating to structure

Alcohols contain the hydroxyl group. The high electronegativity of oxygen and the shapes of the molecules mean alcohol molecules will be polar.

Figure 2.1.3: *Methanol and ethanol*

Hydrogen bonds will be able to form between the hydroxyl groups of adjacent alcohol molecules.

Figure 2.1.4: *Hydrogen bonds can form between the hydroxyl groups of adjacent alcohol molecules*

Hydrogen bonding helps explain many of the physical properties of the alcohols.

Boiling points of alcohols

The bar chart shows the boiling points of primary alcohols with up to 4 carbon atoms. They are:

CH_3OH	CH_3CH_2OH	$CH_3CH_2CH_2OH$	$CH_3CH_2CH_2CH_2OH$
methanol	ethanol	propan-1-ol	butan-1-ol

They are compared with the equivalent alkanes (methane to butane) with the same number of carbon atoms.

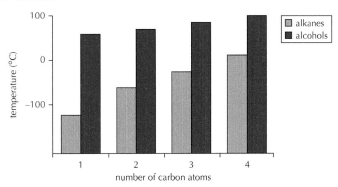

Figure 2.1.5: *Boiling points of alcohols compared to alkanes*

Notice that:

- The boiling point of an alcohol is always much higher than that of the alkane with the same number of carbon atoms.

- The boiling points of the alcohols increase as the number of carbon atoms increases.

The patterns in boiling point reflect the patterns of intermolecular attractions. The intermolecular forces that exist between alkane molecules are London dispersion forces. The larger the alkane molecule the more electrons it will have and the more sites there will be on adjacent molecules where London dispersion forces will exist. Because there are more electrons the temporary dipoles that give rise to London dispersion forces can be greater. More or greater forces between adjacent molecules will mean more energy will be required to separate molecules, leading to increasing boiling points.

With alcohol molecules as well as more London dispersion forces along the length of the hydrocarbon chains there are hydrogen bonds between the hydroxyl groups. Hydrogen bonds are much stronger than London dispersion forces, meaning more energy is required to separate alcohol molecules.

Alcohols have higher boiling points than corresponding alkanes due to the presence of hydrogen bonds in alcohols.

The trend of increasing boiling points as we go up the alcohol homologous series is due to more and greater London dispersion forces along the hydrocarbon chains.

Similar explanations help explain melting point trends and differences in viscosity and volatility (ease of evaporation) of the alcohols.

Diols and triols

Diols and **triols** have **high boiling points** due to strong **hydrogen bonding** between molecules.

A comparison of the boiling points of alcohols with equivalent fluoroalkanes (molecules containing the same number of electrons) shows the effect of hydrogen bonding in the alcohols. There is no hydrogen bonding between fluoroalkanes, only weaker London dispersion forces.

Table 2.1.2: *Boiling points of alcohols and fluoroalkanes*

Alcohols	Boiling point (°C)	Fluoroalkanes	Boiling point (°C)
ethanol	78	fluoroethane	−37
ethane-1,2-diol	196	1,2-difluoroethane	31
propane-1,2,3-triol	290	1,2,3-trifluoropropane	71

Solubility of alcohols

Table 2.1.3 Shows the solubility of some primary alcohols.

Table 2.1.3: *Solubilities of first eight straight-chain primary alcohols*

Name	Formula	Solubility (gl⁻¹)
Methanol	CH_3OH	miscible
Ethanol	C_2H_5OH	miscible
Propan-1-ol	C_3H_7OH	miscible
Butan-1-ol	C_4H_9OH	90
Pentan-1-ol	$C_5H_{11}OH$	27
Hexan-1-ol	$C_6H_{13}OH$	6
Heptan-1-ol	$C_7H_{15}OH$	1
Octan-1-ol	$C_8H_{17}OH$	0·3

The first three primary alcohols – methanol, ethanol and propan-1-ol – are totally miscible with water, i.e. they will mix completely with water in any proportions.

This is because hydrogen bonds can form between the alcohol molecules and the water molecules.

Figure 2.1.6: *Hydrogen bonds can form between methanol molecules and water molecules*

The solubility of alcohols decreases as the hydrocarbon tail of the alcohol molecule gets bigger. This is because as the size of the hydrocarbon tail increases, the covalent character of the molecules increase.

Carboxylic acids

All carboxylic acids contain the carboxyl (-COOH) functional group.

Propanoic acid and benzoic acid are both examples of carboxylic acids as they both contain the carboxyl functional group.

propanoic acid

benzoic acid

> ### 🔍 Hint
>
> Benzene is a hydrocarbon with molecular formula C_6H_6. The carbons in benzene were found to be joined in a ring structure with a hydrogen joined to each carbon. The circle in the centre of the structural formula represents the electrons not used to bond directly to other atoms in the structure.
>
>
>
> benzene

Naming carboxylic acids

Naming straight-chain carboxylic acids

The structure of the carboxyl group means it will always be on an end carbon. Naming straight-chain carboxylic acids is therefore straightforward. The name simply relates to the number of carbons in the chain.

Table 2.1.4: *Names and shortened structural formulae for first eight straight-chain carboxylic acids*

Carboxylic acid	Shortened structural formula
methanoic acid	HCOOH
ethanoic acid	CH_3COOH
propanoic acid	CH_3CH_2COOH
butanoic acid	$CH_3(CH_2)_2COOH$
pentanoic acid	$CH_3(CH_2)_3COOH$
hexanoic acid	$CH_3(CH_2)_4COOH$
heptanoic acid	$CH_3(CH_2)_5COOH$
octanoic acid	$CH_3(CH_2)_6COOH$

Naming branched carboxylic acids

1. Name the longest carbon chain containing the carboxyl group.

2. Name the branches (side chains). Branches are ordered alphabetically.

> **⚠ Remember this**
> Carboxylic acid names end in –*oic*.

$$\text{e.g. } CH_3 \text{ — methyl;} \qquad C_2H_5 \text{ — ethyl; etc.}$$

Remember about prefixes when there is more than one side chain.

3. Indicate the position of the branches on the main chain, numbering from the carboxyl group as carbon 1.

Worked example

Drawing branched carboxylic acids

Worked example

2,3-dimethylbutanoic acid

1. **butanoic** indicates four carbons in the longest straight chain.
2. **dimethyl** indicates two methyl groups (—CH_3).
3. **2,3** indicates the methyl groups are on carbons 2 and −3 – numbering is from the carboxyl group carbon.

Molecular formula : $C_6H_{12}O_2$

GO! **Activity 2.1.3**

1. Name the compounds with the following structures:

   (i)

   (ii)

2. Draw structures for the following compounds:

   (i) 2,4-dimethylpentanoic acid
   (ii) 3-ethyl-2-methylheptanoic acid

SQA KEY AREA

Reaction of carboxylic acids with bases

Neutralisation reactions

Carboxylic acids show typical acid properties and can be used to neutralise bases to form salts.

The name of the salt formed from a particular carboxylic acid will have the ending -oate. Ethanoic acid will form ethanoate salts.

Ethanoic acid will react with calcium carbonate to form calcium ethanoate, carbon dioxide and water.

$$2CH_3COOH(aq) \ + \ CaCO_3(s) \ \rightarrow \ (CH_3COO^-)_2Ca^{2+}\,(aq) \ + \ CO_2(g) \ + \ H_2O(\ell)$$
calcium ethanoate

Figure 2.1.7: *Kitchen work surfaces made from marble (calcium carbonate) can be damaged if carboxylic acids such as vinegar (ethanoic acid) are spilled on them*

Propanoic acid will react with sodium hydroxide to form sodium propanoate.

$$C_2H_5COOH(aq) \ + \ NaOH(aq) \ \rightarrow \ C_2H_5COO^-Na^+(aq) \ + \ H_2O(\ell)$$
sodium propanoate

Metal oxides would form the same salts as metal hydroxides.

GO! Activity 2.1.4

1. Name the following salts of carboxylic acids:
   (a) $C_3H_7COO^-Na^+$
   (b) $(CH_3CH_2CH_2CH_2CH_2COO^-)_2Ca^{2+}$
   (c) $CH_3CH(CH_3)CH_2COO^-K^+$

2. Write formulae equations for each of the following reactions:
   (a) ethanoic acid reacting with magnesium
   (b) pentanoic acid reacting with sodium oxide
   (c) propanoic acid reacting with calcium hydroxide
   (d) methanoic acid reacting with potassium carbonate

CHEMISTRY IN CONTEXT: SALTS OF CARBOXYLIC ACIDS AS PRESERVATIVES

Some facts about food waste

Each year about 18 million tonnes of food is thrown away and disposed of in landfill. Almost 50% of the food comes from our homes, with the rest being thrown away by food producers and retail outlets. The foods that are thrown away most in the UK are potaoes, bread and milk. On average more than 20 million slices of bread, 5 million glasses of milk and nearly 4.5 million potatoes will be thrown away each day. Other common foods wasted include bananas, tomatoes and cooked ham. The cost to the average household is nearly £700 a year – £60 per month. Most of the food is perfectly good but some of it is thrown away because it has spoiled.

Figure 2.1.8: *Mould grows on food when it becomes contaminated by bacteria and fungal spores*

Mould formation can be inhibited by added preservatives. The salts of some carboxylic acids are used as preservatives.

The sodium, potassium and calcium salts of propanoic acid can be added to breads and bakery products to minimise mould formation.

Sodium benzoate is added to foods with an acid pH such as fizzy drinks, jams and fruit pies as a mould inhibitor.

Figure 2.1.9: *Sodium benzoate is added to fizzy drinks as a preservative*

When the sodium benzoate dissolves the benzoate ions combine with hydrogen ions to give benzoic acid molecules.

$$C_6H_5COO^-(aq) \ + \ H^+(aq) \ \rightleftharpoons \ C_6H_5COOH(aq)$$

The benzoic acid molecules are the active mould inhibitor.

Learning checklist

In this chapter you have learned:

- Carbon chemistry is described as systematic because similar rules and patterns that apply to one set of compounds can often be applied to other sets of compounds.

- Groups of compounds that obey the same general formula and have similar chemical properties are referred to as a homologous series.

- Saturated carbon compounds contain single carbon-to-carbon bonds and unsaturated compounds contain at least one carbon to carbon double bond.

- Bromine solution can be used to distinguish between saturated and unsaturated carbon compounds.

- Isomers – molecules having the same molecular formula but different structural formulae – can belong to different homologous series.

- Physical properties of compounds can be explained in terms of the polarity of the molecules and the types of intermolecular forces that exist between molecules of the compounds.

- To name straight-chain and branched alcohols with up to eight carbons in the main chain indicating the position of the hydroxyl (-OH) group.

- To write molecular formulae and draw structural formulae for straight-chain and branched alcohols with up to eight carbons in the main chain.

- To classify alcohols as primary, secondary or tertiary.

- To classify alcohols with two hydroxyl groups as diols and with three hydroxyl groups as triols.

- To explain the effect that hydrogen bonding has on the physical properties of alcohols.

- Carboxylic acids contain the carboxyl (-COOH) functional group.

- To write molecular formulae and draw structural formulae for straight-chain and branched carboxylic acids with up to eight carbons in the main chain.

- To name the salts formed when carboxylic acids react with bases in neutralisation reactions.

2 Esters, fats and oils

You should already know

- Alcohols contain the hydroxyl functional group (–OH).
- Carboxylic acids contain the carboxyl functional group (–COOH).
- Naming of straight-chain and branched alcohols and carboxylic acids with no more than eight carbons in their longest chain.

(National 5 Chemistry: Nature's chemistry: Everyday consumer products)

Learning intentions

In this chapter you will learn about:

- Making esters.
- Condensation reactions.
- Uses of esters.
- Hydrolysis of esters.
- Fats and oils – naturally occurring esters.
- Saturation and unsaturation in fats and oils.
- Intermolecular bonding in fats and oils.

Making esters

Esters are a group of carbon compounds formed when carboxylic acids (molecules containing a carboxyl, –COOH, group) and alcohols (molecules containing a hydroxyl, –OH, group) react together.

Esters are found naturally and are the compounds mainly responsible for fruit flavours.

In the laboratory an ester can be made by heating a carboxylic acid and an alcohol together. A small amount of concentrated sulfuric acid (H_2SO_4), which acts as a catalyst, is added to the reaction mixture. A paper towel soaked in cold water

Figure 2.2.1: *Esters are the compounds mainly responsible for the flavours of fruit*

SQA KEY AREA

wrapped around the test tube acts as a condenser. Vapours given off during the warming of the reaction mixture condense on the sides of the boiling tube and run back into the reaction mixture.

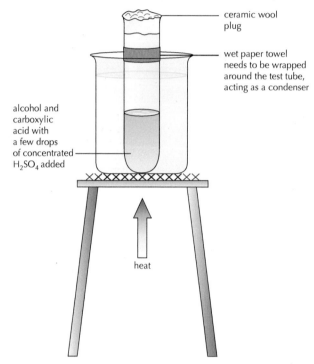

Figure 2.2.2: *Heating an alcohol and a carboxylic acid with concentrated sulfuric acid will produce an ester*

After heating for a few minutes the ester can be isolated by pouring the reaction mixture into a sodium carbonate solution. Unreacted acid will react with the sodium carbonate solution and the unreacted alcohol will dissolve leaving the ester, which is insoluble in aqueous solutions, floating on the surface of the sodium carbonate solution. Esters typically have a pleasant, fruity smell.

Figure 2.2.3: *Esters are insoluble in water and will form a layer on the surface when poured into an aqueous solution*

The name of an ester is derived from the parent alcohol and parent acid.

The first part of the name is derived from the alcohol and ends in -yl; the second part comes from the acid and ends in -oate.

When methanol and ethanoic acid react, methyl ethanoate is produced. The circled group in the ester structure is called the ester link.

methyl ethanoate

GO! Activity 2.2.1

Vitamin C, found in many fruits, can be classed as a cyclic ester.

Figure 2.2.4: *Oranges and other citrus fruits are a good source of vitamin C. Some people get their vitamin C from effervescent tablets*

(a) Identify the ester link in the vitamin C structure.

(b) Unlike most esters, vitamin C is very soluble in water.
Use your knowledge of bonding to explain why vitamin C will be soluble.

Condensation reactions

The type of reaction taking place when an ester forms is known as a **condensation reaction**.

The carboxyl group from the acid and the hydroxyl group from the alcohol react to form an ester linkage by eliminating a water molecule.

$$H-\overset{\overset{\textstyle H}{|}}{\underset{\underset{\textstyle H}{|}}{C}}-\overset{\overset{\textstyle O}{\|}}{C}-O-H \;+\; H-O-\overset{\overset{\textstyle H}{|}}{\underset{\underset{\textstyle H}{|}}{C}}-H \;\rightleftharpoons\; H-\overset{\overset{\textstyle H}{|}}{\underset{\underset{\textstyle H}{|}}{C}}-\overset{\overset{\textstyle O}{\|}}{C}-O-\overset{\overset{\textstyle H}{|}}{\underset{\underset{\textstyle H}{|}}{C}}-H \;+\; H-O-H$$

ethanoic acid   methanol   methyl ethanoate   water

The ⇌ symbol indicates the reaction is reversible. The concentrated sulfuric acid absorbs water and helps more ester form. Although the name of the parent alcohol forms the first part of the name of the ester, the part of the molecule derived from the parent acid tends to be drawn on the left. Table 2.2.1 lists some esters and their parent carboxylic acid and alcohol.

📖 Word bank

• **condensation reaction**
a reaction where molecules join by eliminating a small molecule, such as water, from between them

Table 2.2.1: *Structures and names of some simple esters and their parent acids and alcohols*

Ester	Parent carboxylic acid	Parent alcohol
methyl methanoate	methanoic acid	methanol
propyl ethanoate	ethanoic acid	propan-1-ol
ethyl butanoate	butanoic acid	ethanol
propyl propanoate	propanoic acid	propan-1-ol

Worked example 1 shows how esters can be named and their structures drawn. Worked example 2 shows how the parent alcohol/carboxylic acid of the ester can be identified and named and their structures drawn.

Worked example: 1

The ester that gives apples their flavour can be made in the laboratory from methanol and butanoic acid.

Name the ester, draw its full structural formula and write the molecular formula.

Worked answer:

Methanol gives **methyl** esters. Butanoic acid gives **butanoate** esters. The ester would be named **methyl butanoate**. The acid and alcohol have the following structures:

butanoic acid

methanol

Eliminating a water molecule from between the carboxylic acid and alcohol molecules, as shown above, gives an ester with the following structure:

Molecular formula: $C_5H_{10}O_2$

methyl butanoate

Worked example: 2

Bananas are the most popular fruit in Europe. The ester with the structure shown is used to give foods a banana flavour.

(i) Draw structures for the parent carboxylic acid and alcohol from which the ester is made.

(ii) Name the parent carboxylic acid and alcohol.

Worked answer:

The first thing to do is to identify the ester link.

The C-O bond in the ester link is the new bond that was formed during esterification. Break this bond to produce the alcohol and carboxylic acid fragments.

Add an OH to the acid fragment.

The parent acid is **ethanoic acid**.

Add an H to the alcohol fragment.

The structural formula for the alcohol is:

The name of the alcohol is **3-methylbutan-1-ol**.

The names of esters can appear quite complicated since the structures of the parent alcohol and carboxylic acid may contain branched chains. Some esters are therefore known by traditional names rather than by systematic names. The ester above is often indicated on labelling as isoamyl acetate.

GO! Activity 2.2.2

1. (a) Name the ester formed when ethanoic acid reacts with butan-1-ol.

    (b) Draw structural formulae for the two esters formed when propanoic acid reacts with butan-1-ol and butan-2-ol.

2. When bees sting they deposit a pheromone to attract other bees. The pheromone contains 2-methylbutyl ethanoate.

2-Methylbutyl ethanoate is a bee alarm pheromone (a chemical that will trigger a response from other bees). When bees are disturbed, individual bees will release this pheromone and waft it with their wings alerting other bees.

When a bee stings it deposits the pheromone with the sting and venom sac. This will trigger other bees to sting the victim close to the site of the original sting.

Figure 2.2.5

   (a) Name and draw structural formula for the carboxylic acid from which 2-methylbutyl ethanoate could be made.

   (b) 2-Methylbutan-1-ol has the following structure:

$$\begin{array}{ccccccc} & & H & H & H & H \\ & & | & | & | & | \\ H & - O - & C & - & C & - & C & - & C & - H \\ & & | & | & | & | \\ & & H & | & H & H \\ & & & H - C - H \\ & & & | \\ & & & H \end{array}$$

   Draw a structural formula for 2-methylbutyl ethanoate.

   (c) Describe how this ester could be made in the laboratory.

   (d) State a property of 2-methylbutyl ethanoate that is suggested by bees' actions.

3. The acid and alcohol below can be reacted to give an ester.

   (a) Name (i) the acid and (ii) the alcohol.

   (b) Write the molecular formula for the ester that will be formed from the acid and alcohol.

Uses of esters

Esters as flavourings and fragrances

Esters are used as flavourings and fragrances, as many have pleasant fruity smells.

Although fruit flavours are generally a complex mixture of compounds, many esters give the fruits their distinctive flavour. These pure compounds can be used in artificial flavourings.

pentyl ethanoate (pears)

3-methylbutyl ethanoate (bananas)

octyl ethanoate (oranges)

methylpropyl methanoate (raspberry)

pentyl butanoate (apricot, strawberry)

ethyl butanoate (pineapple)

methyl butanoate (apple)

Figure 2.2.6: *Esters as fruit flavourings*

Esters as solvents

Esters are excellent solvents and are widely used as solvents in industrial applications for non-polar compounds that don't dissolve in water. Ethyl ethanoate is used in nail care products.

> **GO!** Activity 2.2.3
>
> Create a table showing, for each of the esters in figure 2.2.6, the names of the parent acid and alcohol and the flavour of the ester.

Figure 2.2.7: *Ethyl ethanoate is used in nail care products*

Figure 2.2.8: *Many car body paints use esters as solvents*

As well as having good solvent properties esters are also suitable in paint applications as they are volatile and evaporate easily.

CHEMISTRY IN CONTEXT: USING ESTERS AS SOLVENTS

Because the boiling points of many esters are lower than 250°C they are classed as volatile organic compounds (VOCs).

Concerns have been raised about the impact on health of exposure to VOCs. Exposure can result in many adverse health effects depending on the type, level and length of exposure.

Health problems can range from minor ailments to major, long-term health complications including:

- *Eye, nose and throat irritation*
- *Headaches, dizziness and tiredness*
- *Nausea and vomiting*
- *Asthma exacerbation and allergic skin reactions*

- *Memory impairment and loss of coordination*
- *Cancer*
- *Liver damage*
- *Kidney damage*
- *Central nervous system damage.*

Care needs to be taken when using esters as solvents.

GO! Activity 2.2.4

The two isomeric esters shown below are used as solvents for printing inks.

(A)

(B)

(a) Name ester (A)

(b) (i) Draw a structural formula for the parent alcohol of ester (B).

    (ii) Name the parent alcohol.

(c) Explain why the esters can be described as 'isomeric'.

CHEMISTRY IN CONTEXT: DECAFFEINATING COFFEE

Figure 2.2.9: *Coffee beans before roasting*

Caffeine is a stimulant found in coffee and tea. It is also added to high-energy drinks as it can make you feel more alert. However, ingesting too much caffeine can have an adverse effect on the body. It can lead to raised blood pressure, increased heart rate and headaches. For that reason some people prefer to drink decaffeinated coffee or tea.

One of the methods used to decaffeinate coffee uses the ester ethyl ethanoate. The decaffeinated coffee can be termed 'naturally decaffeinated' since the ethyl ethanoate used can be extracted from natural materials. Coffee beans that have been steamed are placed in vats of the solvent. The caffeine is dissolved in the ethyl ethanoate while the water soluble compounds that give coffee its flavour remain in the bean. By repeating the process the caffeine can be removed, leaving the beans ready for drying and roasting. The solvent can then be evaporated, leaving caffeine which can be recycled and added to high-energy drinks.

Hydrolysis of esters

The formation of esters is reversible, i.e. the esters that are formed can be broken down to give the parent acid and alcohol.

The process is known as **hydrolysis** as water is reacting with the ester.

Esters can be hydrolysed by heating the ester under reflux (see figure 2.2.10) with a dilute acid such as hydrochloric acid or a dilute alkali such as sodium hydroxide.

When a dilute acid is used the parent alcohol and parent carboxylic acid are obtained.

When methyl propanoate is hydrolysed using dilute acid, methanol and propanoic acid would be obtained.

Figure 2.2.10: *The laboratory set-up used to heat under reflux. The vapours given off by heating the reaction mixture condense in the Liebig condenser and run back into the reaction mixture*

📖 Word bank

- **hydrolysis**
the breaking down of a molecule into separate molecules by reaction with water

$$\text{methyl propanoate} + \text{H-O-H} \longrightarrow \text{propanoic acid} + \text{methanol}$$

methyl propanoate   propanoic acid   methanol

When a dilute alkali is used to hydrolyse an ester a salt of the carboxylic acid is obtained. When methyl propanoate is hydrolysed using dilute sodium hydroxide solution, methanol and sodium propanoate would be obtained.

$$\text{methyl propanoate} + \text{NaOH} \longrightarrow \text{sodium propanoate} + \text{methanol}$$

methyl propanoate   sodium hydroxide   sodium propanoate   methanol

ⒼⓄ Activity 2.2.5

Draw structural formulae and name the products formed when the following esters are hydrolysed.

(i)   Propyl butanoate using dilute hydrochloric acid.

(ii)   Ethyl ethanoate using dilute sodium hydroxide solution.

(iii)

[structural formula: H–C(=O)(H)–C–O–C–C–C–C–H]

Using dilute hydrochloric acid solution.

(iv)

[structural formula: H–C–C–C(=O)–O–C–C–C–H]

Using dilute sodium hydroxide solution.

CHEMISTRY IN CONTEXT: WINE MAKING

Figure 2.2.11: *A wine producer checking the quality of a wine*

Our tongues only detect five basic tastes: sweet, salt, bitter, sour and umami (savouriness).

When tasting wines, wine tasters swirl the wine in the glass for 10–20 seconds and then smell the wine. The swirling releases some of the volatile molecules that give the wine its flavour. The wine is then sipped. Sometimes air can be drawn in through the mouth and breathed out through the nose. The heat in the mouth helps release more compounds into the air, allowing the taster to gain a fuller experience of the flavour.

As a wine ages, complex reactions involving the formation of esters from the condensation reactions between alcohols and acids created by different yeasts and hydrolysis of esters due to acidity in the wine cause the wine's character to change.

Activity 2.2.6

Methyl 2-aminobenzoate is an ester used to give sweets and
drinks a grape flavour.
(a) Write the molecular formula for methyl 2-aminobenzoate.
(b) Heating the ester with dilute hydrochloric acid breaks the
ester into 2-aminobenzoic acid and methanol.
   (i)   What name is given to this type of chemical reaction?
   (ii) Draw the structure for 2-aminobenzoic acid.

methyl 2-aminobenzoate

Fats and oils

Structure

Edible fats and oils are naturally occurring esters. They are produced in a condensation
reaction when long-chain carboxylic acids, commonly called fatty acids, react with
glycerol (propane-1,2,3-triol).

glycerol (propane-1,2,3-triol)   **stearic acid (octadecanoic acid), a fatty acid**

The hydrocarbon tail in a fatty acid is often shown as a serrated line.

Fats and oils are also called triglycerides.

The structure of a fat or oil can be represented as:

R^1, R^2 and R^3 are long
hydrocarbon chains
in the fatty acids.

Figure 2.2.12: *The shape of fat and oil molecules are very
complicated. They can be simplified as shown in figures
2.2.13, 2.2.14a and 2.2.14b*

Figure 2.2.13: *Simplified structure of a
fat/oil often called the 'tuning fork'
because of its shape*

Note the ester links in each figure.

The fatty acid chains in the molecules can be either saturated or unsaturated. If the fatty
acid chains are mostly saturated then the substance will likely be solid at room temperature

and be termed a **fat**. The greater the proportion of unsaturated fatty acid chains the more likely is the substance to be liquid at room temperature and be termed an **oil**.

In **fats** the shape of the molecules allows molecules to pack closer together with stronger van der Waals forces between the molecules than is the case in oils. In **oils** the presence of double bonds on the fatty acid parts of the molecules cause the hydrocarbon chains of the fatty acids to be more kinked, meaning the molecules are unable to pack as closely. This is shown in the simplified diagrams in figures 2.1.14a and 2.1.14b.

Figure 2.2.14a: *In fats, molecules can pack more closely than in oils. This leads to stronger van der Waals forces between molecules and higher boiling points*

The melting points of pure triglycerides show that the longer the fatty acids chains in the compound, the higher the melting point. The presence of double bonds in the fatty acid chains lowers the melting point.

Figure 2.2.14b: *In oils, double bonds in the fatty acid chains cause kinking, which prevents the molecules from packing as closely as in fats*

$$H_2C—OCO(CH_2)_{10}CH_3$$
$$H_3C(CH_2)_{10}OCO—C—H$$
$$H_2C—OCO(CH_2)_{10}CH_3$$

triaurin
mp 45°C

$$H_2C—OCO(CH_2)_{16}CH_3$$
$$H_3C(CH_2)_{16}OCO—C—H$$
$$H_2C—OCO(CH_2)_{16}CH_3$$

tristearin
mp 71°C

$$H_2C—OCO(CH_2)_7CH=CH(CH_2)_7CH_3$$
$$H_3C(CH_2)_7HC=HC(CH_2)_7OCO—C—H$$
$$H_2C—OCO(CH_2)_7CH=CH(CH_2)_7CH_3$$

triolein
mp −4°C

Classifying fats and oils

Fats and oils can be classified by their source, e.g. vegetable, animal or marine (fish). The proportion of the different fatty acids in the fats and oils depends on the source.

Table 2.2.2: *The composition of eight fats and oils*

Fat or oil	Percentage of fatty acid by type		
	Saturated	Mono-unsaturated	Polyunsaturated
Butter	66	30	4
Beef fat	52	44	4
Lard	41	47	12
Olive oil	14	77	9
Corn oil	13	25	62
Sunflower oil	11	20	69
Coconut oil	94	5	1

Fats and oils are mixtures of triglycerides that contain different fatty acids. From Table 2.2.2 we can see that the triglycerides in fats such as butter, beef fat and lard contain a significant proportion of unsaturated fatty acids and the triglycerides in oils contain a small amount of saturated fatty acids. Coconut oil contains mainly saturated fatty acids. The reason it is liquid at room temperature is that the fatty acid chains are much shorter than in other oils.

Bromine solution can be used to compare the degree of unsaturation of a fat or an oil. Bromine molecules can add across the double carbon to carbon bonds of the fatty acids. The more double carbon-to-carbon bonds in the fatty acids the more bromine molecules can add across.

A simple way to compare two oils to find out which is more unsaturated is to add bromine solution dropwise to equal volumes of each and see which decolourises more bromine solution.

Table 2.2.3 *Common fatty acids in fats and oils*

Molecular formula	Trivial name	Systematic name	Saturated/ Unsaturated
$C_{18}H_{36}O_2$	stearic	octadecanoic acid	saturated
$C_{18}H_{34}O_2$	oleic	9-octadecenoic acid	mono-unsaturated
$C_{16}H_{32}O_2$	palmitic	hexadecanoic acid	saturated
$C_{16}H_{30}O_2$	palmitoleic acid	9-hexadecenoic acid	mono-unsaturated
$C_{18}H_{32}O_2$	linoleic	9,12-octadecadienoic	polyunsaturated

The quick way to determine from a formula if a fatty acid is saturated is to look at the numbers of hydrogen and carbon atoms. A saturated fatty acid has twice as many hydrogens as carbons. For every two Hs that the fatty acid is short of this figure, there will be a double bond in the structure.

Fats, oils and health

Fats and oils are an essential component of a healthy human diet.

Fats and oils are a concentrated energy source, and are involved in the transport and storage of vitamins within the body.

Fats and oils as an energy source

Fats and oils provide more than twice the energy given by the equivalent mass of carbohydrates. Fats provide the body with 37 kilojoules of energy (9 food calories) per gram whereas carbohydrates only give 17 kilojoules of energy (4 food calories) per gram. In the UK 25%–50% of the energy in our diets will come from fats and oils in our foods.

Fats and oils are a necessary part of our diet but are also mainly responsible for one of the biggest health issues affecting the western world – obesity! Too much fat and oil in our diet leads to weight gain. Our body stores the extra fats as fatty tissue.

Medical research recognises that having a greater proportion of unsaturated fatty acids than saturated fatty acids in our diets has health benefits. In particular, polyunsaturated fatty acids (those with more than one carbon to carbon double bond in the chain) are thought to be beneficial.

Fat soluble vitamins

Fats and oils are also essential for the transport and storage of vitamins A, D, E and K in our bodies.

The structures of these vitamins mean that they will not be soluble in water but will be soluble in fats and oils.

Fat soluble vitamins

vitamin A: part of the visual pigment
$C_{20}H_{33}O$

$C_{29}H_{50}O_2$ **vitamin E: an antioxidant**

vitamin D_2: calcium metabolism
$C_{28}H_{44}O$ & bone growth

vitamin K_1: a blood clotting factor
$C_{31}H_{46}O_2$

Figure 2.2.15: *Good sources of vitamin A include cheese, eggs, yoghurt and liver*

CHEMISTRY IN CONTEXT: FAT SOLUBLE VITAMINS AND HEALTH

Vitamin A *is also known as* **retinol** *and has several important functions. These include strengthening our immune systems, keeping our skin and the linings of some parts of the body, such as the nose, healthy, and helping vision in low light conditions.*

Vitamin D *is sometimes referred to as the sunshine vitamin as our bodies make vitamin D when exposed to the sun's rays.*

Very few foods are good sources of vitamin D. Oily fish are among the best food sources. Vitamin D increases the amount of calcium and phosphate that can be absorbed through the small intestine. Calcium and phosphate are needed for the development and maintenance of strong bones and teeth.

A lack of vitamin D can lead to bone deformities such as rickets in children and bone pain and tenderness in adults.

In 2011 it was reported in the Daily Telegraph that the number of children admitted to hospital with rickets had risen by 140% from 2001 to 2008. Rickets was thought to be a condition that died out in the 1930s but research showed that 20% of young children showed some signs of the disease.

Children spending more time indoors watching television and playing computer games was thought to mean that their bodies were making less vitamin D.

In response the breakfast cereal producer Kellogg's announced that it would add vitamin D to all its children's cereals by the end of 2012.

Vitamin E acts as an antioxidant preventing red blood cells and essential fatty acids from being destroyed and helps maintain cell structure by protecting cell membranes.

Vitamin E is found in a wide variety of foods. The richest sources are plant oils such as soya, corn and olive oil. It is also found in cereals and cereal products.

Vitamin K is produced naturally by bacteria in our intestines. It is needed for normal blood clotting. There is increasing evidence that vitamin K is also needed to help build strong bones.

Vitamin K is found in green leafy vegetables, such as broccoli and spinach, vegetable oils and cereals.

Figure 2.2.16: *A child with rickets caused by lack of vitamin D*

CHEMISTRY IN CONTEXT: OMEGA-3 OILS

Dietary advice is that foods rich in omega-3 oils should be included in our diets. Oily fish such as herring, salmon, sardines and tuna are a rich source of omega-3 fatty acids.

Omega-3 fatty acids are fatty acids with a carbon to carbon double bond on the third last carbon of the hydrocarbon chain.

Omega-3 and omega-6 fatty acids are important components of cell membranes and are used by the body to make other compounds such as those involved with regulating blood pressure. The body can make all the omega-3 and omega-6 fatty acids it needs with the exception of two, linoleic acid and linolenic acid. These are known as essential fatty acids.

Figure 2.2.17: *Olive oil is a rich source of vitamin E*

Figure 2.2.18: *Oily fish such as sardines are a good source of omega-3 fatty acids*

linoleic acid $C_{18}H_{32}O_2$

linolenic acid $C_{18}H_{30}O_2$

The omega-3 oils have been linked to lowered cholesterol levels in the blood, reduced risk of heart attacks and improved brain function.

People from Mediterranean countries, Japan and Greenland have diets high in omega-3 oils and have a much lower incidence of heart disease than western countries. There is also growing interest in the role of omega-3 fatty acids in the prevention of diabetes and certain types of cancer.

Health experts suggest eating fish twice a week, with one of the times recommended to be eating oily fish.

GO! Activity 2.2.7

Internet research activity

Linoleic acid is an example of an omega-6 fatty acid. Oleic acid is an example of an omega-9 fatty acid.

Carry out an internet search to find out more about omega-3, 6 and 9 fatty acids, their importance to health and sources of these fatty acids in our diet.

Learning checklist

In this chapter you have learned:

- An ester can be identified from the presence of the ester group $-\overset{\overset{\displaystyle O}{\|}}{C}-O-$.

- The ester name is in the form -yl -oate where the first part of the name is derived from the parent alcohol and the second part from the parent carboxylic acid.

- Esters can be named given the names of the parent alcohol and carboxylic acid or the structural formula of the ester.

- Molecular formulae can be written and structural formulae drawn for esters given the name of the ester or structural formulae of their parent alcohol and carboxylic acids.

- Esters have characteristic smells and are used as flavourings and fragrances.

- Esters are used as solvents for non-polar substances.

- Esters can be made by reacting alcohols with carboxylic acids.

- Ester formation is an example of a condensation reaction.

- The ester link is formed when the hydroxyl group of the alcohol reacts with the carboxyl group of the acid eliminating a small molecule of water in the process.

- Esters can be broken down to the parent alcohol and parent carboxylic acid.

- The breakdown of an ester to an alcohol and a carboxylic acid is an example of hydrolysis.

- During hydrolysis a molecule breaks down to two smaller molecules by reacting with water.

- The products of hydrolysis of an ester can be named.

- Molecular formulae can be written and structural formulae drawn for the products of hydrolysis of an ester.

- Edible fats and oils are naturally occurring esters formed from the condensation reaction between glycerol and three fatty acid molecules.

- Fatty acid molecules can be saturated or unsaturated.

- The lower melting point of oils is related to the degree of unsaturation in the fatty acid molecules.

- Molecules in oils cannot pack as closely as those in oils, leading to weaker intermolecular attractions (van der Waals forces) and lower melting points.

- Bromine solution can be used to determine the degree of unsaturation of fats and oils.

- Fats and oils are an essential part of our diet, providing a concentrated source of energy.

- Fats and oils are needed to transport fat soluble vitamins in our bodies.

3 Soaps, detergents and emulsions

You should already know

- Edible fats and oils are naturally occurring esters.
- Esters can be hydrolysed.

(Higher Chemistry: Nature's chemistry: Esters, fats and oils)

Learning intentions

In this chapter you will learn about:

- Hydrolysis of fats and oils to produce soaps.
- The cleaning action of soaps, related to their structure.
- The development of detergents to overcome difficulties of using soaps.
- Emulsions and emulsifiers.

CHEMISTRY IN CONTEXT: A SHORT HISTORY OF SOAP MAKING

In ancient civilisations, such as Babylon, Egypt and Rome, it was known that mixing animal fats with ashes from burned wood produced a substance that helped to clean clothes. These civilisations were actually using soaps. Roman legend has it that the word 'soap' is derived from Mount Sapo, where animal sacrifices were made to the Roman gods, and from where rainwater washed a mixture of melted animal fats and wood ashes into the river below. There, the soapy mixture was found to be useful for washing clothing and skin. In the early beginnings of soap making the technique was only known to a few individuals. In the middle ages it is believed that crusaders returning to Europe brought with them soap from Aleppo in Syria. Soap-making factories were established in cities in Spain and Italy. Although soap was expensive, it was still in great demand. In Spain soap was made from olive oil. The soap was white and became known as Castile soap and was particularly favoured by royalty.

In Northern Europe the soaps were made from animal fats and were not as pleasant. It wasn't until 1791 when a Frenchman named LeBlanc discovered a chemical process for making soap, that the cost of production became significantly lower. In 1865 an American, William Sheppard, took out a patent for a liquid soap. Nowadays liquid soaps are increasing in popularity.

Figure 2.3.1: *Marseille in France became famous for its soap. The soap was traditionally made by heating sea water from the Mediterranean, olive oil and alkaline chemicals in a large cauldron for several days*

Hydrolysing fats and oils

In the chapter **Esters, fats and oils** you learned that edible fats and oils are naturally occurring esters.

An ester can be broken down (hydrolysed), to an alcohol and a carboxylic acid by heating the ester with either an alkali or with a dilute acid. When an ester is hydrolysed using an alkali a salt of the carboxylic acid is obtained.

When fats and oils are hydrolysed using alkali, salts of the long-chain fatty acids are formed. These are soaps.

Making soap

Soaps are made by hydrolysing a fat or oil using sodium or potassium hydroxide.

Fats and oils are triglycerides, naturally occurring esters of glycerol and long-chain fatty acids.

Figure 2.3.2: *Student making soap in the laboratory*

Hydrolysis breaks the ester linkages in the triglycerides.

3 NaOH

triglyceride

soap molecules

glycerol

When brine, a solution of sodium chloride, is added to the mixture the soap forms a solid crust that can be skimmed off from the surface of the mixture. This process is known as salting out.

Structure of soap molecules

A soap molecule has a long covalent hydrocarbon part, often referred to as the tail, and an ionic part, often referred to as the head.

The tail being covalent and non-polar is insoluble in water. It is termed **hydrophobic**, which means 'water hating'.

When soap is mixed with water, the soap breaks down (dissociates) in water to give soap ions with negatively charged heads and sodium ions. The negatively charged head of the soap ion is termed **hydrophilic**, which means 'water loving'.

The structure of soap ions helps us understand the cleaning action of soap.

hydrophilic head

hydrophobic tail

Figure 2.3.3: *Structure of a soap molecule*

When soap is used to clean oil or grease from a surface, the hydrophobic tails of the soap ions bury into the oil and grease. Agitation causes small grease droplets (micelles) to form in the water. The negative charges on the heads prevent the globules of oil from recombining. This allows the oil or grease to be washed off the surface.

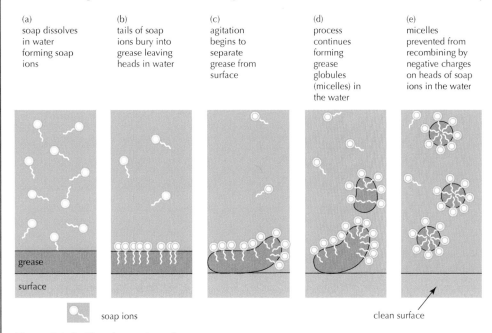

(a) soap dissolves in water forming soap ions

(b) tails of soap ions bury into grease leaving heads in water

(c) agitation begins to separate grease from surface

(d) process continues forming grease globules (micelles) in the water

(e) micelles prevented from recombining by negative charges on heads of soap ions in the water

grease

surface

soap ions

clean surface

Figure 2.3.4: *Cleaning action of soap*

Hard water

Hard water is water that contains dissolved calcium or magnesium ions. These ions can leach into the water if the water flows over or percolates through rocks such as chalk, limestone or dolomite.

When soap is used in hard water areas the calcium and magnesium ions combine with the soap ions to form an insoluble precipitate known as scum, making the soap much less effective. The deposits also clog fabrics and make them feel stiff.

To overcome this chemists have developed (soapless) detergents.

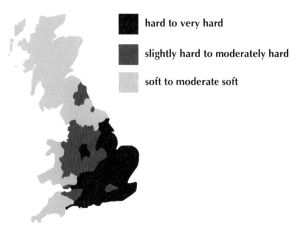

hard to very hard

slightly hard to moderately hard

soft to moderate soft

Figure 2.3.5: *A map of water hardness in the UK showing Scotland is a soft water area*

Detergents

A shortage of fats and oils during the First World War, and a need to develop a cleaning product that could be used in hard water areas where the water was rich in dissolved minerals, led to the development of the first synthetic detergents in Germany in 1916.

They were made by reacting long-chain hydrocarbons obtained from crude oil with sulfuric acid and then neutralising the product with sodium hydroxide to give molecules with a similar structure to soap. The molecules have a hydrocarbon part that is hydrophobic and an ionic part that is hydrophilic.

Figure 2.3.6: *Molecular structure of the detergent sodium dodecyl sulfate (sodium lauryl sulfate)*

One major benefit of detergents is they do not form a scum with hard water. Again, during the Second World War, a shortage of fats and oils for soap making led to further research and the development of more detergent products. Since then further research has led to the introduction of more and more cleaning detergent products including biological washing powders, fabric softeners and liquid hand-washes.

Sodium *p*-dodecyl benzene sulfonate and sodium dodecyl sulfate are detergents which act in a similar way to soap. The detergent ions have a **negative charge**. Detergents with this type of structure are referred to as **anionic** detergents.

$$H_{25}C_{12}-O-SO_2-O^-Na^+$$

**sodium lauryl sulfate or
sodium n-dodecyl sulfate**

(The *p*- in the name simply indicates where the hydrocarbon chain is attached to the ring of carbon atoms.)

60% of the detergents in use are anionic detergents and have a similar structure.

CHEMISTRY IN CONTEXT: OTHER TYPES OF SOAPLESS DETERGENTS

Other soapless detergents with a different structure have been developed. Some have no charge on the head and are termed **non-ionic detergents,** *while others have a positive charge on the head and are termed* **cationic detergents.**

Non-ionic detergents are included in washing-up liquids.

Figure 2.3.7: *A polyethylene ethoxylate – a non-ionic detergent used in washing-up liquids*

Polyethylene ethoxylates are a common type of non-ionic detergent. The head has repeating units containing oxygen atoms. It is uncharged but the presence of the oxygen atoms make the head end of the molecule polar.

The head is hydrophilic because hydrogen bonds can form between water molecules and the oxygen atoms in the chain.

Cationic *detergents are used in fabric softeners.*

Figure 2.3.8: *Trimethyldodecylammonium chloride – a cationic detergent*

The positive heads can bond to negative areas in fabric, leaving the tails on the surface of the fabric, giving a soft feel.

123

CHEMISTRY IN CONTEXT: WHAT'S IN THE BOX?

Not all dirt and stains are the same. Table 2.3.1 shows some common types of stain.

Table 2.3.1: *Types of stain*

Particulate	Greasy	Enzymatic	Oxidisable
metal oxides	vegetable oil	blood	fruits
rust	animal fat	egg	vegetables
clays	sweat	milk	wine
carbon	waxes	grass	coffee/tea

Figure 2.3.9: *There are many different types of stain that detergents will remove*

Garments might have stains from different sources. Removing different types of dirt and stains requires different chemicals and cleaning methods. In order to achieve this, particular cleaning formulations, containing different types of detergent molecules, also known as **surfactants**, *needed to be developed.*

Modern laundry cleaning products are complex mixtures of chemicals.

Table 2.3.2: *Types of compound in modern laundry cleaning products*

Types of compound	Function
builders	soften water
bleaches	oxidise coloured stains to colourless
surfactants	basic cleaning agents
enzymes	break down proteins and starches
fillers	help detergent disperse more evenly
optical brighteners	make clothes cleaner
polymers	break down soils and stop them being redeposited on fabrics

Emulsifiers

Oil and water do not normally mix and if shaken together will quickly separate. They can be made to mix by adding another substance. Substances that will allow liquids that are normally immiscible to mix are known as **emulsifiers**. When the two liquids mix in this way an **emulsion** is formed. The word emulsion comes from a Latin word meaning 'to milk'. Milk is a natural emulsion of milk fat and water. A protein in milk called casein acts as an emulsifier, stopping the milk fat and water separating.

Emulsifiers are one of the most widely used types of food additive.

The table shows foods in which emulsifiers are most commonly used.

Table 2.3.3: *Foods containing emulsifiers*

Figure 2.3.10: *Milk is a natural emulsion*

Foods containing emulsifiers		
biscuits	toffees/caramels	bread
breakfast cereals	chewing gum	margarine
cakes	chocolate	low-fat spreads
desserts/mousses	ice-cream/sorbets	peanut butter

📖 **Word bank**

• **emulsifier**

a substance that allows two normally immiscible substances to mix

• **emulsion**

mixture which contains small droplets of a liquid dispersed in another liquid

Emulsifiers have a structure related to soaps in that the molecules have a part that is hydrophilic and a part that is hydrophobic.

The most common emulsifiers used in food production are lecithin, E322, and mono- and di-glycerides of fatty acids, E471.

Lecithin is found naturally in egg yolks and soya beans. The molecules in lecithin have both a negatively charged atom and a positively charged atom.

Figure 2.3.11: *A molecule in lecithin showing the negative and positive parts of the molecule*

In lecithin the part of the molecule that has electrical charges is soluble in water, i.e. hydrophilic, while the fatty acid part is soluble in oils and fats.

Figure 2.3.12: *Lecithin is added to chocolate. It allows the chocolate to be moulded into bars*

Mono- and di-glycerides are grouped under E number, E471. They are commonly used as emulsifiers in bakery products.

These are made by reacting fatty acids, or oils and fats with a high content of the desired fatty acid, with glycerol.

In a mono-glyceride, one of the hydroxyl groups of a glycerol molecule has been replaced by a fatty acid chain. In di-glycerides, two of the hydroxyl groups of the glycerol molecule have been replaced by fatty acid chains.

a di-glyceride of palmitic acid

The presence of hydrophilic hydroxyl groups and hydrophobic fatty acid residues mean that mono- and di-glycerides can act as emulsifiers.

Adding mono- and di-glycerides to breads and cakes improves the texture and volume of the products. They keep cakes and bread soft, improving shelf life.

Figure 2.3.13: *Using emulsifiers improves the texture of baked goods*

Figure 2.3.13a: *Part of an ingredients label from a low fat spread showing the presence of emulsifiers*

Emulsifiers are useful in the processing of many foods, helping maintain their quality and freshness. In low-fat spreads, emulsifiers help prevent the growth of moulds, which would happen if the oil and fat separated.

Activity 2.3.1

One problem with chocolate is that it can develop a bloom when stored at too high a temperature. An emulsifier, sorbitan tristearate, can be added to help prevent this.

sorbitan tristearate

Explain why the structure of sorbitan tristearate allows the molecule to act as an emulsifier.

Figure 2.3.14: *Chocolate that has been stored at too high a temperature can develop a bloom*

CHEMISTRY IN CONTEXT: MAKING MAYONNAISE

The emulsifying effect of lecithin can be demonstrated by preparing a homemade mayonnaise.

If some olive oil and lemon juice are whisked together they soon separate. Whisking the lemon juice with two egg yolks and then whisking in the oil a small amount at a time will create a homemade mayonnaise. The lecithin in the egg yolks will prevent the oil separating.

Homemade mayonnaise recipe

2 large egg yolks

3 tablespoons lemon juice
1/4 teaspoon salt

pinch of white pepper
1 cup oil

Figure 2.3.15: *Mayonnaise is an example of an emulsion*

Learning checklist

In this chapter you have learned:

- Hydrolysis of edible fats and oils in alkaline conditions produces soaps.

- Soap molecules have an ionic head and a hydrocarbon tail.

- The ionic head is hydrophilic and dissolves well in water.

- The hydrocarbon tail is described as hydrophobic, water hating, and dissolves well in grease and oil.

- How to explain the cleaning action of soap.

- Hard water contains calcium and magnesium ions which forms a scum with soap.

- Detergents were developed to combat hard water conditions.

- Detergents clean in the same way as soaps.

- Emulsifiers are compounds that allow two normally immiscible liquids to mix.

- Emulsions are formed when two normally immiscible liquids mix.

- Emulsifier molecules have both hydrophilic and hydrophobic parts in their structure.

- Emulsifiers are widely used in the food industry and can be made by reacting edible oils with glycerol.

- When emulsifiers are made, only one or two fatty acid groups are linked to each glycerol backbone.

4 Proteins

SQA KEY AREA

You should already know

- Carboxylic acids contain the carboxyl functional group (–COOH).
- The names of the straight-chain carboxylic acids up to C_8.
- Condensation reactions involve molecules joining by eliminating a small molecule.

(Higher Chemistry: Nature's chemistry: Systematic chemistry, alcohols and carboxylic acids)

(Higher Chemistry: Nature's chemistry: Esters, fats and oils)

Learning intentions

In this chapter you will learn about:
- The importance of proteins.
- Amino acids.
- Dietary proteins.
- Condensation of amino acids to make proteins.
- The peptide link.
- Digestion.
- Enzymes as biological catalysts.
- Enzyme hydrolysis of dietary proteins.

The importance of proteins

Proteins are the major structural materials of animal tissue and are needed in our diet for the growth and repair of body tissue. However, as well as forming our body tissues, proteins are responsible for many of the biological processes that take place in our bodies.

Table 2.4.1: *Proteins have many different functions in our bodies*

hair and nails	a protein called alpha-keratin forms your hair and fingernails, and also is the major component of feathers, wool, claws, scales, horns and hooves
muscles	muscle proteins called actin and myosin enable all muscular movement — from blinking to breathing to rollerblading
cellular messengers	receptor proteins stud the outside of your cells and transmit signals to partner proteins on the inside of the cells
antibodies	antibodies are proteins that help defend your body against foreign invaders, such as bacteria and viruses
blood	the haemoglobin protein carries oxygen in your blood to every part of your body
brain and nerves	ion-channel proteins control brain signalling by allowing small molecules into and out of nerve cells
enzymes	enzymes in your saliva, stomach, and small intestine are proteins that help you digest food
cellular construction workers	huge clusters of proteins form molecular machines that do your cells' heavy work, such as copying genes during cell division and making new proteins

CHEMISTRY IN CONTEXT: MYOGLOBIN AND WHALES

The average human can remain underwater for one to two minutes. Japanese pearl fishers can hold their breath for about two minutes. The record for a human holding their breath underwater is held by Aleix Segura who, on 28 February 2016, held his breath for 24 minutes and 3 seconds at the 17th Mediterranean Dive Show in Barcelona. But many marine animals such as whales can hold their breath for much longer.

Figure 2.4.1: *A pod of sperm whales swimming off the coast of Sri Lanka*

The reason whales can hold their breath is to do with a protein called myoglobin. Whales have developed a highly specialised breathing system. A whale's lungs work in the same way as ours do, but they absorb a much higher percentage of the oxygen from the air that they breathe. A human absorbs about 15% of the oxygen inhaled. A whale, however, can absorb as much as 90% of the oxygen it breathes in. The oxygen carried in the blood by haemoglobin binds to the protein myoglobin found in muscle cells. In whales the muscle cells contain greater amounts of myoglobin than the muscle cells of other animals. This enables whales to absorb and store larger amounts of oxygen in their cells than other animals. Whales also use oxygen more efficiently. When whales dive, they can slow their heart rate. Pressure also constricts their blood vessels, slowing blood flow to certain organs without decreasing blood pressure. The sperm whale's respiratory system is among the most efficient in the world. It can hold its breath for 80 to 90 minutes diving to a depth of 3 kilometres in search of its primary food source, squid.

Amino acids

Proteins are natural polymers made up of amino acid units. Each amino acid has two functional groups, an amino group $-NH_2$ and a carboxyl group $-COOH$. The amino acids are sometimes termed α-amino acids because the amino group is attached to the α-carbon, the carbon next to the carboxyl group. The amino acids differ in the side chain (R) that is attached to the α-carbon.

Glycine (aminoethanoic acid) is the simplest amino acid.

glycine (aminoethanoic acid)

Alanine, 2-aminopropanoic acid, is the next simplest amino acid.

alanine (2-aminopropanoic acid)

There are 20 amino acids required for synthesis of body proteins.

Ten of the amino acids can be made in our bodies by biochemical processes involving enzymes but the other ten cannot be made by our bodies and must be obtained through our diet. These ten amino acids are known as **essential amino acids**.

Unlike fats and oils, amino acids cannot be stored by the body.

When two amino acid units join together they do so by eliminating a molecule of water from between them. This is an example of a condensation reaction.

The structure joining the amino acid units together is an **amide link**. In the chemistry of proteins the amide link is more commonly referred to as a **peptide link** since the amino acids join to form peptides. The peptide link has structure

Chains of amino acids joined together are known as peptides.

When two amino acids join a dipeptide is formed.

Three amino acid units joining together would be referred to as a tripeptide.

> 📖 **Word bank**
>
> • **essential amino acid**
>
> an amino acid that cannot be made by our bodies and that must be obtained from dietary proteins

Figure 2.4.2: *The condensation reaction between two amino acids*

> 📖 **Word bank**
>
> • **peptide link**
>
> the amide link formed when the carboxyl group of one amino acid molecule reacts with the amino group of another amino acid molecule

Many amino acid units joining together would be referred to as a polypeptide.

Proteins are polypeptides. The different proteins in the body are formed from different sequences of amino acids joined together.

SQA KEY AREA

Dietary proteins

If we were asked, most of us would be able to name protein-rich food – meat, fish, cheese, eggs, etc.

The amount of protein we require in our diet will depend on our age and our body mass. Nutritionists use a formula to calculate the mass of protein required in a person's diet.

Mass of protein required (grams) = Body mass (kg) × 0·8

Figure 2.4.3: *Protein-rich foods*

Table 2.4.2: *Recommended daily protein intake*

Age (years)	1–3	4–6	7–10	11–14	15–50	Over 50
Recommended protein requirement (grams)	15	20	28	42	55	53

Proteins in our diet provide the essential amino acids needed to make the different proteins required by our bodies.

Table 2.4.3: *The 20 amino acids needed to make proteins*

Non-essential amino acids (can be made by the body)		Essential amino acids (must be obtained in our diets)	
Name	Common symbol	Name	Common symbol
Alanine	Ala	Arginine	Arg
Asparagine	Asn	Histidine	His
Aspartic acid	Asp	Isoleucine	Ile
Cysteine	Cys	Leucine	Leu
Glutamine	Gln	Lysine	Lys
Glutamic acid	Glu	Methionine	Met
Glycine	Gly	Phenylalanine	Phe
Proline	Pro	Threonine	Thr
Serine	Ser	Tryptophan	Trp
Tyrosine	Tyr	Valine	Val

Just as different words are made by joining letters of the alphabet in different order, different proteins are formed by different combinations of the different amino acids.

alanine

alanine residue in a protein chain

Lysozyme, an enzyme found in tears and saliva, and which breaks down the cell walls of bacteria, contains residues of all 20 amino acids. (An amino acid residue is simply the part of the amino acid that is in the chain.)

There are 129 amino acid residues in the polypeptide chain of lysozyme. Notice that crosslinks (disulfide bridges) can form between cysteine amino acid residues in the chain.

cysteine

a disulfide bridge between cysteine residues

Figure 2.4.4: *The amino acid sequence in lysozyme*

Activity 2.4.1

The amino acid residues in part of a polypeptide chain have the following sequence:

Ala   Ala   Cys   Val

alanine

cysteine

valine

Draw the section of the polypeptide chain with this amino acid residue sequence.

Enzymes

Enzymes are responsible for the many chemical reactions that take place in our bodies. Most enzymes are **proteins**. Enzymes are described as **biological catalysts** since they speed up these biochemical reactions. Recent research has shown that there is a link between enzyme levels in our bodies and our general health. People who are sick show lowered levels of certain enzymes in their bodies.

> 📖 **Word bank**
>
> • **enzyme**
> A substance produced by living organisms that will act as a catalyst in a specific biochemical reaction. Most enzymes are proteins.

Digestive enzymes

Enzymes are responsible for the digestion of our food. Proteins are hydrolysed to amino acids.

Amylase is an enzyme produced by our salivary glands and pancreas. It is responsible for the breakdown of carbohydrates in our diet.

Pepsins are enzymes produced in the stomach that are responsible for the breakdown of protein. They are active in low pH environments.

Proteins are also broken down in the small intestine by **trypsins** produced by the pancreas.

Lipases are enzymes which break down fats.

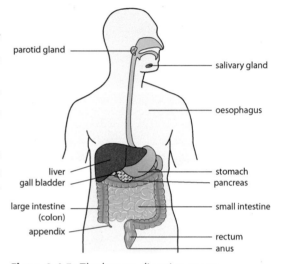

Figure 2.4.5: *The human digestive system*

Protein digestion

An inactive protein, pepsinogen, is made and stored in the lining of our stomachs. When we eat, pepsinogen is released into the stomach where it reacts with hydrochloric acid and rapidly produces the enzyme pepsin. Pepsin begins to break down proteins in our food and its activity is greatest at low pH (1·5–2·5), which is the normal pH of the gastric juices in our stomachs.

The pepsin can break the peptide link between certain amino acids and breaks proteins down into smaller peptide units (sequences of a few amino acids joined together). When the stomach contents pass into the small intestine the gastric juices are neutralised and the pepsin becomes inactive. The peptides are either absorbed through the wall of the intestine or broken down further to amino acids by the enzymes chymotrypsin and trypsin, which are released by the pancreas.

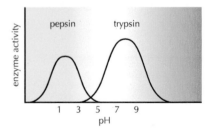

Figure 2.4.6: *Pepsin works best at low pH; the optimum pH for trypsin activity is at neutral pHs*

GO! Nobel Prize winners

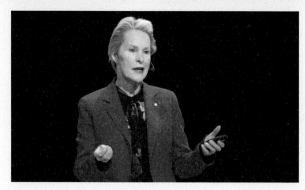

In 2018 Professor Frances H. Arnold won a share of the Nobel prize 'for the directed evolution of enzymes'. This involved genetically changing enzymes (proteins) to produce biological catalysts which are used to produce everything from biofuels and plastics to pharmaceuticals in a more environmentally friendly way. In many of the processes the enzymes have replaced toxic chemicals.

Figure 2.4.7: *Frances H. Arnold*

Protein structure

Protein structures are very complicated. The polypeptide chains have many N—H bonds and C═O along their length. Hydrogen bonds can form between the N—H of one amino acid and the C═O bond of another. Protein molecules vary in length from around 5000 atoms to several million. In the 1940s Linus Pauling and Robert Corey proposed that protein molecules could have one of two orderly arrangements both held together by hydrogen bonds. One arrangement is where there is a regular coiling of the protein chain into the shape of a helix (figure 2.4.8). The second arrangement is a folding of the chain to make

coloured patches = —C— of the different amino acids (with R above and H below the C)

Figure 2.4.8: *Hydrogen bonds forming between N—H of one amino acid residue and the C═O of another along a polypeptide chain* pleated sheets (figure 2.4.9). These structures were later confirmed by X-ray crystallography. The hydrogen bonds form between the –N-H group of one peptide link and the –C=O of another. Details of the bonding which holds protein molecules in particular shapes can be found on page 64.

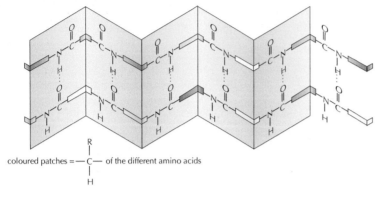

coloured patches = —C— of the different amino acids

Figure 2.4.9: *Hydrogen bonding (red dotted lines) between parallel chains in pleated sheet protein*

Protein chains can then twist and fold into the characteristic shape of a particular protein. The specific shape of the protein allows it to carry out specific functions.

Figure 2.4.10: *A model representing pepsin. The protein folds and twists into a specific shape*

Denaturing proteins

Proteins work best at specific temperatures and pHs. Changes in temperature and pH can cause hydrogen bonds to break and the protein to change shape. The protein is then unable to carry out its specific function. The protein is then said to be **denatured**. The denaturing of proteins in foods causes the appearance and texture of food to change during cooking.

Normal protein

Denatured protein

Figure 2.4.11: *Protein structures unravel when the protein is denatured*

📖 Word bank

- **denature**

to cause the shape/appearance of a protein to change and the activity of an enzyme to decrease

CHEMISTRY IN CONTEXT: COOKING FOOD

During cooking, the proteins in meat begin to change when the temperature rises above 44°C.

At temperatures above 44°C, the muscle protein loses moisture and shrinks. This causes the meat to become tougher. However, connective tissue, the protein collagen, that holds meat to bone, etc., only starts to denature and soften at temperatures above 54°C. The molecular gastronomy approach to cooking meat is to use a water bath. The technical term is cooking 'sous vide'. Cuts such as fillet of beef, venison or chicken breast that contain little collagen need only be cooked for a short while at low temperature. Cuts that contain more collagen need to be cooked much longer to give the time for the connective protein to denature and turn to jelly. Pieces of meat are cooked in a vacuum sealed bag to retain the juices. These can be reabsorbed by the meat as some of the proteins in meat have the ability to renature, i.e. return to their original form. This is why when roasting meat the advice is always to allow the meat to rest before serving.

Another example of proteins denaturing is cooking an egg. Albumin in egg is a globular protein, i.e. the protein chains are clumped together in small balls.

When the egg is heated the strands unwind as hydrogen bonds are broken. New bonds form between protein strands leading to an interconnected structure and the albumin taking on the familiar white colour and texture of cooked egg.

Figure 2.4.12: *Tough beef ribs cooked for 48 hours sous vide*

Figure 2.4.13: *Egg albumin has a globular structure*

Figure 2.4.14: *When an egg is cooked the albumin turns white as the protein becomes denatured*

Hydrolysing proteins in the laboratory

Proteins can be hydrolysed to amino acids in the laboratory. The protein needs to be heated with fairly concentrated acid to break the peptide links between amino acid units.

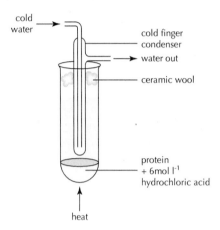

Figure 2.4.15: *Hydrolysing a protein sample*

When a peptide link breaks, a hydrogen from the water adds to the —NH and an —OH from the water adds to the —C=O.

To identify and draw structures for the products formed by hydrolysis, first identify the amide link. Then break the link adding a hydrogen to the —NH and an —OH to the —C=O.

Worked example

1 Identify the peptide links in the structure.

2 Break the bond between the carbon and the nitrogen and add OH to the CO and H to the NH.

Activity 2.4.2

The sequence of amino acid residues in part of a polypeptide chain is

(a) Use table 2.4.3 to name the amino acids that have formed this section of the polypeptide chain.
(b) The section of the polypeptide chain, in the order shown above, has the following structure.

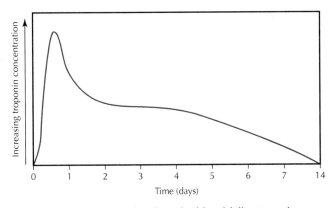

Draw the structural formulae for the three amino acids.

CHEMISTRY IN CONTEXT: HEART ATTACKS

Heart attacks can be detected, and their severity assessed, by measuring the levels of an enzyme, troponin, in the blood.

Figure 2.4.16: *Troponin levels in the blood following a heart attack*

During a heart attack troponin, a protein that regulates the contraction of the heart, is released into the bloodstream from heart muscle cells that have been damaged during the heart attack.

GO! Nobel Prize winners

Bovine insulin was the first protein to have its amino acid sequence worked out. The sequence was worked out by the English biochemist Frederick Sanger who began his research in 1944.

Sanger heated the insulin with 6 mol l⁻¹ hydrochloric acid for 24 hours. He then identified the amino acids using a technique called two-way chromatography. A sample of the hydrolysed protein was spotted onto chromatography paper and a chromatogram run using a suitable solvent. The chromatogram was then removed, dried, turned through 90° and the chromatogram run in a second solvent to further separate the amino acid spots.

Sanger spent 10 years working out the sequence of amino acids in bovine insulin. He received the Nobel Prize in 1958 for his work.

In 1980 he shared the Nobel Prize in Chemistry with two American scientists for his pioneering work on DNA and became the only scientist to have been awarded the Nobel Prize for Chemistry twice.

In 1986 Sanger was awarded the Order of Merit. He declined a knighthood as he did not want to be known as 'Sir'. Frederick Sanger died in 2013 at the age of 95.

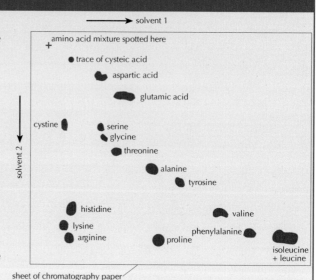

Figure 2.4.17: *Two-way chromatogram showing amino acids produced by hydrolysing insulin*

Figure 2.4.18: *Frederick Sanger, the only scientist to have won the Nobel Prize for Chemistry twice*

⁜ Make the Link

How chromatography can be used to separate components in a mixture is described in Chapter 3.5.

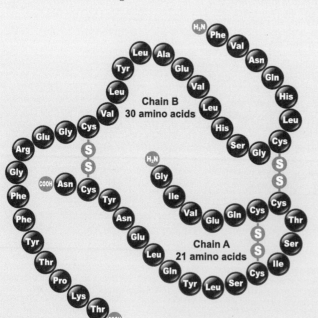

Figure 2.4.19: *Seventeen different amino acids are required to make the hormone insulin*

Learning checklist

In this chapter you have learned:

- Proteins have many different functions in our bodies.

- Proteins are made from amino acids.

- Amino acids contain an amino group ($-NH_2$) and a carboxyl group ($-COOH$).

- There are 20 different amino acids needed to make the proteins in our bodies.

- Ten of the amino acids must be obtained from dietary proteins and are referred to as essential amino acids.

- Amino acids join by a condensation reaction to form proteins.

- Given the structure of amino acids, show how they join to form part of a protein structure.

- The link joining amino acid residues in polypeptide chains is a peptide (amide) link ($-CONH-$).

- Most enzymes are proteins and act as biological catalysts.

- During digestion, enzymes break proteins into smaller peptide chains and amino acids.

- The breakdown of proteins during digestion is an example of hydrolysis.

- The structural formulae of amino acids obtained on hydrolysis of protein can be identified from the structure of a section of the protein.

- Protein chains can form spirals and sheets held together by intermolecular forces including hydrogen bonds.

- When proteins are heated intermolecular forces are broken allowing the proteins to change shape.

- Protein molecules that have changed shape are described as denatured.

- When food is cooked, denaturing of proteins causes its appearance and texture to change.

5 Oxidation of food

You should already know

- Ion-electron equations for oxidation and reduction reactions.

(National 5 Chemistry: Chemistry in society: Metals)

- Oxidising and reducing agents.

(Higher Chemistry: Chemical changes and structure: Oxidising and reducing agents)

Learning intentions

In this chapter you will learn about:

- Oxidation of alcohols.
- Oxidation and reduction of carbon compounds in terms of oxygen to hydrogen ratios within molecules.
- Aldehydes and ketones as carbonyl compounds.
- Naming and drawing straight-chain and branched aldehydes and ketones with up to eight carbons in the main chain.
- Reactions that distinguish aldehydes and ketones.
- Oxidation of aldehydes.
- Aldehydes and ketones as flavour molecules.
- Oxidation of food.
- Antioxidants.

Oxidation of alcohols

When a square of copper metal is placed in a Bunsen flame the surface turns black as a coating of copper(II) oxide forms. If the heated square is dropped into an evaporating basin containing a small volume of ethanol, the copper metal turns reddish-brown again and a faint vinegary smell can be detected.

When the heated square is dropped into ethanol, a primary alcohol, the copper(II) ions are reduced to copper atoms.

Figure 2.5.1: *A coating of copper(II) oxide forms on copper when it is heated*

$$Cu^{2+}(s) + 2e^- \rightarrow Cu(s)$$

The **ethanol** is **oxidised** to the aldehyde, **ethanal**, during the reaction.

The ion-electron equation for the oxidation is:

$$\underset{\text{ethanol}}{C_2H_5OH} \rightarrow \underset{\text{ethanal}}{CH_3CHO} + 2H^+ + 2e^-$$

The electrons appear on the right of the equation, i.e. have been lost by the reactants. Loss of electrons is oxidation. When primary alcohols are oxidised, aldehydes are formed.

Another way of deciding if oxidation has taken place is to look at the oxygen to hydrogen ratio of the reactant and product molecules.

ethanol	ethanal

oxygen:hydrogen ratio   1:6   1:4

When an alcohol is oxidised there is an **increase** in the oxygen to hydrogen ratio.

Conversely, when a carbon compound is reduced there will be a **decrease** in the oxygen to hydrogen ratio in going from reactant to product.

When an alcohol is oxidised the hydrogen from the hydroxyl group and a hydrogen from the carbon that the hydroxyl group is attached to are removed.

> ### 🔍 Hint
>
> Confused about ratios? Think in fractions!
>
> Remember 1:6 (1/6 = 0·167)
>   1:4 (1/4 = 0·25)
>   0·167 < 0·25
>
> Therefore going from 1:6 to 1:4 represents an increase in the oxygen to hydrogen ratio.

If the heated square is dropped into propan-2-ol, a secondary alcohol, it again turns reddish-brown and a faint smell of nail varnish is detected.

When propan-2 ol is used the product is propanone. Propanone is an example of a ketone. Comparing the oxygen to hydrogen ratios shows that the propan-2-ol has been oxidised.

propan-2-ol	propanone

oxygen:hydrogen ratio   1:8   1:6

The oxygen to hydrogen ratio has increased from propan-2-ol to propanone therefore the propan-2-ol has been oxidised. When secondary alcohols are oxidised, ketones are formed.

Tertiary alcohols cannot be oxidised. If a heated square of copper is dropped into 2-methylpropan-2-ol the square remains black. The copper(II) ions are not reduced therefore the alcohol cannot have been oxidised.

Another way of carrying out the oxidation of alcohols is to use acidified potassium dichromate solution as the **oxidising agent**.

In the traditional definition **oxidation** is defined as **loss of electrons** by a substance. An oxidising agent is defined as a substance that will help oxidation to take place by accepting the electrons that the substance being oxidised is losing.

> ### 📖 Word bank
>
> • **oxidising agent**
>
> substance that accepts electrons and helps oxidation to take place

SQA KEY AREA

An **oxidising agent** is therefore defined as an **electron acceptor**.

Dichromate ions in acid conditions accept electrons and change to chromium(III) ions. Acidified potassium dichromate turns from orange to green during the reaction as the orange dichromate ions are reduced to green chromium(III) ions.

$$Cr_2O_7^{2-}(aq) + 14H^+(aq) + 6e^- \longrightarrow 2Cr^{3+}(aq) + 7H_2O(\ell)$$

orange   green

Figure 2.5.2: *During the oxidation of primary and secondary alcohols using acidified potassium dichromate, the colour changes from orange to green. Tertiary alcohols do not change the colour*

Naming and drawing aldehydes and ketones

Aldehydes and ketones both contain a carbonyl group.

carbonyl group

In aldehydes the carbonyl group is on an end carbon. Propanal is an example of an aldehyde.

propanal

In ketones the carbon of the carbonyl group is attached to two other carbons. The simplest ketone is propanone.

propanone

Aldehydes

The straight-chain aldehydes are simply named by removing 'e' and adding **'al'** to the corresponding alkane name.

methanal   ethanal   propanal

Figure 2.5.3: *The formulae for the three simplest aldehyde molecules*

> ⚠️ **Remember this**
>
> Aldehydes have their carbonyl group on the end of the molecule.

For branched aldehydes, systematic names are given by:

1. naming the longest hydrocarbon chain;
2. naming the branches (side chains). Branches are ordered alphabetically
   e.g. CH_3 — methyl; C_2H_5. — ethyl; etc.

   Note: Prefixes are used if there is more than one side chain of the same type (e.g. di- is used if there are two of the same type, tri- if there are three, etc.);
3. indicating the position of the branches on the main chain, numbering from the carbonyl group as carbon 1.

Worked example 1

Name the aldehyde with the following structure:

Step 1: The longest chain has 5 carbons.

The molecule name is based on pentanal.

Step 2: There is one methyl branch. This will be shown by putting the prefix methyl in front of pentanal.

methyl**pentanal**

Step 3: The methyl side chain is on the fourth carbon in the chain counting from the carbonyl carbon.

The name of the aldehyde would therefore be **4-methylpentanal.**

Worked example 2

Draw the structure of 2,3- dimethylhexanal.

Step 1: The main chain has six carbons with one of the end carbons a carbonyl group.

Step 2: The chain is numbered from the carbonyl group.

Step 3: Methyl groups are attached to carbons 2 and 3 of the chain.

Step 4: The structure is therefore:

Molecular formula: $C_8H_{16}O$

Ketones

The straight-chain ketones based on alkanes are named in the same way as straight-chain alcohols, by simply identifying the position of the carbonyl group in the chain. The name ending is **-one**. For propanone and butanone the position is not specified as there is only one possible structure.

propanone   butanone

Pentanone has two possible structures. The carbonyl group can be at position two or three in the chain.

pentan-2-one   pentan-3-one

For branched ketones, systematic names are given by:

1. naming the longest carbon chain containing the carbonyl group;
2. numbering the chain from the end that the carbonyl group is nearer to;
3. naming any branches (side chains). Branches are ordered alphabetically
    e.g. CH_3 — methyl; C_2H_5. — ethyl;   etc.

    Note: Prefixes are used if there is more than one side chain of the same type (e.g. di- is used if there are two of the same type, tri- if there are three, etc.);
4. indicating the position of the branches on the main chain.

Worked example 1

Name the ketone with the following structure:

Step 1: The longest chain containing the carbonyl group has 6 carbons: hexanone

SQA KEY AREA

Step 2: The carbonyl is at position 2:   hexan-2-one

Step 3: There are two branches: CH_3—methyl;
C_2H_5—ethyl

Step 4: The ethyl is joined to the carbon 3:   3-ethyl

The methyl is joined to the carbon 5:   5-methyl

The name of the ketone is therefore: 3-**e**thyl-5-**m**ethylhexan-2-one

(Note: the side chains are arranged in alphabetical order in the name.)

Worked example 2

Draw the full structural formula for 3-ethyl-4-methylpentan-2-one.

Step 1: The main chain has 5 carbons.

C—C—C—C—C

Step 2: The corbonyl group is at position 2 in the chain.

Step 3: There is an ethyl group, $-C_2H_5$, attached to carbon 3 and a methyl group, $-CH_3$, attached to carbon 4.

Step 4: The full structural formula is:

Molecular formula: $C_8H_{16}O$

Activity 2.5.1

1. Draw structural formulae for the following molecules:

   3-ethylpentan-2-one

   2,4,4-trimethylheptanal

2. A student named the following structure 4-ethylpentan-2-al.

   (a) The student has made two mistakes in the naming. What are they?

   (b) Give the correct name for the compound.

3. Draw and name all the straight-chain and branched aldehydes and ketones that have molecular formula $C_6H_{12}O$. There are 3 straight-chain and 11 branched isomers to find and name.

Reactions that distinguish aldehydes and ketones

Aldehydes and ketones both contain the carbonyl functional group but have different chemical properties.

Aldehydes can be **oxidised** whereas ketones cannot.

When an aldehyde is oxidised a carboxylic acid is formed.

For example, ethanal would be oxidised to ethanoic acid.

ethanal   ethanoic acid

O:H ratio   1:4   2:4

The oxygen to hydrogen ratio has increased therefore ethanal has been oxidised.

The ion-electron equation for this reaction is:

$$CH_3CHO(\ell) + H_2O(\ell) \longrightarrow CH_3COOH(\ell) + 2H^+(aq) + 2e^-$$

Since electrons appear on the right-hand side of the equation, i.e. are lost from the reactants, the equation shows that the reaction is an oxidation.

Three reagents can be used to distinguish aldehydes and ketones: acidified potassium dichromate, Fehling's solution and Tollen's reagent. A few drops of the compound to be tested are added to about 5 cm^3 of the chosen reagent in a test tube and the test tube placed in a hot water bath. Each of the reagents gives a distinctive result with aldehydes. There is no reaction with ketones.

Figure 2.5.4: *Orange dichromate ions are reduced to green chromium(III) ions when an aldehyde is added*

Figure 2.5.5: *Blue copper(II) ions are reduced to red-brown Cu(I) ions when an aldehyde is added*

Figure 2.5.6: *Colourless silver ions are reduced to grey silver metal when an aldehyde is added*

Acidified potassium dichromate

A colour change is observed with aldehydes. Orange dichromate ions are **reduced** to green chromium(III) ions (figure 2.5.4).

Fehling's solution

Fehling's solution is an alkaline solution containing copper(II) ions. When Fehling's solution is used a brick red precipitate is formed with aldehydes (figure 2.5.5).

The blue copper(II) ions are **reduced** giving a precipitate of copper(I) oxide.

$$2Cu^{2+}(aq) + H_2O(\ell) \longrightarrow Cu_2O(s) + 2H^+(aq) + 2e^-$$
$$\text{blue} \qquad\qquad\qquad \text{reddish–brown}$$

Tollen's reagent

Tollen's reagent is ammoniacal silver nitrate and contains silver(I) ions. Aldehydes **reduce** the silver ions to the metal and a very thin layer of silver metal is deposited on the test tube. For this reason the test is often referred to as the 'silver mirror test'.

$$Ag^+(aq) \quad + \quad e^- \longrightarrow Ag(s)$$
$$\text{colourless} \qquad\qquad\qquad\quad \text{silver mirror}$$

Aldehydes as flavour molecules

Why is it that there are only five basic tastes but many different flavours? Flavour is a combination of taste and smell.

Many of the flavours and aromas we enjoy are due to aldehydes.

Table 2.5.1

Aldehyde	Flavour/Aroma
Hexa-2,4-dienal	grassy
citronellal	lemon
benzaldehyde	almonds
vanillin	vanilla
cinnamaldehyde	cinnamon

> **Hint**
>
> You do not have to know the names of the aldehydes and ketones with complicated formulae like the ones in table 2.5.1 but you should be able to identify them as aldehydes or ketones from their functional group.

In high concentrations aldehydes can be unpleasant but in low concentrations they contribute to many pleasant flavours.

Ketones also contribute to the flavours we enjoy.

methyl 2-pyridyl ketone / popcorn

ionone / roses

carvone / spearmint

Figure 2.5.7: *Some ketones that contribute to flavour*

GO! Nobel Prize winners

Figure 2.5.8: *Richard Axel (left) and Linda Buck won a Nobel Prize for their work on how we detect smell*

In 1991, Richard Axel and Linda Buck published research that shed light on how the brain interprets smell. In 2004 they were awarded the Nobel Prize in Medicine for their research on odorant receptors and the organisation of the olfactory system, i.e. how our bodies detect smells.

We have about 1000 different smell receptors but they allow us to distinguish more than 10 000 different smells!

This is because a specific volatile molecule can trigger more than one receptor. Axel and Buck discovered that it is the combined response from these receptors that we perceive as a certain smell.

CHEMISTRY IN CONTEXT: RASPBERRY KETONE

frambinone - note the position of the carbonyl group indicating it is a ketone

Figure 2.5.9: *Compounds extracted from raspberries can be used to add fragrance to cosmetics and flavour and colouring to foods such as ice cream and fizzy drinks*

Over 200 molecules have been identified as contributing to the flavour of raspberries but the distinctive flavour of raspberries is due to one particular ketone, frambinone, commonly referred to as raspberry ketone.

Claims have been made that this compound can aid weight loss.

In 2005 Japanese scientists reported that obese male mice fed a high-fat diet lost weight and fat when given raspberry ketone as part of their diet. It was concluded that raspberry ketone was in some way aiding lipolysis, the breakdown of fat, in the bodies of the mice.

Figure 2.5.10: *Studies with mice indicated that raspberry ketone might aid weight loss*

During a television show in 2012 raspberry ketone was described as a 'miracle fat burner in a bottle'. Since then, a whole new industry has grown up supplying raspberry ketone supplements as an aid to weight loss.

No human studies have as yet been carried out on the effects of raspberry ketone. Online articles on the use of raspberry ketones indicate that it is not known if they are harmful or beneficial. There are anecdotal reports of people taking raspberry ketones suffering from jitteriness, raised blood pressure and rapid heartbeat. Advice given online is that you should talk to your doctor if you are thinking about taking any supplements or if you have any concerns about your weight or weight loss.

SQA KEY AREA

Oxidation of food

One of the main causes of food spoilage is the oxidation of compounds in food.

When meat is cut it takes on a pink-red colour as oxygen reacts with myoglobin, the oxygen binding protein in meat. Further oxidation causes the oxymyoglobin to change to metmyoglobin which gives the meat a brown colour. Although the brown colour is off-putting it does not necessarily mean the meat is 'off', i.e. unfit to eat.

One indicator that foods may have gone off is smell.

Figure 2.5.11: *The surface of meat can turn brown*

Oxygen can react with fats and oils in food releasing free fatty acids. These in turn can react further with oxygen. The fatty-acid chains break at double carbon to carbon bond positions within the chain. This can release volatile aldehyde molecules such as ethanal. The free fatty acids and the aldehydes being given off can give the foods an unpleasant smell. Oils with a high number of double bonds are particularly susceptible to oxidation. When a fat or oil has oxidised in this way it is often described as having turned **rancid**.

Figure 2.5.12: *One indicator that a food has gone off is smell*

📖 Word bank

- **rancid**
  having an unpleasant flavour or taste due to the oxidation of edible oils in food

Antioxidants in foods

Antioxidants are compounds that can be added to foods to prevent oxidation. These compounds oxidise in preference to the food.

Adding antioxidants to foods and beverages will extend their shelf life. Compounds with E numbers E3XX are used as antioxidants. Some examples are given in table 2.5.2.

Table 2.5.2: *E numbers for some common compounds used as antioxidants*

E number	Compound	Use	Food
E300	vitamin C	helps to prevent cut and pulped foods from going brown by preventing oxidation reactions that cause the discolouration	jams, chopped fruit
E306	tocopherols	reduces oxidation of fatty acids and some vitamins	pies
E320	BHA (butylated hydroxyanisole)	helps to prevent the reactions that break down fats and cause the food to go rancid	butter, chewing gum, baked goods e.g. biscuits
E330	citric acid	reduces discolouring	jams, biscuits

Some antioxidants are compounds made up of molecules that contain the hydroxyl functional group.

Figure 2.5.13: *Vitamin C is an antioxidant containing the hydroxyl group*

When vitamin C oxidises the reaction involves hydroxyl groups.

The hydroxyl groups attached to the two carbons in the ring are oxidised to carbonyl groups.

$$\text{vitamin C} \longrightarrow \quad + \quad \boxed{2H^+ + 2e^-}$$

O:H ratio   6:8 (3:4 = 0·75)   6:6 (3:3 = 1)

The ion-electron half-equation and the oxygen to hydrogen ratio both indicate that the process is oxidation.

CHEMISTRY IN CONTEXT: ACTIVE PACKAGING

As well as adding antioxidants to foods, chemists are developing 'active packaging' – packaging that will improve the shelf life of foods and medicines by controlling amounts of oxygen and moisture and combatting microbes.

The most widespread type of active packaging involves the addition of oxygen scavengers. In the food industry, these scavengers help prevent oils and fats turning rancid and meat discolouring.

An effective scavenger should:

- *be able to absorb large quantities of oxygen*
- *be inexpensive*
- *be able to be recycled*
- *not react to produce any potentially toxic chemical.*

Figure 2.5.14: *Small packets containing iron are added into some food packing to absorb oxygen*

One of the most effective means of removing oxygen from within a package is the inclusion of small sachets containing powdered iron and sodium chloride. The oxygen is absorbed through the material of the sachet and reacts with the iron. 1 g of iron will react with 300 cm³ of oxygen.

In the 1980s the compounds BHA, butylhydroxyanisole (E320) and BHT, butylhydroxytoluene (E321), which prevent fats and oils in breakfast cereals from oxidising, began to be incorporated into the wax packaging in cereal boxes.

butylhydroxyanisole (BHA) **butylhydroxytoluene (BHT)**

Researchers are investigating ways in which polymer technology can create plastics suitable for use in active packaging. These include:

- *incorporating antioxidant molecules into the polymer structure of plastics used for packaging*
- *using copolymers, i.e. polymers where two different types of monomer, one of which acts as an antioxidant, are used to create the polymer chain*
- *incorporating thin films of metal into plastic.*

Learning checklist

In this chapter you have learned:

- Primary and secondary alcohols can be oxidised to aldehydes and ketones respectively.

- Tertiary alcohols cannot be oxidised.

- Hot copper(II) oxide or acidified potassium dichromate can be used to oxidise primary and secondary alcohols.

- Oxidation in carbon compounds is indicated by an increase in the oxygen to hydrogen ratio.

- Aldehydes and ketones contain the carbonyl functional group.

- The carbonyl group has structure

- The carbonyl functional group is on an end carbon in aldehydes.

- The carbonyl functional group is joined to two other carbons in ketones.

- Given the name for straight-chain and branched aldehydes and ketones with up to eight carbons in the main chain a structural formula can be drawn.

- Given a structure for a straight-chain or branched aldehyde or ketone with up to eight carbons in the main chain it can be named.

- Aldehydes can be oxidised further to carboxylic acids.

- Aldehydes and ketones can be distinguished using acidified potassium dichromate, Fehling's solution or Tollen's reagent as oxidising agent.

- Many flavour molecules are aldehydes.

- Oxidation is the major cause of food spoilage.

- Oxygen can react with the fatty acids in fats and oils causing them to become rancid.

- Antioxidants are molecules which prevent other substances from oxidising.

- Antioxidants can be identified as the substance being oxidised in a redox equation.

6 Fragrances

You should already know

- Alkenes are unsaturated hydrocarbons.

(National 5 Chemistry: Nature's chemistry: Homologous series)

Learning intentions

In this chapter you will learn about:

- Essential oils obtained from plant materials.
- Properties, uses and products of essential oils.
- Terpenes, a class of compounds that are commonly found in essential oils.
- Oxidation of terpenes in plants.

SQA KEY AREA

Essential oils

Fragrance – the word evokes thoughts of pleasant, sweet smells and conveys thoughts of luxury and relaxation. Fragrances have been known and used since ancient times. Ancient civilisations were aware that burning certain plant materials released pleasing odours.

People then began to develop ways of extracting the oils in the plants that were responsible for the smells. These oils we know as **essential oils**. They are essential since they have been derived from plant essences. The essential oils obtained are used to give **fragrance** to **perfumes and cosmetic products**, to **cleaning products** and are used as **flavourings** in food.

Figure 2.6.1: *Burning incense*

CHEMISTRY IN CONTEXT: AROMATHERAPY: THE USE OF ESSENTIAL OILS FOR THERAPEUTIC PURPOSES

Throughout history oils have been used to create pleasant aromas. They may also have been an important constituent of many herbal remedies used in the past for the treatment of illnesses and ailments.

In places such as ancient Egypt people were familiar with many essential oils. Essential oils were viewed as being more precious than gold. Analysis of mummies and ancient tombs show that oils such as those extracted from cedarwood, cinnamon and myrrh were used to embalm bodies in the mummification process. Myrrh is known to have anti-bacterial properties and would have helped preserve bodies. In 1922, when King Tutankhamun's tomb was opened, 50 alabaster jars that contained residues of essential oils were discovered.

The term aromatherapy was coined in the early twentieth century by a French chemist, René-Maurice Gattefossé. Following an accident in his lab when he severely burned his hands, he is reputed to have plunged them into a jar of lavender oil. His burns healed exceptionally well and he then began to research the use of essential oils in medicine. During the Second World War Dr Jean Valnet pioneered the use of essential oils for antiseptic purposes.

The late twentieth century has seen an increase in interest in aromatherapy and the use of essential oils for therapeutic purposes.

Figure 2.6.2: An alabaster jar from an Egyptian tomb which contained essential oils

CHEMISTRY IN CONTEXT: EXTRACTING ESSENTIAL OILS

Essential oils are found in more than 2000 plant species. Different parts of the plants can contain the essential oils. Oil of Bergamot, which gives Earl Grey tea a distinctive flavour, is obtained from the flowers of the plant. Vetiver oil, used in aftershaves to give a woody aroma and a cooling effect, is obtained from the roots of the plant. Essential oils can be obtained from fruits, nuts and seeds, the wood and bark of trees, and the roots and rhizomes of plants.

Figure 2.6.3: A roadside distillation arrangement in Vietnam, used to extract essential oils from the leaves of trees grown locally

Different methods have been used to extract essential oils from plant material. When you dig your fingernails into an orange in order to peel it, you may be aware of a fine spray being released. This is the essential oil from the orange which is released as the cells are damaged. Simply pressing plant materials can release these essential oils. One of the first methods used to extract essential oils was to crush the plant material and mix it with olive oil or animal fats. The essential oils would infuse into the oils and fats and give them the smell of the essential oils. This process was known as **enfleurage**, which literally means 'saturating with the perfume of flowers'. The same process is used to infuse oils used in the kitchen with flavours such as garlic and chilli.

steam generator   shredded plant material   essential oils

Figure 2.6.4: An apparatus that can be used to obtain essential oils by steam distillation

*The most common method used nowadays to extract essential oils is **steam distillation**. This can be adapted for use in a school chemistry laboratory.*

*Steam from a generator is passed through shredded plant material in a heated flask. The **volatile essential oils** vaporise and are carried over by the steam and condensed, forming an oily layer of top of the water.*

SQA KEY AREA

Composition of essential oils

Essential oils are concentrated mixtures of volatile, non-water soluble compounds obtained from plants.

The essential oils are composed mainly of a class of compounds known as **terpenes**.

Terpenes are unsaturated compounds that can be viewed as being based on isoprene, 2-methylbuta-1,3-diene, units joined together.

Figure 2.6.5: *Structure of isoprene (2-methylbuta-1,3-diene)*

Isoprene is a gaseous hydrocarbon which is naturally produced by different plants and emitted through their leaves into the atmosphere. Plants use isoprene to create terpenes by a complex biochemical process.

The term terpene is not only used to refer to hydrocarbons consisting of isoprene units, it is often used to include terpene derivatives such as terpene alcohols or aldehydes and ketones based on terpenes. These types of compounds are also referred to as terpenoids. The name ending will normally indicate the functional group present. For example, -ene will indicate it is a hydrocarbon; -ol will indicate it contains a hydroxyl functional group; -al will indicate it contains a carbonyl (aldehyde) group, etc.

myrcene

a terpene found in bay leaves

geraniol

a terpene **alcohol** found in essential oils from rose

Figure 2.6.6: *Terpenes can contain different functional groups*

Myrcene and geraniol are **linear** terpenes – they are open chains. As well as forming linear terpenes, the isoprene units can be joined as **cyclic** terpenes.

For complex molecules it is sometimes easier to represent molecules as skeletal structures. In the skeletal structure for limonene only the bonds between the carbons are shown. Sometimes end carbons are shown.

Figure 2.6.7: *Structural formula for limonene, a cyclic terpene and its skeletal structure alongside*

Since terpenes can have different functional groups they are classified according to the number of isoprene units that are joined together.

Table 2.6.1: *Classes of terpenes*

Class of terpene	Number of isoprene units	Formula
monoterpenes	2	$C_{10}H_{16}$
sesquiterpenes	3	$C_{15}H_{24}$
diterpenes	4	$C_{20}H_{32}$
sesterterpenes	5	$C_{25}H_{40}$
triterpenes	6	$C_{30}H_{48}$
tetraterpenes	8	$C_{40}H_{64}$
polyterpenes	many	$(C_5H_8)n$

🔍 Hint

You do not need to be able to name different terpenes but you should be able to identify the isoprene units in a structure and the number of units within a molecule.

The main classes of terpene in the essential oil plants are monoterpenes, sequiterpenes and diterpenes. The different terpenes give essential oils their particular fragrance.

Tetraterpenes include beta-carotene, which gives many fruits their orange-red colour.

beta-carotene

Figure 2.6.8: *Orange fruits and vegetables are good sources of beta-carotene*

Polyterpenes include natural rubber.

Table 2.6.2: *Some monoterpenes in essential oils*

Compound name	Fragrance	Natural occurrence	Skeletal representation
myrcene	woody	bay leaf	
geraniol	rose	geranium, lemon	OH
geranial	lemon	lemongrass	O
linalool	lavender	lavender	HO
limonene	orange	orange, lemon	

Animals also produce terpenes, for example squalene and lanosterol.

Figure 2.6.9: *A skeletal representation of lanosterol, a triterpene consisting of six isoprene units*

Lanosterol is the terpene from which all steroids are made. Squalene is used in the body to produce lanosterol.

Shark liver oil is a rich source of squalene.

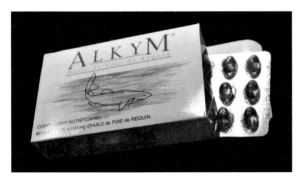

Figure 2.6.10: *Capsules containing shark liver oil, a source of squalene*

$$H_3C \diagup \underset{CH}{\overset{CH_3}{\underset{|}{C}}} = CH \diagup CH_2 \diagup \underset{CH}{\overset{CH_3}{\underset{|}{C}}} = CH \diagup CH_2 \diagup \underset{CH}{\overset{CH_3}{\underset{|}{C}}} = CH \diagup CH_2 \diagup \underset{\underset{CH_3}{|}}{C} = CH \diagup CH_2 \diagup \underset{\underset{CH_3}{|}}{C} = CH \diagup CH_2 \diagup \underset{\underset{CH_3}{|}}{C} = CH \diagup CH_3$$

Figure 2.6.11: *Squalene is a triterpene consisting of six isoprene units*

GO! Activity 2.6.1

1. (a) The systematic name for isoprene is 2-methylbuta-1,3-diene.

Draw a structural formula for isoprene.

(b) Limonene is a cyclic terpene

  (i) Write a molecular formula for limonene.

  (ii) Copy the structure and circle an isoprene unit.

2. Humulene and neocembrene are both terpenes. Humulene is found in hops and contributes to the flavour of beers. Neocembrene is a terpene used by termites to mark trails.

humulene   neocembrene

(a) Use table 2.6.1 to identify the classes of terpene to which humulene and neocembrene belong.

(b) Use coloured pens to identify the isoprene units making up humulene and neocembrene.

Oxidation of terpenes

Terpenes can oxidise easily. **Oxidation** of terpenes in plants is often responsible for the distinctive **aroma** of spices.

Common terpenes in spices formed by oxidation in plants include citral, camphor, pinene, eugenol, anethol, thymol, geraniol and menthol.

Since terpenes oxidise easily, spices when ground can lose their aroma since the greater surface area means greater exposure to oxygen of the air. This is one reason why it is advised that spices such as nutmeg should be ground when they are required rather than stored in the ground form.

Figure 2.6.12: *Whole spices retain their fragrance longer than ground spices*

CHEMISTRY IN CONTEXT: USING ESSENTIAL OILS

Figure 2.6.13: *Essential oils should be stored in dark glass bottles to extend their shelf life*

Essential oils have a limited shelf life. To improve shelf life it is important that essential oils are stored out of direct sunlight, preferably in a dark glass bottle and at a low temperature as this will slow down oxidation of the oil.

Citrus oils are particularly prone to oxidation.

Limonene can oxidise in the air.

Figure 2.6.14: *Oxidation products from limonene*

The initial fragrance of oils containing limonene will deteriorate as oxidation takes place. Limonene has a smell of oranges. Carveol and carvone, the oxidation products, smell of spearmint.

Limonene and its oxidation products can irritate the skin. Limonene-1,2-oxide is a known skin sensitiser.

To prevent skin irritation essential oils need to be diluted in carrier oils before being applied to the skin. Carrier oils are fatty oils obtained from plants. In aromatherapy, to prevent skin reactions, only a few drops of the essential oil are dissolved in a carrier oil, such as almond or grapeseed oil, before being applied to the skin.

Tea tree oil products have become very popular and are marketed as having benefits for several skin conditions due to tea tree oil having anti-bacterial properties. The oil contains several terpenes.

The most active compound in tea tree oil is the terpene, terpinen-4-ol. Another terpene, 1,8-cineole is thought to be mainly responsible for allergic reactions to tea tree oil products.

Figure 2.6.15: *Tea tree oil is included in a range of skin care products*

Figure 2.6.16: *Terpenes in tea tree oil*

Learning checklist

In this chapter you have learned:

- Essential oils are concentrated extracts of the volatile, non-water-soluble aroma compounds from plants.

- Essential oils are used to give fragrance to perfumes, cosmetic and cleaning products, and are used as flavourings in food.

- Essential oils contain terpenes.

- Terpenes are molecules based on isoprene (2-methylbuta-1,3-diene) units joined together.

- Isoprene units in terpene molecules can be identified and the number of units joined stated.

- The term terpene is used to include compounds containing different functional groups.

- Oxidation of terpenes in plants is responsible for the aroma of many spices.

7 Skin care

Learning intentions

In this chapter you will learn about:

- The damaging effect of ultraviolet radiation (UV) on skin.
- The action of sunblocks.
- The effect of UV radiation on bonds – formation of free radicals.
- Free radical scavengers:
  - in cosmetic products
  - in food products
  - in plastics.

The damaging effect of ultraviolet radiation (UV) on skin

It has been estimated that on average a woman will spend £22 000 over her lifetime on cosmetics and skincare products. Increasingly, men are also using skincare products such as moisturisers to protect their skin.

Figure 2.7.1: *The use of skincare products by women and men is increasing*

As we age our skin gradually loses its youthful appearance. Lines and wrinkles begin to appear. While some of the factors causing this are natural and unavoidable, much of the change can be associated with exposure to the sun's rays. Premature ageing of the skin due to exposure to the sun is known as photoageing.

Our skin is made up of three layers – the outer layer, the epidermis; the middle layer, the dermis; and the basement layer, the subcutis.

Figure 2.7.2: *The skin is made up of three layers*

The dermis is primarily made up of two fibrous proteins, collagen and elastin, which work together. Collagen gives the skin rigidity and elastin allows the skin to stretch and return to its original shape.

The sun's rays contain harmful **ultraviolet** (UV) radiation. Ultraviolet radiations are invisible, high-energy radiations that lie beyond the violet end of the visible spectrum. There are different types of UV radiation: UVA, UVB and UVC. Very little UVC reaches the surface of the Earth.

Figure 2.7.3: *UVA and UVB rays form part of the electromagnetic spectrum of radiations*

UVB radiation is responsible for sunburn, which occurs in the epidermal layer of the skin. This type of radiation damages DNA in cells. The UV radiation has sufficient energy to break bonds between atoms. A small proportion causes DNA structures to be changed. Although our bodies can repair the damaged DNA some of the damage can result in melanomas (skin cancers). About 11 000 people are diagnosed with melanomas in the UK each year.

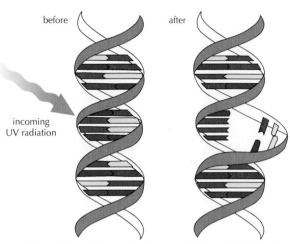

before   after

incoming
UV radiation

Figure 2.7.4: *Ultraviolet radiations can damage DNA molecules in living organisms in different ways. Bonds between the stands of DNA can be broken.*

The **UVA radiation** is more penetrating than UVB radiation and damages collagen in the dermal layer of the skin. Over time the continual damage to collagen results in wrinkling of the skin. Cells in the dermis produce **melanin** for the epidermis. This melanin is the pigment that gives our skin a tanned appearance, but it is being produced by the skin to try to protect the skin from the harmful UV radiations.

The action of sunblocks

Sunblocks are used to protect the skin from damaging UV radiation. There are two different types of sunblock, those which physically prevent UV radiation reaching the skin and chemical sunblocks that absorb the UV radiation.

Physical sunblocks usually contain zinc oxide or titanium oxide. These compounds reflect the UV radiation, preventing it reaching the skin. The downside of using them is that they leave a white appearance on the skin. Manufacturers try to minimise these effects by using the physical blockers in the form of very small particles known as nanoparticles. There is concern that these may be absorbed through the skin and accumulate in body tissues. Physical sunblocks also are easily wiped off meaning that they have to be re-applied on a regular basis.

Chemical sunblocks absorb the UV radiation. They are made by dissolving chemicals in oils. When these chemicals absorb UV radiation electrons in the molecules jump into higher energy levels. This is described as being excited. However, the sunblock molecules cannot remain like this and release the absorbed energy either by releasing lower energy radiations or by interacting with other molecules.

Figure 2.7.5: *Many cricketers apply physical sunblocks to their faces to prevent sunburn*

The effect of UV radiation on bonds – formation of free radicals

Reactions that are caused by UV radiation being absorbed are termed photochemical reactions.

When a molecule absorbs UV radiation electrons in bonds become excited, i.e. raised to a higher energy level. This can result in the molecule breaking apart.

When a chlorine molecule absorbs UV radiation the electrons in the bond jump into higher electron energy levels. The bond breaks forming two highly reactive atoms that have unpaired electrons. The atoms are said to be excited, since the unpaired electrons are in a higher energy level than normal, and are termed **free radicals**.

📖 **Word bank**

• **free radicals**
atoms or molecules that are highly reactive due to the presence of unpaired electrons

$$Cl_2(g) \xrightarrow{\text{UV}} Cl \cdot (g) + Cl \cdot (g)$$

Figure 2.7.6: *Formation of chlorine free radicals*

The formation of free radicals also occurs during the reaction of hydrogen with chlorine.

Hydrogen and chlorine are mixed and placed in a plastic bottle. The two gases do not react until a bright light is shone at them. When the light is shone at them the gases react explosively.

Figure 2.7.7: *Hydrogen and chlorine react explosively when exposed to bright light*

The UV light splits the chlorine molecule into two chlorine free radicals. This step in the reaction sequence is termed **initiation**.

$$Cl_2(g) \rightarrow 2Cl \cdot (g)$$

The chlorine radicals then react with hydrogen molecules forming hydrogen free radicals.

$$Cl \cdot (g) + H_2(g) \rightarrow HCl(g) + H \cdot (g)$$

The hydrogen free radical formed can react with a chlorine molecule.

$$H \cdot (g) + Cl_2(g) \rightarrow HCl(g) + Cl \cdot (g)$$

Steps where free radicals react to produce other free radicals are termed **propagation** steps.

The reaction continues until all the molecules have been used up and the remaining free radicals have combined together. The term used to describe this step is **termination**.

$$H \cdot (g) + Cl \cdot (g) \rightarrow HCl(g)$$

The reaction of chlorine with hydrogen is an example of **a free radical chain reaction**.

There are three stages in a free radical chain reaction: **Initiation; Propagation; Termination**.

Initiation: The initial step where free radicals are formed when a molecule absorbs radiation.

Propagation: Steps where free radicals react to form further free radicals that can themselves react.

Termination: Step in which free radicals combine, slowing the rate and stopping the reaction.

GO! Activity 2.7.1

1. Chlorine will react with methane in a free radical chain reaction. Some steps in the reaction are shown.

   (i) $CH_3 \cdot (g) + Cl_2(g) \rightarrow CH_3Cl(g) + Cl \cdot (g)$

   (ii) $CH_4(g) + Cl \cdot (g) \rightarrow CH_3 \cdot (g) + HCl(g)$

   (iii) $Cl_2(g) \rightarrow 2Cl \cdot (g)$

   (iv) $CH_3 \cdot (g) + CH_3 \cdot (g) \rightarrow C_2H_6(g)$

   (v) $CH_3Cl(g) + Cl \cdot (g) \rightarrow CH_2Cl \cdot (g) + HCl(g)$

   State the term used to describe each of the steps shown.

2. Alkanes such as hexane (C_6H_{14}) will decolourise bromine solution when UV light is shone on a test tube containing the liquids. The reaction takes place slowly.

The coloured bromine molecules are split into free radicals by the UV light and react with the hexane to give colourless bromohexane.

(a) What term is used to describe a reaction initiated by light?

(b) The initiation step of the reaction involves bromine molecules breaking into free radicals.

Figure 2.7.8: *Bromine solution being decolourised by hexane in UV light*

(i) Write an equation to describe the initiation step.

(ii) Complete the equation for:

1. the propagation step

$$C_6H_{14} + Br \cdot \rightarrow X + Y$$

2. the termination step.

$$C_6H_{13} \cdot + Z \rightarrow C_6H_{13}Br$$

CHEMISTRY IN CONTEXT: TYRIAN PURPLE – AN EARLY EXAMPLE OF A PHOTOCHEMICAL REACTION

Tyrian purple was a dye that was highly prized in ancient times. It was made in the ancient Phoenician city of Tyre and obtained from the mucus of sea snails. Twelve thousand snails were required to produce 1·4 g of the dye, making the dye very expensive. The dye was a sign of status. Robes dyed with Tyrian purple were worn by Alexander the Great and Roman emperors such as Julius Caesar.

The cloth was immersed in the dye and exposed to a strong light. It turned successively green, blue, red, deep purple-red and, finally by washing in soap and water, a permanent shade of bright crimson. Unlike other dyes Tyrian purple did not fade with age or exposure to light. In fact, the colour became richer. Photochemistry in action!

Figure 2.7.9: *An image of the Roman emperor Justinian dressed in a robe dyed with Tyrian purple*

CHEMISTRY IN CONTEXT: THE 'OZONE HOLE'

What is ozone?

Ozone is a form of oxygen with the formula O_3. It is a pale blue gas with a sharp, irritating odour and is toxic even in very small concentrations.

The presence of ozone in the stratosphere (the layer of the atmosphere 12 to 50 km above the Earth's surface) is vital to protect us from harmful UV radiation coming from the Sun. Ozone absorbs a lot of this harmful radiation and stops it reaching us. Life as we know it would be impossible if ozone in the stratosphere was destroyed. There has been concern about an ozone 'hole' that has developed in the atmosphere over Antarctica in recent years.

How is ozone formed?

In the stratosphere a series of reactions that absorb UV radiation take place.

Oxygen molecules absorb radiation and break apart to give oxygen radicals (excited atoms).

$$O_2 \rightarrow 2O \cdot$$

The oxygen radicals then react with other oxygen molecules to form ozone.

$$O \cdot + O_2 \rightarrow O_3$$

Ozone itself could react with oxygen radicals and reform oxygen molecules.

$$O \cdot + O_3 \rightarrow 2O_2$$

The ozone can also break down into oxygen molecules and oxygen atoms by absorbing UV radiation.

$$O_3 \rightarrow O_2 + O \cdot$$

This reaction is the main screening reaction preventing harmful UV radiation reaching the Earth's surface.

Ozone is being made and destroyed all the time in a chain reaction. A point is reached where ozone is being made as fast as it is being used up:

rate of ozone production = rate of ozone breaking down

At this point the concentration of ozone in the stratosphere should be constant.

From knowledge of the rates of reaction chemists are able to estimate what the concentration of ozone should be at different altitudes at different times of the day and year.

However, when chemists compared their calculated concentrations with the actual measured values they found the actual ozone concentration to be much less than expected. This suggested that the ozone was being removed faster than expected.

What's causing the loss of ozone?

In the early 1970s Professor Sherry Rowland and Dr Mario Molina predicted that a group of compounds known as chlorofluorocarbons (**CFCs**) would damage the ozone layer. CFCs were widely used as the propellants in aerosols, the cooling agent in refrigerators, in the manufacture of expanded polystyrene and as a cleaning solvent in the electronics industry.

One of the main properties of CFCs was that they were extremely stable – it was difficult to break them down. Rowland and Molina were interested in what might happen to CFCs when they were released into the environment – in the 1970s an estimated 1 million tonnes of CFCs were being released into the atmosphere every year. Although CFCs are extremely stable Rowland and Molina wanted to know what would happen to CFCs in the stratosphere where UV radiation would break them down. As Rowland himself said: 'everything is broken down there'. They knew that chlorine atoms would be produced and calculated that they were about a thousand times more likely to react with ozone than anything else. They also calculated that each chlorine atom could destroy 100 000 ozone molecules. They initially thought there must be a mistake in their calculations but they were quickly confirmed by other scientists.

How do chlorine atoms destroy ozone?

When chlorine-containing compounds reach the stratosphere they absorb high-energy radiation. Chlorine molecules absorb a quantum of radiation and break down to form chlorine free radicals. The symbol 'hυ' is used to indicate a quantum of radiation.

$$CF_3Cl + h\upsilon \rightarrow CF_3 \cdot + Cl \cdot$$

The chlorine radicals react with ozone to form chlorine monoxide (ClO •) and oxygen.

$$Cl \cdot + O_3 \rightarrow ClO \cdot + O_2$$

Figure 2.7.10: *Chlorofluorocarbons are compounds containing chlorine, fluorine and carbon*

Figure 2.7.11: *Professor F. Sherwood Rowland*

The chlorine monoxide is also a free radical so is very reactive and can react with oxygen atoms to form more chlorine atoms, which can then go on to react with more ozone molecules.

$$ClO \cdot + O \cdot \rightarrow Cl \cdot + O_2$$

Chemists have carried out experiments in the laboratory, under conditions similar to those found in the stratosphere, to compare the rate of reaction of ozone with chlorine radicals to the rate of reaction with oxygen radicals.

$$Cl \cdot + O_3 \rightarrow ClO \cdot + O_2 \qquad \text{reaction 1}$$

$$O \cdot + O_3 \rightarrow 2O_2 \qquad \text{reaction 2}$$

Removal of ozone by reaction with chlorine radicals takes place 1500 times faster than reaction with oxygen radicals.

The activation energy for the reaction of chlorine radicals with ozone, reaction 1, is much lower than the reaction between oxygen radicals and ozone, reaction 2. This means more particles in reaction 1 have energy greater than the activation energy so the reaction will be faster than reaction 2. Note: activation energy is covered in Chemistry in society: Controling the rate.

Figure 2.7.12: Potential energy diagrams showing $Cl + O_3$ has a lower activation energy than $O + O_3$ so will be faster

What is the 'hole' in the ozone layer?

What is described as a hole in the ozone layer is actually a thinning of the ozone layer in the stratosphere. This is most apparent in the Antarctic during October, which is springtime in the southern hemisphere. The weather conditions at this time of the year are such that the reactions which cause ozone depletion happen at the fastest rate. The British Antarctic Survey (BAS) has been monitoring the atmosphere over the Antarctic since the 1950s. In 1981 a team of scientists started measuring the concentration of ozone in the stratosphere and over two to three years their results showed that there were alarmingly low levels of ozone. At first they thought there was something wrong with their instruments but replacement instrumentation gave the same results – there was a hole developing in the ozone layer. At the same time NASA satellites were taking measurements from above the Earth. Many of the readings were initially ignored because their computers were programmed to ignore readings which seemed impossibly inaccurate.

Satellite images of the ozone hole above the Antarctic can be taken hourly every day. Readings taken in September 2019 showed the maximum size of the ozone hole reached 6·3 million square miles. Scientists however cautioned that this was not an indication that atmospheric ozone was on a fast track to recovery, stating that the main reason for the hole being smaller was due to higher temperatures in the stratosphere. In September 2000 the readings indicated that the size of the hole was nearly 19 million square miles.

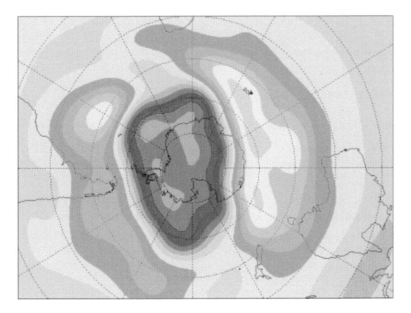

Figure 2.7.13: A NASA satellite image showing the ozone layer in September 2006. The grey and pink areas show the thinnest layers of ozone

What has been done to stop the problem?

The CFCs released into the atmosphere are likely to be active for many years to come. However, as early as 1975, as a result of Rowland and Molina's work, the state of Oregon banned CFCs as propellant gases in aerosols. They were joined in the following few years by the whole of the USA, Canada, Norway and Sweden. Unfortunately Europe and Japan continued the use of CFCs until the Montreal Protocol in 1987. The Montreal Protocol was a worldwide agreement for restricting the production and release of CFCs into the atmosphere. The publication of ozone depletion rates following the Montreal agreement led to subsequent meetings in London in 1990, Copenhagen in 1992 and again in Montreal in 1997. These strengthened the agreement to stop the production and release of CFCs and other similar chemicals into the atmosphere. By 1998 the developed nations had almost phased out their use of CFCs. A special fund was also set up to help developing countries to move away from using CFCs.

DAILY NEWS

world - business - finance - lifestyle - travel - sport

Healing the Ozone Layer: Chemist Says Treaty Is Working

The Montreal Protocol, enacted in 1987, put controls on the use of aerosol CFCs.

Johnna Rizzo
National Geographic News
Published 16 April 2013

'The Montreal Protocol is working,' says chemist Mario Molina, who shared the Nobel Prize for his work on the effects of chlorofluorocarbons (CFCs). 'CFCs are a global environmental problem that is being solved by society.'

The international treaty, which opened for signature in 1987, created controls on the use of CFCs, gases used as coolants in refrigerators and to propel aerosols like hair spray out of cans. The problem was that CFCs spread out in the stratosphere, where they led to a hole in the ozone layer.

When Molina started studying CFCs in the 1970s and discovered their role in ozone depletion, each US household averaged 30 to 40 spray cans. Since the late 90s, CFC production has all but stopped, making modern spray cans ozone safe.

The ozone layer itself? Though scientists say it will take until beyond 2050 to return to pre-1980s levels of CFCs – they take about a hundred years to decompose – the amounts in the atmosphere are steadily decreasing. (See chart below.)

Atmospheric abundance of CFC-12*, *parts per trillion*

*CFC-12, COMMONLY CALLED FREON-12, WAS A POPULAR REFRIGERANT AND AEROSOL PROPELLANT.

Figure 2.7.14: *From* National Geographic – *April 2013*

The former United Nations (UN) General Secretary Koffi Annan once described the Montreal Protocol and subsequent agreements as 'perhaps the most important international agreement to date' because of the unprecedented worldwide support for the action.

Despite these moves to stop the release of CFCs into the atmosphere those CFCs that are there will be there for many years. It has been estimated that it will not be until 2065 that ozone levels will return to pre-1970 levels. Hydrofluorocarbons (HFCs), which were used as replacements for CFCs, are now thought to contribute to global warming and agreement on phasing them out was reached between the USA and China, the biggest users, in June 2013, as reported in 'The Economic Times':

DAILY NEWS

world - business - finance - lifestyle - travel - sport

US, China agree to work jointly on phase down of hydrofluorocarbons

The Economic Times, 9 June 2013

Figure 2.7.15: *US President Barack Obama*

WASHINGTON: For the first time, the US and China, the world's top two greenhouse-gas emitters, have agreed to work together and with other countries to phase down the consumption and production of hydrofluorocarbons (HFCs) as an important new step to combat global climate change.

'On Sunday, President (Barack) Obama and President Xi (Jinping) agreed on an important new step to confront global climate change. For the first time, the United States and China will work together and with other countries to use the expertise and institutions of the Montreal Protocol to phase down the consumption and production of hydrofluorocarbons (HFCs), among other forms of multilateral cooperation,' the White House said in a press statement.

CHEMISTRY IN CONTEXT: FREE RADICALS AND HEALTH

Free radicals can be particularly damaging to our health.

Increased UV radiation reaching the Earth's surface results in increased free radical formation at ground level. Ozone is formed in the lower atmosphere by the action of UV light on nitrogen oxides and hydrocarbons produced in vehicle engines. Ozone is thought to affect crop growth, damages materials like rubber, and irritates the lungs, causing coughing.

UV radiation can also cause the formation of oxygen radicals in the body. These radicals are often termed reactive oxygen species (ROS).

Reactive oxygen species (· unpaired electrons)

$Ö::Ö$	$·Ö::Ö$	$·Ö::Ö·$	$·Ö:H$	$:Ö:H$
oxygen	superoxide anion	peroxide	hydroxyl radical	hydroxide ion
O_2	$·O_2^-$	$·O_2^{2-}$	$·OH$	OH^-

Figure 2.7.16: *Oxygen forms reactive oxygen species with unpaired electrons, free radicals, readily*

Figure 2.7.17: *Cigarette smoke is a major source of free radicals and ROS. Cigarette packets must, by law, carry a health warning*

Superoxide and peroxide radicals are oxygen molecules that have gained electrons. A hydroxyl radical has one fewer electron than a hydroxide ion.

Formation of radicals happens naturally during respiration. Some of the oxygen we breathe in is converted to superoxide as part of the normal respiratory process. This in turn can, under certain conditions, form other ROS such as hydroxyl radicals. These radicals can damage cell membranes. Each day every cell in our bodies is exposed to ten thousand million (10^{10}) superoxide radicals and the DNA in each cell will suffer 10 000 attacks from radicals causing damage. Our bodies have a remarkable ability to repair damage to DNA. However, repairs are not always perfect and these can lead to mutations as we get older. There is increasing evidence that ROS are linked to the ageing process and the development of cancers and Alzheimer's disease.

SQA KEY AREA

Free radical scavengers

Our bodies produce chemicals which will react with free radicals that might otherwise cause damage to cells. These substances are termed **free radical scavengers**. These substances work by reacting with free radicals to form stable molecules. Removing the free radicals stops free radical chain reactions, which would damage cells, taking place. The process doesn't completely prevent damage and becomes less effective as we grow older.

Until the mid-1990s the main focus of research on antioxidants related to the role of vitamins and minerals. Studies have suggested that the antioxidants that occur naturally in fresh fruits and vegetables have a protective effect. For example, vitamin E and beta-carotene appear to protect cell membranes; vitamin C removes free radicals from inside cells.

vitamin C

vitamin E

B-carotene

Figure 2.7.18: *Vitamins and minerals protect cells from damage by free radicals*

Plants have developed many substances that protect themselves from free radical damage.

Free radical scavengers in food

In 1995 studies into the health benefits of a class of compounds called polyphenols and, in particular, compounds known as flavonoids began to appear.

Current evidence strongly supports a contribution from polyphenols to the prevention of heart and coronary artery disease, cancers and osteoporosis (weakening of the bones).

parsley   thyme   luteolin

Figure 2.7.19: *The herbs thyme and parsley are good sources of the flavonoid, luteolin*

Research is increasingly showing that those who eat antioxidant-rich foods reap health benefits.

There are thousands of different substances contained in foods that have antioxidant properties. It is thought that eating a varied diet rich in many different antioxidants is better than taking supplements, which might only contain a few.

Food rich in antioxidants include:

- Berries such as blueberries, blackberries, raspberries, strawberries and cranberries
- Beans such as kidney beans
- Fruits such as apples, avocados, cherries, pears, plums, pineapple, oranges and kiwi
- Vegetables such as spinach, red cabbage, potatoes, sweet potatoes and broccoli
- Beverages such as green tea, coffee, red wine and many fruit juices
- Nuts such as pistachios, pecans, hazelnuts and almonds
- Dark chocolate.

Antioxidants, which act as free radical scavengers, are also added to certain foods to help prevent the food from spoiling. They play an important role in extending the shelf life of foods. They ensure that foodstuffs retain their colour and taste, and remain edible for longer. This is particularly true for foods with a high fat content. Antioxidants are added to help prevent fatty acid chains from breaking down and releasing unpleasant odours associated with fats turning rancid. They also prevent vitamins and amino acids, which oxidise easily when exposed to air, from being destroyed.

Figure 2.7.20: *Foods rich in antioxidants can benefit our health*

Free radical scavengers in cosmetic products

Many cosmetics, such as anti-ageing creams, contain antioxidants, which act as free radical scavengers.

To be effective the antioxidants need to be able to penetrate into the epidermal and dermal layers of the skin. Many creams contain compounds derived from vitamin C and vitamin E. Vitamins C and E are powerful free radical scavengers. However the effectiveness of compounds derived from them is disputed. Recent research has focused on polyphenols. They have been found to be able to pass into the epidermis and dermis, which demonstrates their potential to be used as active ingredients in anti-ageing cosmetic products.

One cosmetics company is marketing and making claims for cosmetic ingredients consisting of polyphenols obtained from different plant sources.

Figure 2.7.21: *Many skincare products incorporate antioxidants in the formulation*

Table 2.7.1: *Sources and claims for some cosmetic ingredients*

Source of compounds	Compounds	Properties	Use
strawberry plant leaves	rich in polyphenols in particular from the flavonoid family	brightens the complexion, smoothes skin texture and gently lightens the skin	developed for dull skins, anti-ageing products and for oily skins with dilated pores
oregano leaves	rich in polyphenols in particular from the hydroxycinnamic acid family	has lightening and antioxidant properties, and a good photostability	for lightening treatments, correction of pigmentary disorders and to combat ageing spots
bilberry leaves	rich in polyphenols in particular from the chlorogenic acid family	prevents redness, improves microcirculation	can be incorporated into anti-ageing care products to improve microcirculation and acts on wrinkles and dark circles

Free radical scavengers in plastics

Free radicals created in the atmosphere by UV radiation can cause plastics to degrade. Plastics such as polypropene and LDPE (low density polyethene) can discolour and crack. Oxygen reacts with carbons in the polymer chains, forming carbonyl groups and weakening the plastics. Free radical scavengers are added to the plastics as UV stabilisers during the manufacturing process.

Figure 2.7.22: *The durability of plastics used to make children's playground furniture and traffic cones is improved by incorporating free radical scavengers into plastics during the manufacturing process*

One common UV stabiliser added to plastics is benzophenone. It will react with reactive oxygen species preventing damage to the polymer chains.

benzophenone

CHEMISTRY IN CONTEXT: A PROBLEM WITH PLASTICS

Figure 2.7.23: *A 1930s shoehorn made of celluloid showing signs of degradation*

Figure 2.7.24: *A piece of 20-year-old polyurethane-based plastic. The plastic has yellowed significantly and lost flexibility since it was manufactured*

While the plastics industry searches for solutions to the problem of plastics waste, such as the development of biopolymers, museum curators are trying to develop ways to preserve exhibits made from plastics.

Many plastic materials are showing signs of deterioration. These include discolouration, crazing and cracking, warping, becoming sticky and in extreme cases, turning completely to powder. Unique and beautiful pieces are being lost through degradation from museum collections across the world.

By 1992 acrylic based paintings worth millions of pounds by leading artists of the 1960s including David Hockney and Jackson Pollock had begun to suffer discolouration, cracking and greyness. To date no method has been found to clean them and prevent further degradation. There are a vast variety of artefacts from early radios to spacesuits in museums and art galleries that need to be preserved. Museums are controlling lighting levels and the atmosphere in which exhibits are stored to try to control degradation.

The film industry is also having to deal with the degradation of irreplaceable archive films recorded using cellulose nitrate film. This was the plastic that was originally used for film recording. Low temperature storage slows down the degradation processes. Promising results have also been obtained by coating cellulose nitrate with epoxydised soya bean oil (ESBO). The National Film Archive transfers material recorded using cellulose nitrate and cellulose triacetate film onto more stable polyester at the rate of a million metres a year.

Learning checklist

In this chapter you have learned:

- UV radiation is a high energy radiation.

- Excessive exposure to UV radiation can lead to skin damage including photoageing and skin cancers.

- Sunblocks can physically protect by reflecting UV radiation.

- Sunblocks can chemically protect by absorbing UV radiation.

- UV radiation causes harmful free radicals that react with proteins in our skin to form wrinkles.

- Free radicals are single atoms or groups of atoms with unpaired electrons and are very reactive.

- The formation of free radicals initiates chain reactions.

- The three stages of a free radical chain reaction are initiation, propagation and termination.

- Free radical scavengers react with free radicals preventing free radical chain reactions taking place.

- Free radical scavengers react with free radicals to form stable molecules.

- Free radical scavengers are added to cosmetic products to prevent free radical damage to skin tissue.

- Free radical scavengers are added to foods to prevent them from spoiling and improve shelf life.

- Free radicals are added to plastics to slow down degradation due to exposure to sunlight.

3

Chemistry in society

1 Getting the most from reactants

You should already know

- How to balance chemical equations.
- The gram formula mass (GFM) of a substance is its formula mass measured in grams and can be calculated using relative atomic masses.
- The gram formula mass of a substance is known as the mole.
- How to carry out calculations involving mass (m) into moles (n) and moles into mass:

$$m = n \times GFM$$

$$n = m \,/\, GFM$$

- The connection between volume (V), concentration (C) and moles (n) of solution:

$$n = C \times V \quad C = n \,/\, V \quad V = n \,/\, C$$

- A balanced equation tells you the mole ratio of reactants and products.

(National 5 Chemistry: Chemical changes and structure: Formulae and reaction quantities)

- How to calculate the masses of the reactants used up and products formed when a fuel burns, using balanced equations.

(National 5 Chemistry: Nature's chemistry: Energy from fuels)

Learning intentions

In this chapter you will learn about:

- How industrial chemical processes are designed to maximise profit and minimise the impact on the environment.
- Factors influencing process design include: availability, sustainability and cost of feedstock(s); opportunities for recycling; energy requirements; marketability of by-products and product yield.
- How 'green chemistry' involves practices such as minimising waste; avoiding the use or production of toxic substances and reducing the number of steps in a chemical process.
- How to measure the efficiency of a reaction by calculating the percentage yield and atom economy.

- How to use mole ratios of reactants and products in balanced equations to calculate moles and masses reacting and being produced and concentrations and volumes of solutions reacting and being produced.
- How to calculate volumes of gases reacting and being produced, from balanced equations.
- How to calculate which reactant is in excess and the limiting reactant in a chemical reaction.

Chemists and the chemical industry

Our world is changing fast. Global population is rising rapidly and there is growing pressure on resources. Rising energy prices and climate change have created a need for new lower carbon energy sources. All of this is driving the transition towards a resource and energy efficient economy, and the chemical industry has a central role to play in enabling this shift.

The chemical industry is worldwide. Global chemical sales is in excess of six trillion US dollars which makes the chemical industry the world's second largest manufacturing industry after the automotive sector. However, most of the world's chemical production is accounted for by only a handful of industrialised nations. The United States, Europe and Asia-Pacific are the world's biggest chemical trading regions. It has been estimated that by 2030 China will account for almost 50% of global chemical sales.

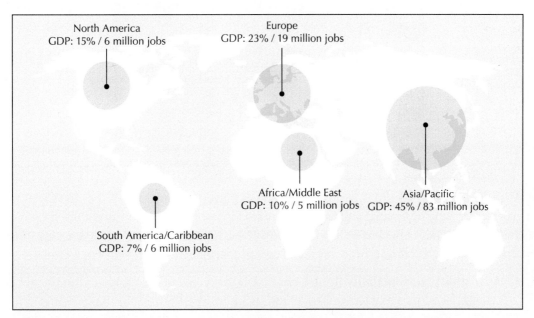

Figure 3.1.1: *Map of the chemical industry's total global economic impact by region in 2017 GDP (Gross Domestic Product) is a measure of the worth of goods produced by a country*

Source: icca-chem.org (March 2019)

At one time in the twentieth century the UK's chemical industry was the world leader in many sectors. Although other countries like China and India now hold that position the chemical industry in the UK still employs hundreds of thousands of people and is worth billions of pounds to the nation's economy. INEOS Grangemouth is one of the UK's largest manufacturing sites. It produces synthetic ethanol, ethene and propene for use in the manufacture of polyethene and polypropene. It is also home to Scotland's only crude oil refinery and produces the bulk of fuels used in Scotland.

Chemicals are the building blocks for our modern world. They are essential for the manufacture of many of the products we use today and in the technologies that will drive us towards a more sustainable future. The work of chemists and the chemical industry has a massive impact on the quality of our lives. Walk into any supermarket and practically everything you see has involved chemists in some way. The quality and availability of the fruit and vegetables is dependent on the use of synthetic fertilisers produced industrially on a large scale. The shelf life of other foodstuffs depends on the inclusion of preservatives and antioxidants in the foods themselves. The cardboard packaging, the metal shelving, plastic flooring and the paint on the walls are all made by chemical processes. Even the gases in the strip lighting and the coolants used in the refrigerators and freezers have been produced by industrial chemists.

Figure 3.1.2: *Many of the items found in a supermarket have been made by industrial chemists*

When making new products industrial chemists have to think about the cheapest and most efficient way of making the product to maximise profit. At the same time they have to think about health and safety issues to protect workers and the environment in general.

Key factors influencing industrial process design include:

- **Availability**, **sustainability** (long term supply) and **cost** of **feedstocks** – the chemicals which have to be reacted or processed in some way in order to make a product.

- **Product yield** – the quantity of chemical produced by a particular chemical process.

- **Marketability of by-products** – often there are other products formed in addition to the intended product, which can be used elsewhere in the process or sold to other companies and used rather than being wasted.

- **Recycling** – if unreacted chemicals can be fed back into the reactor this improves the efficiency and profitability of the process and reduces potential environmental pollutants being released into the environment.

- **Energy requirements** – the cost of energy sources like gas and electricity are increasing all the time so low energy processes are more profitable and ways of using energy released during chemical reactions need to be found.

Environmental considerations include the following:

- **Reducing waste**

A typical chemical process generates products and waste from raw materials such as reactants, solvents and reagents. Recycling of reactants is well established in industry. If, in addition, most of the reagents, the solvent and the catalyst can be recycled, then fewer are needed in the process and there is less waste. This is shown diagrammatically in figure 3.1.3.

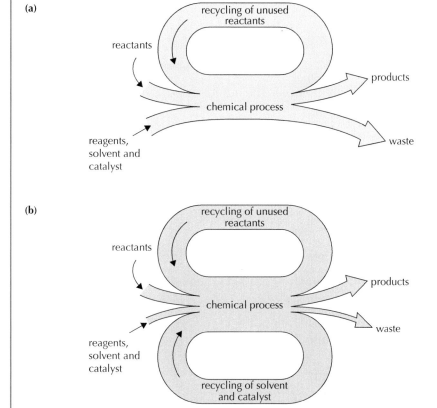

Figure 3.1.3: *Green chemistry processes (b) recycle reagents, solvents and catalysts, which reduces the amount of waste compared to non-green processes (a)*

- **Using fewer toxic chemicals**

Chemical syntheses which use less toxic reagents are preferred in green chemistry. An example is the preparation of a type of polycarbonate used where high optical properties combined with strength are needed. The polycarbonate is manufactured by a condensation reaction between bisphenol A and either carbonyl chloride or diphenyl carbonate.

Carbonyl chloride is a very poisonous gas, manufactured from other toxic gases, carbon monoxide and chlorine:

$$CO(g) + Cl_2(g) \longrightarrow \begin{array}{c} Cl \\ \diagdown \\ C{=}O \ (g) \\ \diagup \\ Cl \end{array}$$

(COCl$_2$)

carbonyl chloride

Diphenyl carbonate, however, is produced from dimethyl carbonate, which is manufactured from methanol, carbon monoxide and oxygen, in the presence of copper(II) chloride, $CuCl_2$:

$$2CH_3OH(\ell) + \tfrac{1}{2}O_2(g) + CO(g) \xrightarrow{CuCl_2} \begin{array}{c} CH_3O \\ \diagdown \\ C{=}O(\ell) \\ \diagup \\ CH_3O \end{array} + H_2O(\ell)$$

dimethyl carbonate

Dimethyl carbonate, when heated with phenol in the liquid phase, forms the diphenyl carbonate:

Although the dimethyl carbonate route also uses carbon monoxide, overall the process is less hazardous than that using toxic chlorine and carbonyl chloride.

- **Biodegradable products**

Household detergents never used to degrade naturally in sewage works. This resulted in foaming, which made the sewage difficult to manage. The modern biodegradable detergents we now use required a lot of research to develop.

Pesticides which break down in sunlight in 2–3 days and which are much less toxic to humans than phosphorus or chlorine-based pesticides have been developed.

CHEMISTRY IN CONTEXT: GREEN CHEMISTRY

*In recent years the chemical industry has become more aware of **green chemistry** – the design of chemical products and processes that reduce or eliminate the use and production of hazardous substances.*

In 1998 Paul Anastas and John Warner of the US Environmental Protection Agency formulated some simple rules for how sustainability can be achieved in the production of chemicals – these are the 12 principles of green chemistry:

1. *Waste prevention instead of cleaning it up after waste is formed.*
2. *Improve the atom economy (see page 228) to reduce wasteful by-products.*
3. *Use of fewer hazardous and toxic chemicals.*
4. *Safer products designed.*
5. *Harmless solvents, separation agents, etc., used.*
6. *More energy efficient processes designed.*
7. *Use of renewable raw materials (feedstocks).*
8. *Fewer steps in a process to avoid unwanted by-products.*
9. *Use of more specific catalysts.*
10. *Design products to undergo degradation in the environment.*
11. *Improved analytical methods for pollution prevention during a process.*
12. *Design of safer processes.*

Implementing these green chemical principles is likely to be costly compared to the current, relatively inexpensive chemical processes, which will have to be redesigned. However as raw materials become more expensive and energy costs increase, such an investment should be paid back in the future. The development of greener processes can therefore be seen as an investment for the future.

- ### Designing safer products

Chemicals need to be as useful as possible but also be safe for us to use and safe for the environment. For example, polymers have been developed which are much less flammable than better known polymers but still have useful properties such as toughness. One polymer which has these properties is polyphenylsulfone, which is now widely used inside aircraft and has been introduced into underground trains where it is also very important to use non-flammable materials.

Figure 3.1.4: *The plastics used to make modern aircraft seats are tough and non-flammable*

Figure 3.1.5: *Many modern paints are water based to avoid using potentially harmful volatile solvents*

- *Safer solvents*

Reactions that occur in the gas phase are preferable as they avoid the use of solvents to bring the reactants together. Examples include the manufacture of ammonia and ethene. Water is widely used as a solvent in industrial processes and although water itself is safe it is essential to ensure it is not wasted and that it is cleaned up before being discharged into the waste system.

Other reactions use organic solvents like hydrocarbons, many of which are toxic and easily evaporate into the atmosphere. Wherever possible alternative solvents are used which are not harmful. One example is the development of water-based paints, which are replacing paints that use these volatile solvents. Liquid carbon dioxide is widely used as a solvent in the extraction of caffeine from coffee beans and in the latest dry cleaning equipment it replaces toxic solvents such as perchloroethene, C_2Cl_4 (see page 60).

- *Renewable feedstocks*

There are many developments aiming to reduce the dependence of the chemical industry on oil and using renewable resources instead. Surfactants which are added to detergents to remove dirt from skin can be made from renewable plant-derived resources such as carbohydrates (sucrose, glucose) or plant oils. Ethene, used to make poly(ethene), can be made from bioethanol produced from carbohydrate sources (see page 201).

- *Reducing the number of steps*

Another way of reducing waste and energy use is by reducing the number of steps in a chemical process. A good example of this is in the production of ibuprofen, a medicine which reduces inflammation and gives pain relief. Ibuprofen was first made in the 1960s by chemists working for Boots. It was initially developed for the treatment of rheumatoid arthritis. The Boots process involved six separate steps from start to finish – the more steps the more reactants, solvents, reagents, catalysts and energy are used. In the 1990s an improved synthesis route was developed by a company called BHC, which only involved three steps. As a result of fewer steps there is less wastage and lower energy consumption. The yield of the final product is also improved. An additional problem with a synthesis that takes several steps (a multi-step synthesis) is that it produces a low overall yield. Imagine each step has a yield of 90%. A one-step process would have a 90% yield, a two-step process a yield of $100 \times (0.9 \times 0.9) = 81\%$, so a three-step process would give a yield of $100 \times (0.9 \times 0.9 \times 0.9) = 73\%$. Applying this calculation to a six-step process, as in the original Boots synthesis, if each step gave a 90% yield then the overall yield would be $(100 \times (0.9)^6) = 53.1\%$.

Figure 3.1.6: *A diagrammatic summary of the Boots six-step synthesis and the BHC three-step synthesis of ibuprofen*

A two-step reaction, in which the first step gave, say, a 75% yield and the second step only gave a 50% yield, would only have an overall yield of $100 \times (0.75 \times 0.5) = 37.5\%$.

• **Catalysis**

Catalysts have played a huge part in the development of more sustainable processes for the manufacture of chemicals. There are many advantages in developing and using catalysts for industrial reactions, some important ones being:

• lower temperature and pressure can often be used;
• they enable alternative reaction pathways to be used, which results in fewer unwanted by-products, which reduces waste.

Recovering the catalyst used is an important element of green chemistry. It not only reduces waste, it also cuts costs. An example is the production of alkylbenzene sulfonates, an active surfactant in many detergents. Aluminium chloride was used as the catalyst in the reaction between benzene and a long-chain alkene. The aluminium chloride could not be recycled. Now a solid zeolite catalyst is used which can be reused so there is no waste product.

New Zealand has huge reserves of natural gas but little oil. The methane obtained from natural gas can be converted into methanol which can be converted into petrol by passing it through the synthetic zeolite ZSM-5. The petrol molecules are driven out of the zeolite and it can be reused.

Figure 3.1.7: *Zeolite ZSM-5 catalyst converts methanol made from methane into petrol*

Other examples of green chemistry:

- *The use of carbon dioxide as the blowing agent for expanded polystyrene production. Expanded polystyrene is a common material used in packing and food transportation. Hundreds of millions of tonnes are produced throughout the world, each year. Traditionally, CFCs and other ozone-depleting chemicals were used in the production process which caused a serious environmental hazard. Not using hazardous substances also allows the polystyrene to be more easily recycled. The CO_2 used in the process is reused from other industries, so overall the carbon released from the process is zero.*

Figure 3.1.8: *Reusing carbon dioxide as the blowing agent in the manufacture of expanded polystyrene reduces the use of ozone depleting chemicals*

- *The use of waste glycerol from biodiesel production to make propylene glycol, which can be used as a cheaper replacement for the more toxic ethylene glycol in antifreeze used in motor vehicles. The synthesis involves using a catalyst which allows the conversion temperature to be lowered while at the same time raising the efficiency of the distillation process.*

Figure 3.1.9: *The propylene glycol used in aircraft deicer is less toxic than ethylene glycol and can be made from waste glycerol from biodiesel production*

- *The manufacture of succinic acid from glucose obtained from renewable feedstocks. Succinic acid is an important chemical in the production of a number of everyday products including polyesters. It is also used as an acidity regulator in the food and beverage industry. Traditionally succinic acid is produced from oil-based feedstocks. The production of succinic acid by the fermentation of renewable feedstocks takes place at a lower temperature and is cheaper than the traditional method, and the carbon dioxide produced as a by-product is captured rather than being emitted into the atmosphere.*

GO! Nobel Prize winners

In 2005 Yves Chauvin, Robert H. Grubbs and Richard R. Schrock were collectively awarded the Nobel Prize in Chemistry for their work on alkene metathesis. Metathesis means 'changing places'. Alkene metathesis involves the double-bonding atom groups changing places with one another. The scientists worked out the reaction mechanism and discovered a variety of very efficient and selective catalysts which work at low temperatures. Because of the relative simplicity of alkene metathesis, fewer undesired by-products and toxic wastes are produced, compared to alternative reactions.

A simple example of alkene metathesis is two propene molecules reacting to form butene and ethene.

propene   propene   butene   ethene

Metathesis is becoming more important in the industrial synthesis of pharmaceuticals, plastics and chemicals needed for medical research. Metathesis is making their production cheaper and more environmentally friendly.

The synthesis of a complex substance Y, needed in cancer research, from molecule X is shown below. Substance X contains a long chain of carbon atoms in which a carbon has been replaced by an oxygen. In the synthesis of Y the long chain has become a large ring, which is required for the anti-cancer activity. To make the large ring, catalytic metathesis has been used with one of the catalysts discovered by the Nobel scientists. From the two double bonds at the ends of the chain (circled) two new double bonds have been obtained. One of these has been used to join two carbon atoms and form the large ring. The other double bond turns up in the by-product, ethene. Synthesising the large ring in any other way is very complicated and requires many more reaction steps.

X   Y   ethene

CHEMISTRY IN CONTEXT: THE BHOPAL DISASTER

*The **Bhopal disaster** was a gas leak incident in India, considered the world's worst industrial disaster. It occurred on the night of 2–3 December 1984 at the Union Carbide India Limited (UCIL) pesticide plant in a city called Bhopal. Over 500 000 people were exposed to methyl isocyanate (MIC) gas and other chemicals. The toxic chemicals leaked into the shanty towns located near the plant. Estimates vary* *on the exact death toll but it is known that thousands of people died on the night of the leak and thousands more are thought to have died in the months and years following. It has been estimated that in the years following the gas leak, hundreds of thousands have been affected in some way. Apart from MIC, the gas cloud may have contained phosgene, hydrogen cyanide, carbon monoxide, hydrogen chloride and oxides of nitrogen, either produced in the MIC storage tank or in the atmosphere. The toxic gas cloud was denser than the surrounding air and so stayed close to the ground and spread outwards through the surrounding community. It is still not clear exactly what happened but a number of failures in the safety systems were identified. It is thought that water managed to get into the MIC storage tank which started a number of reactions which produced the toxic gases.*

Figure 3.1.10: *Bhopal's death toll – initial death toll (official) (3–6 December): more than 3000; initial toll (unofficial): 7000–8000; total deaths to date: over 15 000; number affected: nearly 600 000; compensation: Union Carbide paid $470m in 1989*

GO! Activity 3.1.1

(a) In industry, suggest why gas phase reactions are often preferred to reactions which happen in solution.

(b) Suggest why pesticides which deteriorate within a few days are preferred to ones which last several weeks.

(c) Suggest why biodegradable detergents are preferred by operators of sewage works.

(d) Suggest why using plant material to produce ethanol is seen as a better source than crude oil in the future.

CHEMISTRY IN CONTEXT: INDUSTRIAL CASE STUDIES

Case study 1: The petrochemical industry in Scotland

INEOS to invest £1 billion in UK

This was one of the headlines announcing that INEOS, one of the largest chemical companies in the world, was to invest £1 billion in the UK, £350 million of it at its Grangemouth site. The company owns and operates Scotland's only oil refinery, producing a range of fuels including petrol and aviation fuel and supplies 70% of the fuel for Scotland's filling stations. INEOS also owns and operates the petrochemical plant on the Grangemouth site. Petrochemicals are chemicals derived from oil. The main petrochemicals produced at

Grangemouth are ethene and propene made by steam cracking ethane and propane. Ethene and propene are basic feedstocks – ethene is used to make industrial grade ethanol and poly(ethene) and propene is the monomer for the production of poly(propene).

Figure 3.1.11: *Flow diagram showing the processes taking place and products made at the INEOS Grangemouth site*

CHEMISTRY IN CONTEXT: WHY IS THERE OIL REFINING AND PETROCHEMICAL PRODUCTION AT GRANGEMOUTH?

Figure 3.1.12: *Grangemouth petrochemical plant produces ethene and propene for manufacturing plastics*

The site at Grangemouth was developed by British Petroleum (BP) in the 1920s to refine imported oil to produce fuels. The reasons for siting the refinery at Grangemouth were that there was an extensive flat area for building, good communications links and, most importantly, a skilled workforce from when shale was mined and processed to produce oil. The refinery was forced to close during the Second World War as the importing of oil dropped. In 1946 it reopened and the world demand for refined oil products led to the growth of the petrochemical industry. BP sited a new petrochemical plant next to its refinery because it produced the feedstocks needed for the plant. The oil needed by the refinery was shipped in from abroad and transported through a pipeline from the Finnart Ocean Terminal on the west coast of Scotland. In 1975 a new source of crude oil feedstock in the shape of North Sea oil further increased the opportunities for the site. The Forties Pipeline System has been the key to Grangemouth's continuing success. The fact that it provides direct access to raw materials for refinery and petrochemicals use has been the major factor in maintaining employment, investment and expansion across the whole complex. Oil has provided advantages previously only experienced in areas such as the Middle East.

Figure 3.1.13: *The Grangemouth site has good communications links and a skilled workforce*

Why does Grangemouth matter?

The petrochemical plant, along with its neighbouring oil refinery, makes up one of Scotland's largest industrial sites and is estimated to be 8% of Scotland's manufacturing industry. The complex employs more than 1300 people, as well as an estimated 2000 contractors, and another 10 000 jobs indirectly rely on the site. One of Scotland's largest modern apprenticeship schemes is based at the site. The refinery

Fracking is short for hydraulic fracturing and involves drilling down to the rocks and then injecting high pressure water to fracture the rocks and extract gas and oil from shale beds. Methane can also be released from coal seams by fracking.

Figure 3.1.14: *An INEOS Dragon ship brings fracked shale gas from the USA to Grangemouth*

📖 **Word bank**

• **decarbonisation** reducing and ultimately eliminating carbon dioxide emissions

supplies 70% of the fuel to Scotland's filling stations and the petrochemical plant uses *by-products* from the refinery to manufacture a range of products, from plastics to pharmaceuticals. The *steam and power* which runs BP's Kinneil terminal and the Forties pipeline, which delivers a third of the UK's oil output, comes from the Grangemouth site. The plant is also close to the shale deposits which were the basis of the modern chemical industry in the nineteenth century. Although shale is no longer mined and processed for oil, there is the potential to extract gas from underground shale deposits by a controversial process known as *fracking*. This is the same process used to extract the shale gas that INEOS imports from the USA. There is great potential to have a *relatively cheap* raw material, close to the Grangemouth site, *available* to produce the feedstocks needed for our petrochemical industry.

Over 60% of gas used in the United States is obtained in this way. In 1996 America was extracting 0·3 trillion cubic feet of shale gas. By 2011 this had risen to 7·8 trillion cubic feet. Attention is now returning to the area where the oil was first

□ possible area for exploration

□ exploration licence already granted

Figure 3.1.15: *A number of sites in Scotland have already been identified for fracking exploration*

discovered in Scotland. More than 20 000 square kilometres covering the entire central belt and a part of the southwest of Scotland have been identified for possible extraction of gas by fracking.

INEOS has most of the fracking licences issued by the Government (as of 2019). However, the Scottish Government does not support fracking or any other gas extraction process as it is not part of their decarbonisation policy.

Case study 2: Ethanol production in the UK

Bioethanol plant major boost to UK farmers

This was one of the headlines which announced the first tanker load of bioethanol leaving what was Europe's largest wheat bio-refinery at Wilton, Teesside, in the north of England in March 2010. The bioethanol is mixed with petrol which results in a greener fuel in motor vehicles. The UK government has made a commitment that by 2020, 13% of fuel sold should come from renewable sources. However, continued delay by the government in making a decision regarding supplementing petrol with ethanol has put the continued production of bioethanol at Wilton in jeopardy.

Since its opening in 2010 the plant has been taken over several times and had to stop production in April 2012 blaming a poor harvest, rising energy costs and the slow development of the market for bioethanol in the UK and Europe. In July 2013 the plant was bought over by CropEnergies, a major bioethanol producer in Germany, Belgium and France. The takeover secured the jobs of 100 workers at the plant and an estimated 2000 related jobs. Production was paused in 2018 but restarted in 2019.

> **KEEP UP TO DATE!**
> You can keep up to date with the government's policy on the use of bioethanol and bioethanol production at Wilton, by looking up 'UK Government's policy on bioethanol' and 'Bioethanol production at Wilton, Teesside' on the internet.

Figure 3.1.16 : *The bioethanol plant at Wilton on Teesside is one of the biggest bioethanol plants in Europe*

The bioethanol is produced by fermentation of animal grade wheat which is a renewable resource.

wheat (carbohydrate) → ethanol + carbon dioxide

The carbon dioxide by-product is collected and sold to the food and drinks industry. This is not just good economics but also stops the carbon dioxide being released into the atmosphere where it contributes to global warming. An additional benefit is the fermentation process results in unfermented grain and protein being left behind which is processed into animal feed products.

Ethanol is also manufactured in the UK by the direct catalytic hydration of ethene in the presence of steam, using phosphoric acid adsorbed on the surface of a solid (silica), as a catalyst. The reaction is reversible and exothermic:

$$C_2H_4(g) + H_2O(g) \;\overset{catalyst}{\rightleftharpoons}\; C_2H_5OH(g)$$

To achieve acceptable reaction rates, a temperature of *around 300°C is used*. Increasing the pressure produces more ethanol but also causes polymerisation of the ethene and higher pressure also means increased costs. In practice, the process is generally operated under a pressure of 60–70 atm.

Higher ethene conversion can be obtained using an excess of water (steam). But at high pressures the catalyst takes up water, its activity drops and it becomes diluted, draining away from the catalyst support.

Great care is taken to minimise the emissions of ethanol from the plant, together with the small amounts of by-products that are produced, mainly ethanal.

Considerable work is being done to improve the catalyst so that the temperature of the furnace can be reduced. This means that less fuel will be used to heat the furnace. With the above conditions, around 5% conversion is obtained. To obtain the 95% yield achieved, unreacted ethene is separated from the liquid products and recycled. The product contains a high proportion of water and is distilled to produce a 95% solution of ethanol. The process has a high atom economy – almost all of the reactants are converted into ethanol with very little by-product.

Table 3.1.1 summarises some of the advantages and disadvantages of making ethanol using non-renewable or renewable resources.

Table 3.1.1

Production method	Ethene and steam	Sugar from plant material
Feedstock	non-renewable	renewable
Type of process	runs all the time (continuous)	stop-start (batch)
Labour force	few workers needed	a lot of workers needed
Rate of reaction	fast	slow
Conditions needed	high temperature and pressure	warm, normal pressure
Purity of product	pure	needs to be purified
Energy needed	a lot	a little

Case study 3: Ammonia and urea production in New Zealand

New Zealand's economy relies heavily on agriculture, sheep and dairy farming and forestry. As a result, the fertiliser industry has become one of New Zealand's biggest economic sectors. The twenty-first century has seen an increase in the production of urea (NH_2CONH_2) used as a nitrogen fertiliser. Urea is made by reacting ammonia with carbon dioxide. The process is carried out at a complex in Kapuni, South Taranaki, and is summarised in figure 3.1.17.

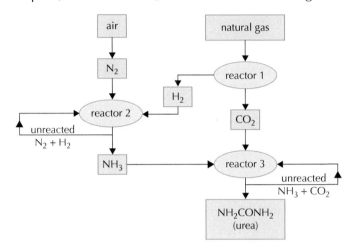

Figure 3.1.17: *Flow diagram showing ammonia and urea production at Kapuni, South Taranaki*

Economic considerations

The process uses three main raw materials: natural gas, air and water. The ammonia plant is situated next to the Kapuni gas treatment plant so natural gas is readily available. Natural gas is used as both fuel gas and as a source of hydrogen for the ammonia process. Carbon dioxide is produced as a by-product and is used in the manufacture of urea in the adjacent site. Air (the source of nitrogen) is, of course, in unlimited supply. Water is pumped from a nearby stream for the boilers, cooling water and process water. The waste water is treated after the process and returned to the stream. All the raw materials are cheap and readily available. Recycling of unreacted chemicals like nitrogen and hydrogen are fundamental to the processes to reduce waste and keep costs down.

Costs are minimised throughout the process by using waste heat boilers and heat exchangers. There are turbogenerators on site, driven by steam produced as part of the processes, which provide around 80% of the power needed to run the plant.

Heat recovery

Most of the heat produced during the various reactions is used to heat water to produce steam which is used to drive the turbo generators and produce energy for the whole plant. Recovered heat is also used to decompose ammonium carbamate to urea and also to evaporate water in the final stage of urea production.

Water recycling

Excess water from the various processes is used to feed the boilers and as the absorbing water for dissolving ammonia. Water evaporated in the concentration of urea is captured and reused.

Carbon dioxide recovery

A solvent called UCARSOL is used to dissolve carbon dioxide produced in the initial ammonia synthesis. The carbon dioxide is recovered from the solvent by heating it. The carbon dioxide and water evaporate. The water is cooled and condenses and the pure carbon dioxide is sent directly to the urea plant where it is used to produce urea. The cleaned UCARSOL is recycled and reused.

Ammonia recovery

At various stages in the processes unreacted and contaminated ammonia are recovered and purified. This is then fed directly into the urea production stage.

Environmental implications

The ammonia and urea complexes are operated in accordance with stringent safety and environmental standards. All effluent is fed into large holding ponds where it is treated and carefully checked before it is discharged. The effluent is sprayed onto fields surrounding the complex. Many waste minimisation measures are carried out during the process, resulting in the plant having minimal effect on the environment.

Ballance, the company which operated the urea plant, have announced a project to produce 'green hydrogen' by using electricity produced from renewable sources to produce hydrogen by electrolysing water. Currently the hydrogen comes from methane. Not only will the hydrogen be used to make ammonia, it can also be used as a fuel for cars and heavy transport. This would result in a drop in the amount of carbon dioxide emitted into the atmosphere. This is in line with the New Zealand government's decarbonisation policy.

KEEP UP TO DATE!
You can keep up to date with the development of green hydrogen by looking up 'Making green hydrogen at Kapuni, New Zealand' on the internet.

Figure 3.1.18: *The Kapuni urea plant showing the fields surrounding the plant*

Chemical analysis

The chemical laboratory plays an important role in monitoring the processes involved in both the ammonia and urea production.

Ammonia production

- The laboratory monitors the gaseous mixtures at each stage in the process using gas chromatography. The concentration of each component during the process is kept at a precalculated figure and laboratory results are compared to these figures. Adjustments are made to the process based on the laboratory results.

- The UCARSOL solution used to capture carbon dioxide is analysed daily to monitor the solution concentration, which must be kept within a certain range.

- The liquid ammonia is analysed to ensure that impurity concentrations are below maximum allowable levels.

Urea production

- The laboratory carries out analysis at various stages of granulation to ensure the granules are the correct size. The process is adjusted to meet the required final product size.
- The pH and moisture content of the final product is analysed.
- Boiler and cooling water is analysed to ensure that the pH is such that corrosion is minimised.

GO! Activity 3.1.2

You may wish to discuss this activity with a partner. You should however present your findings on your own.

Look at the issues (including green issues) industrial chemists have to consider when making a product (pages 187–191). Look at case study 3: Ammonia and urea production in New Zealand. Summarise how the issues are addressed and present the information in a suitable way. This could be in the form of a table, summary paragraphs, etc.

You can repeat the exercise for case studies 1 and 2.

Case study 4: Metals for the twenty-first century – the rare earth elements

CASE STUDY

What are they and why are they important?

The rare earth elements (REEs) are the 15 lanthanides (see the periodic table on page 13) plus yttrium. Scandium is found in most rare earth deposits and is sometimes classified as a rare earth element. It is the industrial uses of rare-earth compounds or mixtures of the rare-earth metals that account for the bulk of the rare earths processed throughout the world. Rare earth metals and alloys that contain them are used in many devices that people use every day, such as computer memory, DVDs, rechargeable batteries, mobile phones, car catalytic converters, magnets, fluorescent lighting and much more.

Since the 1990s there has been an explosion in demand for many items that require rare earth metals – in 2019 it was estimated that there were over 5.5 billion mobile phones in use worldwide. The use of computers and DVDs has grown almost as fast as mobile phones.

Many rechargeable batteries are made with rare earth compounds. Demand for the batteries is being driven by demand for portable electronic devices such as mobile phones, readers, computers and cameras. These devices have a short lifespan and recycling of the rare earth elements is seldom done. Billions are thrown away each year.

Y 39	Yttrium: Lasers, superconductors and microwaves
Nd 60	Neodymium: Magnets, lasers radiation filtering
Eu 63	Europium: Televisions, lasers, nuclear reactors
Tb 65	Terbium: Fuel cells, electronics, sonar systems
Dy 66	Dysprosium: Magnets, lasers, nuclear reactors

Figure 3.1.19: *Rare earth elements and their uses*

Figure 3.1.20: *Tiny amounts of rare earth metals are used in most small electronic devices*

Around 1 kg of rare earth compounds are contained in batteries that power electric vehicles and hybrid-electric vehicles. As these types of vehicles grow in popularity the demand for batteries made with rare earth compounds will grow even faster.

Rare earth elements are used as catalysts for air pollution control, phosphors for illuminated screens on electronic devices and polishing compounds for optical-quality glass. All of these products are expected to experience rising demand. Some large wind turbines need up to two tonnes of rare earth magnets (supermagnets). Rare earth metals are easy to magnetise and hold their magnetism in the solid state.

Availability and sustainability of rare earth elements

The British Geological Survey's risk list ranks the threat to the global supply of the metals and other elements necessary to maintain our economy and lifestyle in our modern society. A number of factors which may affect availability are considered when the list is compiled:

- The natural abundance of elements in the Earth's crust.
- The location of current production and reserves.
- The political stability of the locations.
- Recycling rates and availability of substitute elements.

The *rare earth elements* are at the top of the list. The name rare is misleading as they are quite abundant although tend to be spread out across the Earth's crust and only in mineable quantities in certain parts of the world. China is

Figure 3.1.21: *Close up of a battery in a plug in hybrid car*

Figure 3.1.22: *Some large wind turbines need up to two tonnes of rare earth magnets (supermagnets)*

the biggest producer of rare earth elements, supplying over 90% of the world's supply – in fact China is now the leading global producer of 22 of the 41 elements on the risk list. Competition for resources is growing, particularly in the emerging economies in Asia and South America. Countries with resources are now more likely to use them than export them.

Supply and demand normally determines the market price of a resource. As supplies shrink prices go up. If a single country controls almost all of the production and makes a firm decision not to export then the entire supply of a resource can be quickly cut off. That is a dangerous situation when new sources of supply take so long to develop.

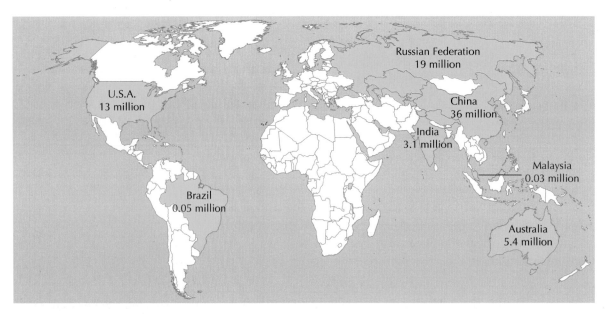

Figure 3.1.23: *World reserves of rare earth elements (tonnes) in 2009*

Write a report on the importance of the rare earth elements. Include the following in your report:

• why they are important

• availability

• sustainability

• the search for alternative sources

• cost.

There is currently no rare earth mining going on in the European Union, which relies almost entirely on Chinese imports. A company called UK Seabed Resources, in partnership with the UK government, holds licences and contracts to explore around 100 000 square miles of the Pacific seabed and collect mineral-rich polymetallic nodules (unusual formations on the ocean floor) which contain rare earths. Similarly, Japanese scientists have found large reserves of rare earth metals on the Pacific seabed that they say can be mined cheaply.

CHEMISTRY IN CONTEXT: CHEMICAL WEAPONS

Chemical weapons used in Syria

This is just one of the newspaper headlines in 2013 which announced to the world that chemical weapons had been used in the civil war in Syria.

Many chemicals can be harmful to living things if handled the wrong way or if you are accidently exposed to them. The chemicals used in weapons of mass destruction however are chemicals which are deliberately made in order to inflict harm on human beings. Under the Chemical Weapons Convention (1993), there is a legally-binding world-wide ban on the production, stockpiling and use of chemical weapons and the chemicals used to make chemical weapons. However, some countries, including Syria, are not signed up to the agreement.

One of the chemicals used in the chemical weapons used in Syria is called mustard gas ($C_4H_8Cl_2S$), which causes large blisters to form on exposed skin and in the lungs. Pure 'sulfur mustards' are colourless, viscous liquids at room temperature. When used in impure form, such as in weapons, they are usually yellow-brown in colour and have a smell resembling mustard plants, hence the name. Mustard gas is an example of a chemical which has no other use to us other than to cause harm to humans.

The war in Syria was not the first time that chemical weapons were used in a war. Mustard gas was used during the First World War along with phosgine and chlorine gas. Mustard gas was first used effectively in the First World War by the German army against British and Canadian soldiers near Ypres, Belgium, in 1917 and later also against the French Second Army. The Allies first used mustard gas in 1917 when it captured German mustard-gas shells. It took the British more than a year to develop their own mustard gas weapon.

Chlorine gas was also used as a chemical weapon in the First World War. This resulted in thousands of deaths and thousands of other people being permanently disabled. Chlorine rapidly put soldiers out of action when inhaled, even in relatively low concentrations.

In October 2013 Syria agreed to destroy all of its facilities for making chemical weapons by 1 November, under the supervision of the Organisation for the Prohibition of Chemical Weapons (OPCW). By mid-2014 it should have destroyed its entire stockpile of chemical weapons.

Figure 3.1.24: *Blisters caused by exposure to mustard gas*

Figure 3.1.25: *A First World War soldier being treated for the effects of mustard gas*

However there have continued to be claims that the Syrian government used chemical weapons against civilians in 2017 and 2018. In September 2019 the US announced that they had concluded that the Syrians had used chlorine as a chemical weapon against civilians on 19 May 2019.

Mole calculations

Mole ratios in a formula

One mole of any substance contains the same number of **atoms** in an element as there are **molecules** or **ionic units** in a compound.

For example, 1 mole of carbon has the same number of atoms as there are molecules in 1 mole of carbon dioxide and ionic units in 1 mole of sodium chloride.

1 mole of molecules contains more than 1 mole of atoms.

For example, 1 mole of carbon dioxide (CO_2) contains 3 moles of atoms – 1 mole of carbon atoms and 2 moles of oxygen atoms. So, 0·5 moles of carbon dioxide contains 0·5 moles of carbon atoms and 1 mole of oxygen atoms, i.e. 1·5 moles of atoms.

1 mole of ionic units has more than 1 mole of ions.

For example, 1 mole of sodium chloride (NaCl) contains 1 mole of Na^+ ions and 1 mole of Cl^- ions, i.e. 2 moles of ions in total. So, 0·5 moles of sodium chloride contains 0·5 moles of Na^+ ions and 0·5 moles of Cl^- ions, i.e. 1 mole of ions in total.

Worked examples 1 and 2 show how this relationship can be used to calculate masses of substances present in everyday foodstuffs.

> ⚠ **Remember this**
>
> Remember the link between moles (n) and mass (m) from National 5:
> 1 mol = gram formula mass (GFM)
>
> Gram formula mass can be calculated from relative atomic masses.
>
> The relationship n = m / GFM can be found in the SQA data booklet. From this,
>
> m = n x GFM.

Worked example: 1

The nutritional information label on a 150 g family bag of potato crisps stated that it contained 0·69 g of sodium. The sodium is in the form of sodium chloride (NaCl).

(a) Calculate the mass of sodium chloride in the 150 g bag of potato crisps.

(b) Calculate the average mass of sodium chloride in a 28 g portion of the crisps.

Worked answer:

(a) Step 1: Calculate the number of moles of sodium ions – this will be the same as the number of moles of chloride ions in NaCl (1:1 ratio). This is also the number of moles of NaCl ionic units.

Gfm of Na = 23 g.

Number of moles of Na = mass/gfm = 0·69/23 = 0·03 mol

The number of moles of NaCl is also 0·03.

Step 2: Calculate the mass of NaCl from the number of moles.

Gfm of NaCl = 23 + 35·5 = 58·5 g.

Mass = moles × gfm

$\qquad$ = 0·03 × 58·5

$\qquad$ = 1·76 g

So, the mass of sodium chloride in the 150 g pack is **1·76 g**.

(b) There are 1·76 g of sodium chloride in the 150 g bag:

$$\begin{array}{ll} 150 \text{ g crisps} & \rightarrow \quad 1·76 \text{ g sodium chloride} \\ \text{So, 28 g of crisps} & \rightarrow \quad \dfrac{1·76}{150} \times 28 = 0·33 \text{ g} \end{array}$$

The mass of sodium chloride in 28 g of crisps is **0·33 g**.

Worked example: 2

A 220 g packet of a low sodium salt contains 66% by mass of potassium chloride (KCl) and 34% by mass sodium chloride (NaCl).

(a) Calculate the mass of potassium in the 220 g packet of the salt.

(b) Calculate the mass of potassium in a 10 g portion of the salt.

Worked answer:

(a) Step 1: Calculate the mass of KCl in the 220 g mixture.

$$\text{Mass of KCl} = \frac{66}{100} \times 220 = 132 \text{ g}$$

Step 2: Calculate the number of moles of KCl in the 132 g.

$$\text{Moles of KCl} = \frac{132}{74 \cdot 6} = 1 \cdot 77 \text{ mol}$$

Step 3: Calculate the mass of potassium from the number of moles of KCl ionic units.

$$1 \text{ mol K} = 39 \cdot 1 \text{ g}$$

So, $1 \cdot 77$ mol $= 39 \cdot 1 \times 1 \cdot 77 = \textbf{69} \cdot \textbf{2 g.}$

(b) There are $69 \cdot 2$ g of potassium in the 220 g packet of salt.

$$220 \text{ g of low salt} \quad \rightarrow \quad 69 \cdot 2 \text{ g of potassium}$$

So, 10 g of low salt $\rightarrow \dfrac{69 \cdot 2}{220} \times 10 = \textbf{3} \cdot \textbf{15 g of potassium.}$

GO! Activity 3.1.4

Use the examples above to help you complete the following calculations.

1. The nutritional information label on a packet of breakfast cereal stated that each 100 g of the cereal contained $0 \cdot 39$ g of sodium. The sodium is in the form of sodium chloride (NaCl).

   Calculate the mass of sodium chloride in a 30 g serving of the cereal.

2. A 215 g packet of a low sodium salt contains 65% by mass of potassium chloride (KCl) and 35% by mass sodium chloride (NaCl).

   (a) Calculate the mass of sodium in the 215 g packet of the salt.

   (b) Calculate the mass of sodium in a 10 g portion of the salt.

Calculating masses reacting and produced

Quantities reacting and being produced can be calculated from balanced equations. We can do this because 1 mole of any substance contains the same number of atoms in an element and molecules or ionic units in a compound.

The numbers in front of the formulae in a balanced equation tell us the mole ratio(s) of reactants and products. The number 1 is never written in front of a formula in an equation – the fact that a formula is written tells you there must be at least 1 mole present. State symbols can be included in equations but do not effect any calculations.

The reaction between hydrogen and chlorine can be used to show how mole ratios can be used:

$$\text{hydrogen} + \text{chlorine} \rightarrow \text{hydrogen chloride}$$

Balanced equation:	$H_2(g)$ +	$Cl_2(g)$	$\rightarrow$	$2HCl(g)$
Mole ratios:	1 mol	1 mol	$\rightarrow$	2 mol
Converting to grams:	2 g +	71 g	$\rightarrow$	73 g $(2 \times 36 \cdot 5)$
So, by proportion,	2 mol	2 mol	$\rightarrow$	4 mol
Converting to grams:	4 g +	142 g	$\rightarrow$	146 g
and,	0·1 mol	0·1 mol	$\rightarrow$	0·2 mol
Converting to grams:	0·2 g +	7·1 g	$\rightarrow$	7·3 g

Worked example: 1

(a) Calculate the number of moles of hydrogen chloride produced when 0·3 mol of hydrogen reacts with excess chlorine (excess means more than enough for complete reaction).

Worked answer:

$$\text{hydrogen} + \text{chlorine} \rightarrow \text{hydrogen chloride}$$

H_2 +	Cl_2 $\rightarrow$	$2HCl$
1 mol	1 mol $\rightarrow$	2 mol

Key relationship **1 mol** $\rightarrow$ **2 mol**

So, 0·3 mol $\rightarrow$ 0·6 mol $(2 \times 0 \cdot 3)$

Moles of hydrogen chloride produced is **0·6 mol**.

Although not asked for in this example, the number of moles of chlorine can be worked out (0·3 mol).

If the question had asked for the answer to be in grams, the number of moles is multiplied by the gram formula mass (GFM):

$$\text{Mass} = \text{moles} \times \text{GFM} \ (m = n \times \text{GFM})$$

$$= 0 \cdot 6 \times 36 \cdot 5$$

$$\text{Mass} = \textbf{21} \cdot \textbf{9 g}$$

(b) Calculate the mass of hydrogen chloride produced when 6·1 g of chlorine reacts with excess hydrogen.

Worked answer:

$$\text{hydrogen} + \text{chlorine} \rightarrow \text{hydrogen chloride}$$

H_2 +	Cl_2 $\rightarrow$	$2HCl$
1 mol	1 mol $\rightarrow$	2 mol

Key relationship **1 mol** $\rightarrow$ **2 mol**

Converting to grams:

71 g	→	73 g
So, 1 g (71/71)	→	73/71 g
So, 6·1 g	→	(73/71) × 6·1
	→	6·27 g

Mass of hydrogen chloride produced is **6·27 g**.

The mass of hydrogen is not asked for in this question but as in example 1 (a) it could be calculated from the balanced equation.

(c) Calculate the mass of hydrogen needed to produce 11·9 g of hydrogen chloride.

Worked answer:

hydrogen + chlorine → hydrogen chloride

$$H_2 + Cl_2 → 2HCl$$

1 mol   1 mol →   2 mol

Key relationship   **1 mol**   →   **2 mol**

Converting to grams:

2 g	→	73 g
So, 2/73 g	←	1 g (73/73)
So, (2/73) × 11·9	←	11·9 g
0·33 g	←	

Mass of hydrogen needed is **0·33 g**.

In this calculation the arrows point right to left in the part of the calculation showing that the mass of hydrogen needed is calculated backwards from the mass of hydrogen chloride produced.

(It is more usual to measure the quantity of gas reacting or produced as volume rather than mass. Converting moles to volume is detailed on page 221.)

Worked example: 2

Calculate the mass of silver metal produced when 2·3 g of Cu is added to excess silver(I) nitrate solution.

Worked answer:

$$Cu + 2AgNO_3 → 2\,Ag + Cu(NO_3)_2$$

1 mol   2 mol   2 mol   1 mol

Key relationship   **1 mol**   →   **2 mol**

Converting to grams:

$$63 \cdot 5 \text{ g} \qquad \rightarrow 215.8 \text{ g } (2 \times 107.9)$$

$$\text{so, } 1 \cdot 0 \text{ g } (63 \cdot 5/63 \cdot 5) \rightarrow 3 \cdot 4 \text{ g } (215.8/63 \cdot 5)$$

$$\text{so, } 2 \cdot 30 \text{ g } (1 \times 2 \cdot 3) \rightarrow 7 \cdot 82 \text{ g } (3 \cdot 4 \times 2 \cdot 3)$$

The mass of silver produced is **7·82 g**

GO! Activity 3.1.5

Use the examples above to help you complete the following calculations.

1. (a) Calculate the mass of water produced when 5·3 g of hydrogen burns in excess oxygen.

    Balanced equation: $2H_2(g) + O_2(g) \rightarrow 2\ H_2O(\ell)$

   (b) Calculate the mass of oxygen needed to burn all of the hydrogen.

2. (a) Calculate the mass of iron(III) sulfide produced when 3·1 g of iron reacts with excess sulfur.

    Balanced equation: $2Fe(s) + 3S(s) \rightarrow Fe_2S_3(s)$

   (b) Calculate the mass of sulfur which would be needed to react with all of the iron.

Calculations involving mass and moles, concentration and volume of solution

The number of moles (n) in solution can be calculated if the concentration (c) and volume (V) of the solution are known, using the relationship: $n = c \times V$. From this,

$c = n / V$ and $V = n / c$.

The relationship $n = c \times V$ can be found in the SQA data booklet so you don't have to remember it.

Calculating the number of **moles** of solution reacting and being produced can be calculated from a balanced equation.

SQA KEY AREA

Worked example: 1

(a) Calculate the number of **moles** of sodium hydroxide needed to completely neutralise 250 cm³ of 0·2 mol l⁻¹ sulfuric acid.

$$2NaOH + H_2SO_4 \rightarrow Na_2SO_4 + 2H_2O$$

Worked answer:

(a) **Step 1:** Work out the key mole relationship from the balanced equation.

$$2NaOH + H_2SO_4 \rightarrow Na_2SO_4 + 2H_2O$$

Key relationship   2 mol   1 mol

From the question, 250 cm³ of 0·2 mol l⁻¹ sulfuric acid reacts completely.

Calculate number of moles: $n = c \times V$

$$= 0·20 \times 0·25$$

$$= 0·05 \text{ mol}$$

The mole ratio shows that twice the number of moles of sodium hydroxide are needed to completely neutralise the sulfuric acid, i.e. 0·10 mol.

(b) If the volume of sodium hydroxide was known in example 1 then the **concentration** of the sodium hydroxide could be calculated using the relationship

$$c = n / V.$$

Let's say 50 cm³ of sodium hydroxide reacted in the above example. The concentration of the sodium hydroxide can be calculated using $c = n / V$.

$$c = 0·10/0·05 = \textbf{2·0 mol l}^{-1}$$

(c) Calculate the **mass** of sodium sulfate (gfm = 142·1 g) produced in **(a)**, assuming complete neutralisation.

Worked answer:

Step 1: Work out the key mole relationship from the balanced equation

$$2NaOH + H_2SO_4 \rightarrow Na_2SO_4 + 2H_2O$$

Key relationship   1 mol   1 mol

From part **(a)** 0·05 mol of sulfuric acid react, so 0·05 mol of sodium sulfate will be produced.

Step 2: Calculate the mass from the number of moles.

Mass of $Na_2SO_4 = n \times GFM = 0·05 \times 142·1 = \textbf{7·1 g}$

The **volume** of solution needed in a reaction can be calculated from the balanced equation.

Worked example: 2

Calculate the **volume** of 0·05 mol l^{-1} sulfuric acid needed to completely neutralise 30 cm^3 of 0·1 mol l^{-1} potassium hydroxide.

$$2KOH + H_2SO_4 \rightarrow K_2SO_4 + 2H_2O$$

Worked answer:

Step 1: Work out the key mole relationship from the balanced equation.

$$2KOH + H_2SO_4 \rightarrow K_2SO_4 + 2H_2O$$

Key relationship   2 mol   1 mol

Moles of potassium hydroxide reacting = $c \times V$ = 0·1 × 0·03
= 0·003 mol

Moles of sulfuric acid reacting = 0·03 × 0·5 = 0·0015 mol (half the number of sulfuric acid moles)

Step 2: Calculate the volume from the number of moles.

$V = n/c$ = 0·0015/0·050 = **0·030 l** (30 cm^3)

GO! Activity 3.1.6

1. Calculate the number of **moles** of sulfuric acid needed to neutralise 20 cm^3 of 0·1 mol l^{-1} sodium hydroxide solution.

$$2NaOH + H_2SO_4 \rightarrow Na_2SO_4 + 2H_2O$$

2. (a) 50 cm^3 of 0·1 mol l^{-1} hydrochloric acid is required to completely neutralise 19·8 cm^3 of sodium hydroxide solution. Calculate the **concentration** of the sodium hydroxide.

$$NaOH + HCl \rightarrow NaCl + H_2O$$

(b) Calculate the **mass** of sodium chloride produced.

3. Calculate the **volume** of 0·5 mol l^{-1} sodium hydroxide needed to completely neutralise 20 cm^3 of 0·3 mol l^{-1} of sulfuric acid.

$$2NaOH + H_2SO_4 \rightarrow Na_2SO_4 + 2H_2O$$

4. Calculate the **mass** of calcium carbonate needed to react completely with 150 cm^3 of 0·1 mol l^{-1} hydrochloric acid.

$$CaCO_3 + 2HCl \rightarrow CaCl_2 + H_2O + CO_2$$

Reactants in excess

All of the previous calculations have assumed that all of the reactants actually react to form products. This is seldom the case. One reactant is usually the **limiting reactant** – one which is completely used up. Other reactants which are not completely used up are in **excess**. Calculations must be based on the quantity of limiting reactant present.

Worked example: 1

25 cm³ of 0·1 mol l⁻¹ sodium hydroxide solution is added to 10 cm³ of 0·2 mol l⁻¹ hydrochloric acid.

$$NaOH + HCl \rightarrow NaCl + H_2O$$

(a) Calculate which reactant is in excess.

(b) Calculate the mass of sodium chloride produced.

Worked answer:

(a) Step 1: Work out the key mole relationship from the balanced equation.

$$NaOH + HCl \rightarrow NaCl + H_2O$$

Key relationship 1 mol   1 mol

Step 2: Calculate the **number of moles** of each reactant from the information in the question.

$n = c \times V$

NaOH: $n = 0·1 \times 0·025$

$= 0·0025$ mol

HCl: $n = 0·2 \times 0·010$

$= 0·0020$ mol

The sodium hydroxide and hydrochloric acid react in a 1:1 ratio, so the hydrochloric acid is the limiting reactant and the sodium hydroxide is in excess.

(b) The number of moles of sodium chloride can be calculated from the mole ratio in the balanced equation using the number of moles of the limiting reactant (hydrochloric acid).

Figure 3.1.26: *Sodium hydroxide being neutralised by hydrochloric acid during a titration*

Step 1: Work out the key mole relationship from the balanced equation.

$$NaOH + HCl \rightarrow NaCl + H_2O$$

Key relationship   1 mol   1 mol

               0·002   0·002

Step 2: Calculate the mass of sodium chloride from the moles produced.

$m = n \times GFM$

   $= 0·002 \times 58·5$

   $= 0·117$ g

Worked example: 2

Hydrogen gas can be produced in the laboratory by reacting zinc with hydrochloric acid. 5·9 g of zinc was added to 250 cm^3 of 0·1 mol l^{-1} of hydrochloric acid.

(a) Calculate which reactant is in excess.

(b) Calculate the mass of hydrogen produced.

$$Zn + 2HCl \rightarrow ZnCl_2 + H_2$$

Worked answer:

(a) Step 1: Work out the key mole relationship from the balanced equation.

$$Zn + 2HCl \rightarrow ZnCl_2 + H_2$$

Key relationship   1 mol   2 mol

Step 2: Calculate the **number of moles** of each reactant from the information in the question.

Zinc: $n = m/GFM$

        $= 5·9/65·4$

        $= 0·090$ mol

Acid: $n = m/GFM$

        $= 0·1 \times 0·25$

        $= 0·025$ mol

Because the mole ratio of zinc:acid is 1:2, the number of moles of acid which would be needed to react with all of the zinc would be $2 \times 0.09 = 0.18$ mol.

The zinc is in excess, so the acid is the limiting reactant.

(b) The mass of hydrogen produced can be worked out using the mole ratios in the balanced equation and using the number of moles of acid, as this is the limiting reactant.

Step 1: Work out the key mole relationship from the balanced equation.

$$Zn + 2HCl \rightarrow ZnCl_2 + H_2$$

Key relationship   2 mol   1 mol

                       0.0250 mol   0.0125 mol

Step 2: Calculate the mass of hydrogen from the moles produced.

$$m = n \times GFM$$

$$= 0.0125 \times 2$$

$$= \textbf{0.025 g}$$

Measuring the mass of a gas is an unusual way of measuring the quantity of gas. Volume is the standard measurement and the method for calculating volumes of gas produced is detailed in the next section.

GO! **Activity 3.1.7**

1. 30 cm³ of 0.1 mol l⁻¹ of sulfuric acid is added to 20 cm³ of 0.2 mol l⁻¹ potassium hydroxide.

$$2KOH + H_2SO_4 \rightarrow K_2SO_4 + 2H_2O$$

(a) Calculate which reactant is in excess.

(b) Calculate the mass of potassium sulfate produced.

2. 4.38 g of magnesium was added to 100 cm³ of 2 mol l⁻¹ of nitric acid.

$$Mg + 2HNO_3 \rightarrow Mg(NO_3)_2 + H_2$$

(a) Calculate the reactant in excess.

(b) Calculate the mass of magnesium nitrate produced.

Calculating volumes of gas

Volumes of gas reacting and being produced can be calculated if the **molar volume (V_m)** is known. Molar volume is the volume occupied by 1 mole of a gas when measured at a given temperature and pressure. This means that the molar volume changes depending on the temperature and pressure at which it is measured. The molar volume for any gas is the same so long as it is measured at the same temperature and pressure.

> ⚠ **Remember this**
>
> For gases, **1 mol** = **molar volume**. The unit for molar volume is **litres mol⁻¹ (l mol⁻¹)**. Measured at standard temperature and pressure (s.t.p = 0°C and 1 atmosphere pressure), molar volume is 22·4 l mol⁻¹. Measured at room temperature and pressure (20°C and 1 atmosphere pressure), molar volume is approximately 24·0 l mol⁻¹.
>
> Converting mass to volume and volume to mass can be done by converting first to moles.
>
> Gram formula mass (GFM)   ↔   1 mole   ↔   molar volume (V_m).

Worked example: 1

Calculate the volume occupied by 0·2 mol of carbon dioxide at room temperature and pressure. Take V_m = 24·0 l mol⁻¹.

Worked answer:

1 mol = 24·0 l mol⁻¹

So, 0·2 mol = 0·2 x 24 = 4·8 l

Worked example: 2

Calculate the number of moles in 7·2 l of carbon dioxide. Take V_m = 23·5 l mol⁻¹.

Worked answer:

23·5 l is the volume occupied by 1 mol of CO_2.

7·2 l will be the volume occupied by $\frac{7·2}{23·5} \times 1 = 0·31$ mol.

Worked example: 3

Calculate the volume occupied by 3·2 g of carbon dioxide. Take V_m = 23·9 l mol⁻¹.

Worked answer:

Step 1: Convert mass to moles.

n = m/GFM

   = 3·20/44·0

   = 0·073 mol

Step 2: Convert moles to volume.

1 mol = 23·9 l mol⁻¹

So, 0·073 mol = 0·073 × 23·9 = 1·74 l

GO! Activity 3.1.8

1. Calculate the volume occupied by 0·1 mol of hydrogen gas at room temperature and pressure. Take V_m = 23·8 l mol^{-1}.

2. Calculate the number of moles in 3·2 l of methane. Take V_m = 23·5 l mol^{-1}.

3. Calculate the number of moles of CO_2 in 250 cm^3 of the gas. Take the molar volume (V_m) to be 24·0 l mol^{-1}.

4. Calculate the volume occupied by 2·2 g of butane (C_4H_{10}) at room temperature and pressure. Take V_m = 24·0 l mol^{-1}.

5. A butane (C_4H_{10}) gas cylinder contains 7 kg of gas. Calculate the volume this mass of gas would occupy at room temperature and pressure. Take V_m = 23·7 l mol^{-1}.

In any calculation involving gases reacting or being produced, the volumes can be worked out from the mole ratio of reactants and products. Gas volumes reacting or being produced can also be calculated when solids and solutions are involved in reactions by knowing the mole ratio from the balanced equation and calculating the number of moles actually reacting and being produced and converting to volumes, provided the molar volume is known.

Worked example: 1

Calculate the volume of carbon dioxide gas produced when 150 cm^3 of methane (CH_4) burns in excess oxygen.

$$CH_4(g) + 2O_2(g) \rightarrow CO_2(g) + 2H_2O(\ell)$$

Worked answer:

Step 1: Work out the key mole relationship from the balanced equation.

$$CH_4 + 2O_2 \rightarrow CO_2 + 2H_2O$$

Key relationship 1 mol   1 mol

Step 2: Use the relationship 1 mol = V_m. This means that if one gas volume is known and the mole ratio is known then the other gas volumes can be calculated by proportion.

Figure 3.1.27: *Natural gas, which is mainly methane, burning in a gas cooker*

$$CH_4 + 2O_2 \rightarrow CO_2 + 2H_2O$$

	1 mol	1 mol
Gas volume relationship	1 vol	1 vol

$$150 \text{ cm}^3 \rightarrow 150 \text{ cm}^3$$

So, 150 cm³ of methane produces 150 cm³ of carbon dioxide.

The question states there is excess oxygen available, which means there is more than enough oxygen available to react with all of the methane. The exact volume of oxygen can be worked out from the mole ratio in the balanced equation – in this case 1:2, so the volume of oxygen used up is 300 cm³.

> ### 🔍 Hint
> vol is the volume of gas given in the question.

Worked example: 2

45 cm³ of methane is reacted with 125 cm³ of oxygen. Show by calculation which reactant is in excess and by how much.

$$CH_4(g) + 2O_2(g) \rightarrow CO_2(g) + 2H_2O(\ell)$$

Worked answer:

Step 1: Work out the key mole relationship and link to volume.

$$CH_4(g) + 2O_2(g) \rightarrow CO_2(g) + 2H_2O(\ell)$$

Key mole relationship: 1 mol   2 mol

Gas volume relationship: $1 \times V_m$ $2 \times V_m$

Step 2: Select one of the reactants, and calculate the volume of this reactant that would be needed to react with the given volume of the other reactant.

Find the volume of O_2 needed for the given volume of CH_4.

$$45 \text{ cm}^3 \text{ CH}_4 \rightarrow 2 \times 45 = 90 \text{ cm}^3 \text{ O}_2$$

Volume of O_2 **needed** = 90 cm³.

Step 3: Calculate volume of excess oxygen gas.

Volume of excess oxygen = volume at start – volume used

$$= 125 - 90$$

Volume of excess oxygen = 35 cm³.

Worked example: 3

Calculate the volume of hydrogen gas produced when 5·5 g of zinc reacts completely with excess hydrochloric acid. Take molar volume (V_m) to be 24 l mol^{-1}.

$$Zn + 2HCl \rightarrow ZnCl_2 + H_2$$

Worked answer:

Step 1: Work out the key mole relationship from the balanced equation.

$$Zn + 2HCl \rightarrow ZnCl_2 + H_2$$

1 mol	1 mol
1 mol	V_m (24 l mol^{-1})

Step 2: Calculate the moles of zinc reacting.

n = m/GFM

  = 5·5/65·4

  = 0·08 mol

Step 3: Calculate the volume of gas produced from the mole: V_m ratio in step 2.

  1 mol $\rightarrow$ V_m (24 l mol^{-1})

So, 0·08 mol $\rightarrow$ 0·08 × 24 = **1·92 l**

Worked example: 4

Nitrogen gas is produced in a car air bag by the rapid decomposition of sodium azide (gfm = 65 g).

$$2\,NaN_3 \rightarrow 2\,Na + 3\,N_2\,(g)$$

sodium azide

Calculate the volume of gas produced when 23 g of sodium azide decomposes. (Take V_m = 24 l mol^{-1})

Worked answer:

Step 1: Work out the key mole relationship from the balanced equation.

Figure 3.1.28: *An inflated airbag under test conditions*

$$2\ NaN_3 \rightarrow 2\ Na + 3\ N_2$$

2 mol   3 mol

2 mol $3 \times V_m$

Step 2: Calculate the moles of sodium azide reacting.

n = m/GFM

  = 23/65

  = 0·35 mol

Step 3: Calculate the volume of gas produced from the mole: V_m ratio in step 2.

2 mol $\rightarrow$ $3 \times V_m$ (24 l mol^{-1})

1 mol $\rightarrow$ $1·5 \times 24$

So, 0·35 mol $\rightarrow$ $0·035 \times 1·5 \times 24$ = **12·6 l**

Worked example: 5

Hint

Density values are found in the SQA data booklet.

Figure 3.1.29: *Neon gas is used in certain types of lighting*

Calculate the molar volume of neon, at standard temperature and pressure (s.t.p), given its density is 0·0009 g cm^{-3}.

Worked answer:

Density of neon = 0·0009 g cm^{-3}, which means 0·0009 g occupies 1 cm^3.

So, 1 g occupies 1/0·0009 = 1111·1 cm^3 = 1·11 l.

gfm of neon = 20·2 g

So, 20·2 g occupies $1·11 \times 20·2$ = 22·4 l.

The molar volume of neon = 22·4 l at s.t.p.

GO! Activity 3.1.9

1. Calculate the volume of carbon dioxide produced when 500 cm³ of butane gas burns in excess oxygen.

$$C_4H_{10}(g) + 6\tfrac{1}{2}O_2(g) \rightarrow 4CO_2(g) + 5H_2O(\ell)$$

2. 60 cm³ of propane is burned in 450 cm³ of oxygen. Show by calculation which reactant is in excess and by how much.

$$C_3H_8(g) + 5O_2(g) \rightarrow 3CO_2(g) + 4H_2O(\ell)$$

3. Calculate the volume of carbon dioxide produced when 2·3 g of calcium carbonate reacts completely with excess hydrochloric acid. Take molar volume to be 24·0 l mol⁻¹.

$$CaCO_3(s) + 2HCl(aq) \rightarrow CaCl_2(aq) + CO_2(g) + H_2O(\ell)$$

4. Calculate the molar volume of Xenon, at standard temperature and pressure (s.t.p), given its density is 0·0059 g cm⁻³.

Experimental determination of molar volume

The molar volume of a gas at room temperature and pressure can be worked out in the laboratory as follows:

1. A flask has the air pumped out of it, then it is weighed on a balance.

2. The flask is filled with a gas and reweighed.

3. The flask is filled with water and the volume of water measured. This gives the volume of the flask.

clip

flask

gas

top pan balance

Figure 3.1.30: *Molar volume at room temperature and pressure can be calculated from its density by first weighing the gas*

The results for three gases are shown in table 3.1.2.

Table 3.1.2

Gas	Oxygen	Nitrogen	Carbon dioxide
mass of 1 mole of gas	32·0 g	28·0 g	44·0 g
mass of empty flask	250·00 g	250·00 g	250·00 g
mass of flask + gas	250·27 g	250·24 g	250·38 g
mass of gas in flask	0·27 g	0·24 g	0·38 g
volume of gas in flask	200 cm³	200 cm³	200 cm³
calculated molar volume	23·70 l	23·33 l	23·16 l

Note that the molar volumes in the table are close to each other but not exactly the same. This is due to experimental error. The main error in the experiment is that not all of the air can be evacuated from the flask and when the gas being investigated is pumped in some air will also be present.

The calculation of the molar volume for oxygen is detailed below:

0·27 g of oxygen occupies 200 cm³

1 g of oxygen occupies 200/0·27 cm³

So, 32·0 g (1 mol) of oxygen occupies 32·0 x (200/0·27) cm³

Molar volume = 23·70 l mol⁻¹.

GO! Activity 3.1.10

1. Use the information in table 3.1.2 to show, by calculation, how the molar volume of nitrogen and carbon dioxide listed in the table were obtained.

2. The molar volume of methane (CH_4) was calculated from experimental data obtained by carrying out an experiment as detailed in the text above.

   Results:
   Mass of empty flask = 250 g
   Mass of flask + gas = 250·134 g
   Volume of gas in flask = 200 cm³

   (a) Calculate the molar volume of methane.
   (b) Suggest why the value obtained was different from the value quoted in reference books (22·4 l mol⁻¹).

Percentage yield and the atom economy

Manufacturers aim to use chemical reactions and processes that make the most effective use of available resources and generate the smallest possible amount of waste material. One way of measuring the efficiency of a process is to calculate the **percentage yield**, which compares the expected product quantity with the actual amount produced.

An example is the manufacture of phenol (C_6H_5OH). It used to be made from benzene (C_6H_6) using sulfuric acid and sodium hydroxide in a multi-step process which can be summarised as:

$$C_6H_6 + H_2SO_4 + 2NaOH \longrightarrow C_6H_5OH + Na_2SO_3 + 2H_2O$$

The chemical equation shows that 1 mol of benzene (78 g) should theoretically yield 1 mol of phenol (94 g). In practice, the actual yield of phenol is found to be 77 g. The percentage yield can be calculated using the following equation:

$$\textbf{Percentage yield} = \frac{\textbf{actual yield}}{\textbf{theoretical yield}} \times \textbf{100\%}$$

So, the percentage yield of phenol $= \dfrac{77}{94} \times 100$

$$= 82\%$$

This percentage yield can be regarded as quite good; however, the calculation doesn't take into account that the reaction also produces 1 mol (126 g) of sodium sulfite as a by-product for each mole of phenol produced. An alternative way to measure the efficiency of a process is the idea of **percentage atom economy**, one of the key ideas in green chemistry (see page 191). The atom economy compares the proportion of reactant atoms that end up in a useful product compared to the number that end up as waste. This can be calculated using the following equation:

$$\textbf{Percentage atom economy} = \frac{\textbf{mass of desired product(s)}}{\textbf{total mass of reactants}} \times \textbf{100}$$

 Hint

The relationships used to calculate percentage yield and atom economy can be found in the SQA data booklet.

The nearer the value is to 100%, the less waste there will be.

For phenol made by the above method:

$$\text{Percentage atom economy} = \frac{94}{78 + 98 \cdot 1 + 80} \times 100$$

$$= 36 \cdot 7\%$$

This calculation gives an atom economy of only 36·7% for the manufacture of phenol by this process, assuming sodium sulfite is waste, which is considered very poor.

An alternative method for the manufacture of phenol has been developed using benzene (C_6H_6) and propene (C_3H_6), which can be summarised as:

$$C_6H_6 + CH_3CH = CH_2 + O_2 \quad \rightarrow \quad C_6H_5OH + CH_3COCH_3$$

The by-product is propanone (CH_3COCH_3) which is a valuable chemical and so the atom economy for this process can be regarded as 100%. Useful by-products are often referred to as co-products.

Ibuprofen became obtainable without prescription in the 1980s. At that stage the method used for production used six steps with an overall atom economy of just 40.1%. In the 1990s BHC developed a new three-stage process with an atom economy of 77.4%, now regarded as a classic example of improving the route to a commercial product.

Some reactions that have 100% atom economy have poor yields and so it is necessary to consider both measures of efficiency, yield and atom economy. Atom economy is calculated in the planning stage, but yield can only be found experimentally.

Some types of reaction have better atom economy than others. Addition and condensation reactions will generally have high atom economies. For example the addition of chlorine to ethene, to form 1,2-dichloroethane, which is an important reaction in the manufacture of poly(chloroethene) (PVC), has an atom economy of 100%:

$$H_2C = CH_2 + Cl_2 \rightarrow ClCH_2CH_2Cl$$

GO! Activity 3.1.11

1. Outline how percentage yield and atom economy are used to estimate how efficient a chemical process is.

2. Iron can be extracted from its ore in a blast furnace. The equation for the reaction taking place in the final step of the process is:

$$Fe_2O_3 + 3CO \rightarrow 2Fe + 3CO_2$$

   (a) Calculate the percentage atom economy of the production of iron.

   (b) In theory for every 10 tonnes of Fe_2O_3 reacted 7 tonnes of iron could be produced. In practice only 4.5 tonnes are produced.

   Calculate the percentage yield of iron.

3. In case study 2 (page 201) ethanol can be made by fermentation of carbohydrate or by the direct hydration of ethene.

   Fermentation: $\quad C_6H_{12}O_6 \rightarrow 2C_2H_5OH + 2CO_2$
   Hydration: $\quad\quad\quad C_2H_4 + H_2O \rightarrow C_2H_5OH$

   (a) Which process has the higher atom economy?

   (b) Explain your answer to (a).

   (c) Give two advantages fermentation has over direct hydration.

4. In case study 3 (page 202) ammonia is made by the Haber process. The hydrogen needed is produced by reacting methane with steam.

$$CH_4 + H_2O \rightarrow 3H_2 + CO$$

(a) Calculate the percentage atom economy for the production of hydrogen.

(b) The carbon monoxide is removed by converting it to carbon dioxide.

What is the carbon dioxide used for?

(c) What would the percentage atom economy be if all of the carbon monoxide was converted to carbon dioxide and made use of?

(d) Hydrogen used to be made by reacting coal (a source of carbon) with steam.

$$C(s) + 2H_2O(g) \rightarrow CO_2(g) + 2H_2(g)$$

This process has a low atom economy and is therefore an inefficient way to make hydrogen.

(i) Calculate the percentage atom economy for the production of hydrogen.

(ii) Suggest another reason for not using coal to produce hydrogen.

5. Benzene (C_6H_6) can be oxidised to make maleic anhydride ($C_4H_2O_3$), an important industrial chemical.

$$C_6H_6 + 4\tfrac{1}{2}O_2 \rightarrow C_4H_2O_3 + 2CO_2 + 2H_2O$$

(a) Calculate the percentage atom economy for the production of maleic anhydride.

(b) Suggest a way in which the carbon dioxide produced could be used.

(c) What would the percentage atom economy be if the carbon dioxide could be used in some way?

Calculating percentage yield

The percentage yield is a way of measuring the efficiency of a chemical reaction. There are a number of reasons why the yield is seldom 100%. The main reasons are:

- The reaction may not go to completion – some of the reactants remain unreacted.

- Side reactions may take place forming by-products.

- Impure reactants.

- Loss of product during purification.

The percentage yield can be worked out by dividing the actual yield by experiment by the theoretical yield worked out by calculation.

$$\textbf{Percentage yield} = \frac{\textbf{actual yield}}{\textbf{theoretical yield}} \times \textbf{100}$$

Calculations from balanced equations give the **theoretical yield**. The **actual yield** is the quantity of the desired product which is actually achieved when the reaction takes place.

Calculate the percentage yield of ammonia if 35·6 tonnes of ammonia is produced when 30 tonnes of hydrogen reacts with excess nitrogen.

(1 tonne = 1000 kg)

$$N_2 + 3H_2 \rightleftharpoons 2NH_3$$

Worked answer:

Step 1: Calculate the **theoretical yield** from the balanced equation.

	N_2 +	$3H_2$	$\rightleftharpoons$	$2NH_3$
Key relationship		3 mol	$\rightarrow$	2 mol
Convert to grams		6 g	$\rightarrow$	34 g
Convert to tonnes		6 t	$\rightarrow$	34 t
		So, 30 t	$\rightarrow$	170 t

The theoretical yield of ammonia is 170 t.

Step 2: Calculate the **percentage yield** of ammonia using:

$$\text{Percentage yield} = \frac{\text{actual yield}}{\text{theoretical yield}} \times 100$$

$$= \frac{35·6}{170} \times 100$$

Percentage yield = 21%

Worked example: 1

Figure 3.1.31: *Industrial production of ammonia*

Calculate the percentage yield of iron if 200 kg of iron(III) oxide produces 120 kg of iron when reduced in a blast furnace.

$$Fe_2O_3 + 3CO \rightarrow 2Fe + 3CO_2$$

Worked answer:

Step 1: Calculate the **theoretical yield** from the balanced equation.

	Fe_2O_3 +	3CO	$\rightarrow$	2Fe	+	$3CO_2$
Key relationship	1 mol		$\rightarrow$	2 mol		
Convert to grams	159·6 g		$\rightarrow$	111·6 g		
	So, 1 g $\left(\dfrac{159·6}{159·6}\right)$		$\rightarrow$	0·7 g $\left(\dfrac{111·6}{159·6}\right)$		
	So, 200 g		$\rightarrow$	140 g		
Convert to kg	200 kg		$\rightarrow$	140 kg		

The theoretical yield of iron is 140 kg.

Worked example: 2

Step 2: Calculate the **percentage yield** of iron using:

$$\text{Percentage yield} = \frac{\text{actual yield}}{\text{theoretical yield}} \times 100$$

$$= \frac{120}{140} \times 100$$

Percentage yield = 86%

If the cost of the feedstocks and the percentage yield for a reaction are known then the cost of the reactants used in the reaction can be calculated.

Worked example: 3

In worked example 2 above the percentage yield of iron from iron ore was calculated as 86%. If the average cost of iron ore (Fe_2O_3) in 2013 was £81 per tonne, calculate the cost of the iron ore needed to produce each tonne of iron (to the nearest £).

(1 tonne = 1000 kg)

Balanced equation: $Fe_2O_3 + 3CO \rightarrow 2Fe + 3CO_2$

Worked answer:

Step 1: Calculate the mass of iron ore needed to produce 1 tonne of iron if the reaction was 100% efficient.

Figure 3.1.32: *Iron being produced in a blast furnace*

	Fe_2O_3 + 3CO	$\rightarrow$	2Fe + $3CO_2$
Key relationship	1 mol	$\rightarrow$	2 mol
Convert to grams	159·6 g	$\rightarrow$	111·6 g
So,	$1·43 \text{ g} \left(\frac{159.6}{111.6}\right)$	$\rightarrow$	$1·0 \text{ g} \left(\frac{111.6}{111.6}\right)$
Convert to kg	1·43 kg	$\rightarrow$	1·0 kg
So,	1430 kg (1·43 t)	$\rightarrow$	1000 kg (1 t)

So, theoretically 1·43 t of iron(III) oxide produces 1 t of iron.

Step 2: Calculate the mass of reactant needed given the % yield of the reaction.

The percentage yield is 86% so the mass of iron(III) oxide needed to produce 1 t of iron is actually 100/86 × 1·43 = 1·663 t.

Step 3: Calculate the actual cost of the reactant.

1 t of iron(III) oxide costs £81, so 1·663 t costs 1·663 × £81 = **£135.**

In order to ensure that a costly reactant is converted into product, an excess of the less expensive reactant(s) can be used.

GO! Activity 3.1.12

1. Aspirin, a common painkiller, can be made by the reaction of salicylic acid with ethanoic anhydride.

$$C_7H_6O_3 \quad + \quad C_4H_6O_3 \quad \rightarrow \quad C_9H_8O_4 \quad + \quad C_2H_4O_2$$

salicylic acid   ethanoic anhydride   aspirin   ethanoic acid

    (a) Calculate the theoretical mass of aspirin which would be produced when 50·4 g of salicylic acid reacted with excess ethanoic anhydride.

    (b) In a laboratory preparation of aspirin, 50·4 g of salicylic acid produced 20·12 g of aspirin.

       Calculate the percentage yield of aspirin.

2. Ethene can be used to produce the ester ethyl ethanoate in a multi-step process involving ethanol and ethanoic acid:

    (1) $C_2H_4 \quad + \quad H_2O \rightarrow C_2H_5OH$

       ethene   ethanol

    (2) $C_2H_5OH \quad + \quad O_2 \rightarrow CH_3COOH \quad + \quad H_2O$

       ethanol   ethanoic acid

    (3) $CH_3COOH \quad + \quad C_2H_5OH \rightarrow CH_3COOC_2H_5 \quad + \quad H_2O$

       ethanoic acid   ethanol   ethyl ethanoate

    (a)   (i) If 69·5 g of ethene was used in the first step, calculate the theoretical yield of ethanol.

        (ii) If 89·9 g of ethanol was actually made, what is the percentage yield for the first step in the synthesis?

    (b)   (i) If all of the 89·9 g of ethanol is used in the second step, what is the theoretical yield of ethanoic acid made in the second reaction?

        (ii) If 101·5g of acid is actually made, what is the percentage yield in the second step?

    (c)   (i) If all the 101·5 g of acid is used in the third step, what is the theoretical yield of ester?

        (ii) If 73 g of ester are actually made, what is the percentage yield of ester actually made?

    (d) Suggest why there is such a low percentage yield of ethyl ethanoate in this.

3. Benzene (C_6H_6) can be oxidised to make maleic anhydride ($C_4H_2O_3$), an important industrial chemical.

$$C_6H_6 + 4\tfrac{1}{2}O_2 \rightarrow C_4H_2O_3 + 2CO_2 + 2H_2O$$

In 2013 the average price of benzene was £933 per tonne.

(a) Calculate the mass of benzene needed to produce 100 kg of maleic anhydride, assuming 100% conversion.

(b) If the reaction is 71% efficient, calculate the actual mass of benzene needed to produce 100 kg of maleic anhydride.

(c) Calculate the cost of the benzene required.
(1 tonne = 1000 kg)

Learning checklist

In this chapter you have learned:

- When making new products industrial chemists have to think about the most economical way to make them to maximise profit and minimise the impact on the environment.

- Factors influencing industrial process design include:

  Availability, sustainability and cost of feedstocks; product yield; marketability of by-products; recyclability of chemicals; energy requirements; use of processes that reduce or eliminate the use and production of hazardous substances.

- Environmental considerations include:

  Waste prevention; avoiding use or production of toxic substances; designing biodegradable products.

- The mole ratio of atoms/ionic units in a compound can be worked out from a chemical formula.

- Chemical equations, using formulae and state symbols, can be written and balanced to show the mole ratio of reactants and products.

- The mass of a mole of any substance, in grams (g), is equal to the gram formula mass (GFM) and can be calculated using relative atomic masses.

- Masses/moles reacting and produced can be calculated from mole ratios in balanced equations.

- Masses, moles, concentrations and volumes of solutions reacting and being produced can be calculated from mole ratios in balanced equations.

- Reactants in excess and the limiting reactant can be calculated from mole ratios in balanced equations.

- In order to ensure a costly reactant is converted to product, an excess of the less expensive reactant(s) can be used.

- Theoretical yield assumes that all of the reactant(s) is converted into product(s).

- Actual yield is the amount of product which is formed under the reaction conditions.

- One mole of any gas occupies the same volume when measured at the same temperature and pressure and is known as molar volume (V_m).

- Molar volume is measured in litres mol^{-1}.

- The volume of a gas can be calculated from the number of moles and vice versa, given the molar volume.

- Volumes of reactant and product gases can be worked out from mole ratios in the balanced equations.

- The percentage yield is a way of measuring the efficiency of a chemical process:

$$\text{percentage yield (\%)} = \frac{\text{actual yield}}{\text{theoretical yield}} \times 100$$

- The percentage atom economy is a way to measure the efficiency of a reaction. It compares the proportion of reactant atoms that end up in a useful product compared to the number that end up as waste.

$$\text{Percentage atom economy (\%)} = \frac{\text{mass of desired product}}{\text{total mass of reactants}} \times 100$$

- If the cost of feedstocks and the percentage yield are known for a reaction then the cost of the reactants can be calculated.

- Reactants with a high percentage yield may have a low percentage atom economy value if large amounts of by-product are formed.

2 Controlling the rate

You should already know

- The rate of a reaction can be increased by increasing the concentration, decreasing the particle size, raising the temperature of the reactants and adding a catalyst.
- The change in rate of a chemical reaction can be followed by measuring the changes in the volume of gas produced, the mass of reactants and changes in other quantities, over time.
- How to draw and interpret graphs of changes in the volume of gas produced, mass of reactants and changes in other quantities, against time.
- The average rate of reaction $= \dfrac{\text{change in quantity}}{\text{change in time}}$
- Rate of reaction can be shown to decrease over time by calculating the average rate at different stages.
- Catalysts speed up reactions but are chemically unchanged at the end of the reaction.

(National 5 Chemistry: Chemical changes and structure: Rates of reaction)

Learning intentions

In this chapter you will learn about:

- Factors controlling the rate of reaction and how collision theory can be used to explain their effects: concentration, pressure, temperature, particle size and collision geometry.
- Activation energy and the activated complex.
- Energy distribution diagrams and the effect of raising temperature.
- The relationship between concentration and rate and temperature and rate.
- Reaction pathways – potential energy changes.
- How catalysts increase the rate of a reaction.

CHEMISTRY IN CONTEXT: EVERYDAY REACTIONS

Preserving paper – slowing down chemical reactions

The paper these words are printed on is undergoing chemical reactions right now as you read. The reactions are extremely slow but they will in time result in the paper deteriorating so much that it will disintegrate and crumble.

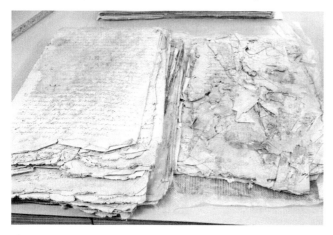

Figure 3.2.1: *Paper from around 1850 onwards was treated with acidic chemicals, which cause the paper to crumble*

Although this is not important for most books and papers such as newspapers, it is an issue for important historical documents that we want to preserve – we want to slow down even further the chemical reactions happening in the paper. The problem stems from the way paper has been made in the last 150 years. Paper is mainly cellulose fibres held together by weak forces of attraction. During the manufacturing process chemicals called sizing agents are added to make the paper less absorbent so that the ink is not smudged on the surface. Traditionally the sizing agent used has been acidic and over time the acid, which dissolves in naturally occurring moisture, reacts with the cellulose causing it to break down (hydrolyse) and eventually crumble. Paper also absorbs acidic pollutants from the air – mainly sulfur and nitrogen oxides. Newspaper is particularly vulnerable to these pollutants and it is the cause of browning of the paper. Cellulose itself has now been found to produce several acids, such as methanoic and ethanoic acid which speed up the deterioration of the paper.

Chemists have been involved in devising preserving methods for important manuscripts. One method known as mass deacidification involves the neutralisation of the acids in the paper by immersing books and manuscripts in a suspension of magnesium oxide (a base) which neutralises the acids. The magnesium oxide permanently 'fixes' in the cellulose fibres on the paper's surface.

Deacidification is used by many libraries, including the National Library of Scotland, to preserve important books and papers. The Library of Congress in the USA also uses this process and aims to preserve an average of 250 000 books and 1 million manuscript sheets every year up until 2020.

Nowadays, alkaline sizing agents can be used to slow down the chemical reactions which cause the deterioration of paper.

Figure 3.2.2: Deacidification sprays containing magnesium oxide as the neutraliser are used to slow down chemical reactions which cause the deterioration of paper

Airbag protection systems – explosively fast reactions

Airbag protection systems are commonplace in most road vehicles and require the bags to be inflated within 60–80 milliseconds of the car's sensors detecting the impact. This requires the gas which fills the bag to be produced in an explosively fast chemical reaction. In many airbag systems two reactions take place. The first, known as the initiator, produces enough energy to ignite a solid propellant – the chemical which produces the gas for the airbag. The gas produced is nitrogen, which is extremely unreactive and non-toxic.

Many airbag systems contain a mixture of sodium azide (NaN_3), potassium nitrate (KNO_3), and silicon dioxide (SiO_2) in the propellant. Within about 40 milliseconds of impact, these components react in three separate reactions that produce nitrogen gas. The reactions, in order, are as follows:

1. *The decomposition of sodium azide, which produces sodium metal and nitrogen gas:*

$$2NaN_3 \rightarrow 2Na + 3N_2$$

2. *The sodium metal is removed by reaction with potassium nitrate. More nitrogen gas is also produced:*

$$10Na + 2KNO_3 \rightarrow K_2O + 5Na_2O + N_2$$

3. *In the final reaction silicon dioxide is used to eliminate the potassium oxide and sodium oxide produced in reaction (2), because Group 1 metal oxides are highly reactive. These products react with silicon dioxide to produce a silicate glass which is a harmless and stable compound:*

$$K_2O + 5Na_2O + 6SiO_2 \rightarrow K_2O_3Si + 5Na_2O_3Si$$

silicate glass

Chemists are carrying out research to find alternative propellant compounds. It is hoped that non-azide reagents will produce less reactive byproducts, which will also have a lower combustion temperature.

Figure 3.2.3: *Inflating an airbag relies on the rapid production of gas from an explosively fast chemical reaction*

Make the Link

You can calculate the volume of gas produced when an airbag inflates – see page 224.

Collision theory

Industry produces a vast range of substances from bulk chemicals such as sodium hydroxide (caustic soda) and ammonia to chemicals made in much smaller quantities such as medicines, chemicals used in the electronics industry and substances of biological origin like vaccines and material for biofuels. Whatever the product, it is important to produce it in the most economical way. This can be achieved through an understanding of the factors that control a chemical reaction. Not only do we need to consider how much of a product a reaction gives and what the energy costs are, we need to know how quickly it can be produced. This is called the rate of the reaction. Rates can vary from incredibly fast, as in the production of gas to inflate an airbag in a car, to very slow, like when paper deteriorates and crumbles.

Generally speaking industrial chemists want to speed up chemical reactions. They need to know how fast they can make a reaction go – and generally the faster the better. However, the rate needs to be controlled. A reaction which is too slow is unlikely to be a commercial success. At the same time, if it is too fast then there is the risk of explosion. One of the most important chemical reactions in the world is the production of ammonia by the Haber process. Without an understanding of the effect of temperature, pressure and catalysts on the rate of reaction, ammonia would not be made at a fast enough rate to make it economically on the large scale which is required. Ammonia is an essential feedstock for the production of fertilisers.

The rates of chemical reactions are affected by:

- The concentration of dissolved reactants and the pressure in gas reactions
- The size of solid reactant particles

SQA KEY AREA

- The temperature at which the reaction takes place
- The collision geometry – the angle at which reactants collide
- The addition of a catalyst.

The effect of each of these factors can be explained by the collision theory. Simple collision theory states that for reactants to form products they must first come in contact with each other (collide). This goes some way to explain the effect of the factors listed above – we can think about the reaction of marble chips (calcium carbonate) with hydrochloric acid to illustrate some of the effects:

calcium carbonate + hydrochloric acid → calcium chloride + water + carbon dioxide

$$CaCO_3(s) \quad + \quad 2HCl(aq) \quad \rightarrow \quad CaCl_2(aq) \quad + \quad H_2O(\ell) \quad + \quad CO_2(g)$$

Concentration

The higher the concentration of the acid the faster the reaction. The more particles there are in a given volume, the more collisions there will be and the greater the chance of reaction and products being formed. So, the higher the concentration the more successful collisions and the faster the reaction.

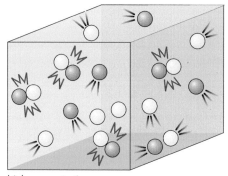

low concentration:
few particles in a given volume

high concentration:
many particles in the same volume

Figure 3.2.4: *Increasing the reactant concentration increases the number of collisions*

Pressure

Increasing the pressure in a reaction involving gases has a similar effect to increasing the concentration of the reactants. The gas molecules are compressed into a smaller space as the pressure is increased so there is a greater chance of them colliding successfully and going on to form products.

Particle size

The smaller the particle size the faster the reaction. When equal masses of small lumps and large lumps are reacted with the same concentration of acid,

low pressure:
molecules are
spread out

high pressure:
volume has been decreased
(at constant temperature),
forcing the molecules
closer together

Figure 3.2.5: *Increasing the pressure of the reactants increases the number of collisions* the small lumps react faster. The small lumps have a greater surface area proportional to their mass than the large lumps, so there are effectively more carbonate ions available for the hydrogen ions to collide with and so the greater the chance of reaction and products being formed.

Temperature

The higher the temperature, the faster the rate of reaction. Acid warmed to 30°C will react much faster with marble chips than acid at room temperature (approximately 20°C). Temperature is a measure of the average kinetic energy of the reactants. As the temperature increases the kinetic energy of the reactants increases, i.e. they move faster. This results in more collisions taking place at a greater speed so the chances of reactants forming products increases, so the rate of reaction increases.

The idea of increased number of collisions leading to reaction on its own is not enough to explain a number of observations. For example, when a gas tap is turned on there are immediately lots of collisions taking place between the gas molecules and oxygen in the air, but there is no observable reaction taking place. However, when the mixture is sparked or a flame held near it there is an explosively fast reaction. This cannot be explained simply by increasing the number or speed of the collisions. Similarly, a relatively small rise in temperature (10°C) is enough to almost double the rate of the reaction between marble chips and acid. Again this cannot be explained simply by an increased number or speed of the collisions. The answer is that not only do collisions have to occur, they have to have a minimum amount of kinetic energy known as the activation energy (E_a).

Collision geometry

Not all collisions between reactants lead to products, even if the molecules have energy equal to or greater than the activation energy. This can be due to the angle at which the molecules collide – the collision geometry. If two diatomic molecules collide 'end-on' this would not be the best alignment to form molecules of product. A better collision geometry would be if the molecules collided 'side-on' or even 'end-to-side':

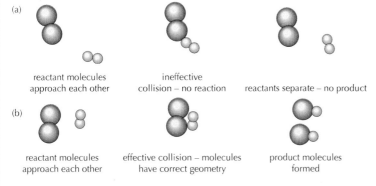

(a)
reactant molecules approach each other

ineffective collision – no reaction

reactants separate – no product

(b)
reactant molecules approach each other

effective collision – molecules have correct geometry

product molecules formed

Figure 3.2.6: *The collision geometry illustrated in (b) is more likely to lead to reaction than if the molecules collide as shown in (a)*

GO! Activity 3.2.1

Magnesium reacts with hydrochloric acid to produce magnesium chloride and hydrogen gas:

$$Mg \quad + \quad 2HCl \quad \rightarrow \quad MgCl_2 \quad + \quad H_2$$

(a) Explain why 2 mol l^{-1} acid reacts quicker than an equal volume of 1 mol l^{-1} acid.

(b) Explain why powdered magnesium reacts much quicker than an equal mass of magnesium ribbon.

(c) Describe how you would carry out an experiment to show how the rate of the reaction changes over time. Include a sketch of the arrangement you would use.

Concentration and rate

The relationship between concentration and rate can be studied in more detail by carrying out a 'clock reaction'. This is where the effect of changing the concentration of one of the reactants in a reaction can be measured by timing how long it takes for a reaction to reach a certain point – usually indicated by a colour change. Because the concentration of only one reactant is being changed the time it takes to reach the same point in the reaction must be due to the one reactant. The longer it takes to reach the same point in the reaction, the slower the rate. The rate of the reaction is related to time (t) and can be measured by calculating the reciprocal of time, i.e. as 1/t and is known as the relative rate.

Take the example of hydrogen peroxide (H_2O_2) reacting with acidified potassium iodide (KI) to form iodine (I_2).

$$H_2O_2(aq) + 2H^+(aq) + 2I^-(aq) \rightarrow 2H_2O(\ell) + I_2(aq)$$

The course of this reaction can be followed by carrying it out in the presence of small quantities of starch and sodium thiosulfate solutions. As the iodine molecules are produced they immediately react with the thiosulphate ions and are converted back to iodide ions:

$$I_2(aq) + 2S_2O_3^{2-}(aq) \rightarrow 2I^-(aq) + S_4O_6^{2-}(aq)$$

During this period the reaction mixture remains colourless. But once the thiosulfate ions have been used up, a blue/black colour suddenly appears because the iodine molecules now get the chance to react with the starch.

Figure 3.2.7: *A clock reaction can be used to show the relationship between concentration and rate*

A series of experiments is carried out in which only the concentration of the iodide ions is varied. The concentrations and volumes of the other chemicals involved are kept constant as is the temperature at which the experiments are performed.

Since the amount of thiosulphate ions initially present will be the same in each experiment, the appearance of the blue/black colour will always represent the same extent of reaction. So if the time (t) it takes for the blue/black colour to appear in each experiment is recorded then we can take 1/t as a measure of the reaction rate.

Example results

Table 3.2.1

Experiment	1	2	3	4	5
Volume of potassium iodide (cm^3)	25	20	15	10	5
Volume of water (cm^3)	0	5	10	15	20
Time (t) (s)	20	26	31	52	104
Relative Rate (1/t) (s^{-1})	0·050	0·038	0·032	0·019	0·010

Note: The concentration of the iodide solution is varied by diluting the original concentration with water, and keeping the total volume the same in each experiment. This allows the volume of iodide solution to be used as a measure of the concentration.

Figure 3.2.8 is a graph of the volume (concentration) of potassium iodide against rate using these results. The straight line shows that the rate of reaction is proportional to the concentration, i.e. if you double the concentration the rate also doubles. This is true for many chemical reactions.

Figure 3.2.8: *The straight line shows that rate is directly proportional to concentration, i.e. doubling the concentration doubles the rate*

Researching chemistry – analysing and communicating results

When plotting experimental results and joining the points in a line graph, a line of best fit is often drawn instead of joining all the consecutive points. This means that some of the points will be on the line, some above and some below. It is highly unlikely that you would ever get experimental results where all the points were on a straight line or fitted a curve.

Temperature and rate

The relationship between temperature and rate can be studied in more detail by studying the 'clock reaction' between oxalic acid and acidified potassium permanganate:

$$5(COOH)_2(aq) + 6H^+(aq) + 2MnO_4^-(aq) \rightarrow 2Mn^{2+}(aq) + 10CO_2(g) + 8H_2O(\ell)$$
$$\text{purple} \qquad\qquad \text{colourless}$$

Initially the reaction mixture is purple in colour due to the presence of the permanganate ions but turns colourless as soon as they are used up. This colour change allows us to follow the course of the reaction.

Figure 3.2.9: *A clock reaction can be used to show the relationship between temperature and rate*

A series of experiments is carried out in which only the temperature of the reaction mixtures was changed. The concentrations and volumes of the reactants were kept constant. Since the amount of permanganate ions initially present will be the same in each experiment, the point at which the purple colour disappears will always represent the same extent of reaction. So if t is the time it takes for the colour change to occur then we can take $1/t$ as a measure of the relative rate.

Example results

Table 3.2.2

Temperature (°C)	Time (t) (s)	Relative Rate (1/t) (s⁻¹)
38	41	0·024
50	20	0·050
57	12	0·083
64	7	0·143

Researching chemistry – general laboratory apparatus

You should know how and when to use glassware such as beakers and thermometers. Thermometers range in accuracy but for general laboratory use mercury or alcohol thermometers reading up to ± 1°C are usually sufficient. In this experiment, where a fairly strong heat is required and no flammable substances are involved, a bunsen burner with a blue flame can be used.

Figure 3.2.10 is the graph of rate against temperature using these results. The curve indicates that the rate of reaction is not directly proportional to the temperature. A close look at the graph shows that the rate of reaction doubles if there is a temperature rise of about 10°C. This experiment supports the idea of activation energy.

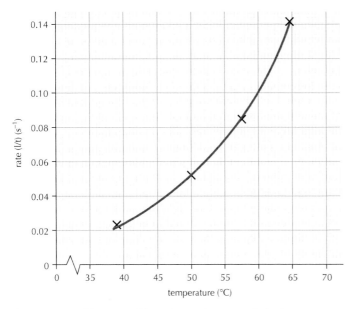

Figure 3.2.10: *The curved line shows that a small rise in temperature results in a big increase in rate*

GO! Activity 3.2.2

The effect of concentration on the rate of a reaction can be investigated by carrying out a 'clock reaction'.

The time it takes for the reaction to reach the same point was measured for different concentrations of one of the reactants.

Results

Table 3.2.3

Concentration of reactant (mol l⁻¹)	Time (s)	Relative Rate (1/t) (s⁻¹)
0·1	7·7	0·13
0·2	3·7	x
0·3	2·6	0·38
0·4	y	0·50

(a) Calculate values for x and y using the information in the table.

(b) Draw a graph of concentration against relative rate including values for x and y.

(c) State the relationship between concentration and relative rate of reaction.

(d) Predict the relative rate when the concentration of thiosulphate is 0·6 mol l⁻¹.

Interpreting rate graphs

The course of a reaction can be followed by measuring the volume of gas given off over time and drawing a graph of volume of gas against time.

Take as an example experiment 1: reacting 40 cm³ of 0·2 mol l⁻¹ hydrochloric acid reacting with excess large marble chips (calcium carbonate):

calcium carbonate + hydrochloric acid → calcium chloride + water + carbon dioxide

$$CaCO_3(s) + 2HCl(aq) \rightarrow CaCl_2(aq) + H_2O(\ell) + CO_2(g)$$

Interpreting the graph for experiment 1:

At 1: The steepest part of the graph – the rate is at its highest. The maximum number of reactant particles are present and the number of effective collisions per second is at its highest.

At 2: The graph is not so steep – the rate of reaction is slowing. Some of the reacting particles have been used up so the number of successful collisions per second will be fewer.

At 3: The graph is horizontal – the reaction has stopped. At least one of the reactants has been used up completely so there can be no further collisions between reactant particles.

Figure 3.2.11: *Graph of volume produced against time for experiment 1*

Figure 3.2.12 shows the graphs obtained from the same reaction but when some of the variables have been changed, e.g. quantities of reactant, particle size and temperature – graph 1 is the original graph.

Experiment 2: 40 cm³ of 0·2 mol l⁻¹ hydrochloric acid reacting with excess large marble chips (calcium carbonate) but at a higher temperature than experiment 1.

Figure 3.2.12: *Graphs 2 and 3 are obtained when the conditions used in experiment 1 are changed*

Interpreting the graph for experiment 2:

The graph is steeper than graph 1 initially, indicating that the reaction is faster. This is because the reaction is taking place at a higher temperature. More particles have energy greater than the activation energy. All the other variables are the same as in experiment 1. The final volume of gas produced is the same in each reaction, although it is produced faster in experiment 2, because the mass of marble chips and the number of moles of acid reacting is the same.

Experiment 3: 40 cm³ of 0·1 mol l⁻¹ hydrochloric acid reacting with excess large marble chips (calcium carbonate) but at the same temperature as experiment 1.

Interpreting the graph for experiment 3:

Initially, the graph is less steep than in experiment 1 indicating the reaction is slower. This is because the concentration of the acid is lower than in experiment 1. The final volume of gas obtained is half that of experiment 1 because the number of moles of acid reacting is half the original.

Activity 3.2.3

(a) Sketch the graph in figure 3.2.11 and add corresponding curves when the reaction is repeated
   (i) at a lower temperature
   (ii) using 20 cm^3 of 0.2 mol l^{-1} hydrochloric acid
   (iii) using powdered marble.
(b) For each of the graphs in (a) explain how you decided the shape of each graph.

Kinetic energy distribution

The need for activation energy explains why the rate of reaction of the molecules in natural gas with the oxygen in the air is so slow. The activation energy for the reaction is high. A spark or flame supplies the energy needed to overcome the activation energy barrier. The reaction is exothermic so once it starts the reaction supplies its own energy. The activation energy needed varies from reaction to reaction. In the Ostwald process colourless nitrogen monoxide reacts quickly with oxygen to produce fumes of brown nitrogen dioxide. The activation energy for the reaction must be low to allow the reaction to happen quickly at room temperature.

Temperature can be considered to be a measure of the average kinetic energy of the particles in a substance. At a given temperature individual molecules of a gas will have different kinetic energies. In other words some molecules will have high kinetic energy and others low kinetic energy. Most particles will have kinetic energy somewhere in-between. This can be shown in an energy distribution diagram:

Figure 3.2.13: *The energy distribution diagram for a reaction at temperature T_1*

The area under the graph in figure 3.2.13 shows the energy distribution of all the reactants at temperature T_1. Only a relatively small number of reactant molecules have energy greater than the activation energy, E_a. This is shown on figure 3.2.14 – the shaded area under the graph indicates the number of molecules with energy greater than E_a.

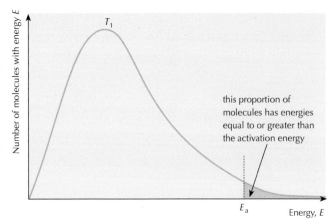

Figure 3.2.14: *The energy distribution diagram for a reaction at temperature T₁*

If the temperature is increased, although there are the same number of molecules, their energy distribution will be different – more molecules will have higher kinetic energy. This is shown in figure 3.2.15 where the energy distribution at T_2 is superimposed on the diagram for temperature T_1.

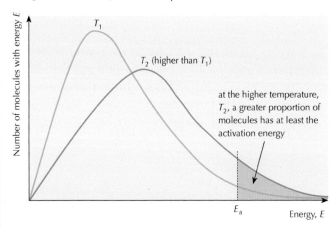

Figure 3.2.15: *Energy distribution diagram for a reaction at temperatures T₁ and T₂*

Notice that the shape of the graph at T_2 is distorted slightly to the right to reflect that more molecules have higher energy. The height of the graph is also lower than the graph at T_1. The shaded area under the graph shows that there are more than twice as many reactant molecules with energy greater than E_a so more than twice as many molecules now have enough energy to react when they collide. This means for a relatively small increase in temperature there is a big increase in the rate of the reaction.

🔵 GO! Activity 3.2.4

1. Explain why, when hydrogen and oxygen gas are mixed, the reaction is so slow that it does not take place at an observable rate, but when a flame is held near the the mixture it explodes.
2. The energy distribution diagrams for a reaction between two gases is shown. Explain the differences in the graphs at 30°C and 40°C.

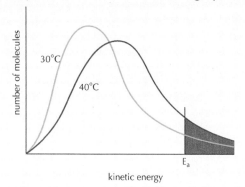

Figure 3.2.16: *Energy distribution diagram for two gases reacting*

Reaction pathways

When chemical reactions occur they are often accompanied by a significant change in energy. When energy is released to the surroundings, usually in the form of heat, the reaction is said to be exothermic. Examples of exothermic reactions you have already come across include the combustion of fuels and the neutralisation of acids with bases. The energy released when new products are formed in an exothermic reaction must have come from the reactants, which have potential energy (PE). Some of this potential energy is released as heat during the reaction. This release of energy is known as the enthalpy change of the reaction. Enthalpy is the name given to stored energy in chemicals and is given the symbol H. The change in enthalpy for a reaction is given by the symbol ΔH. Δ is the Greek symbol delta and means 'change of'. ΔH is measured in kJ and kJ mol^{-1} when one mole of substance is reacted or produced.

Enthalpy changes can be shown in simple potential energy diagrams – Figure 3.2.17 shows the enthalpy change (ΔH) for an exothermic reaction.

Figure 3.2.17: *Simple potential energy diagram for an exothermic reaction*

Figure 3.2.18: *Potential energy diagram for an exothermic reaction, showing the activation energy (E_a)*

The activation energy (E_a) for a reaction can be added to a reaction profile to give a more accurate representation of the energy changes taking place, Figure 3.2.18.

There are reactions in which instead of energy being given out when products are formed, energy is taken in from the surroundings. These are endothermic reactions. An example is when ammonium chloride reacts with barium hydroxide solution. The temperature of the solution drops, indicating that energy is being taken in from the surroundings during the reaction. Figure 3.2.19 shows the potential energy diagram for an endothermic reaction.

Figure 3.2.19: *Potential energy diagram for an endothermic reaction*

If potential energy values are added to the diagrams the enthalpy change (ΔH) for a reaction can be calculated by subtracting the enthalpy of products from the enthalpy of the reactants:

$$\Delta H = H_{(products)} - H_{(reactants)}$$

The activation energy can be calculated by subtracting the enthalpy of the reactants from the energy maximum in the graph.

Worked example

 Hint

Exothermic reactions always have a negative sign in front of the ΔH value to indicate the reaction is exothermic. Endothermic reactions have a positive sign in front of the ΔH value, which is sometimes omitted.

Calculate (i) the enthalpy change and (ii) activation energy, from the potential energy diagram shown.

Worked answer:

(i) $\Delta H = H_{(products)} - H_{(reactants)}$

$\quad\quad = 10 \quad - \quad 30$

$\quad \Delta H = -20$ kJ

(ii) $E_a = 45 - 30$

$\quad E_a = 15$ kJ

Figure 3.2.20: *Potential energy graph*

Figure 3.2.21: *The 'no smoking' warning sign in petrol stations – naked flames and sparks can supply activation energy to ignite the petrol*

The potential energy diagrams show the activation energy as an energy barrier which the reactants have to overcome in order to form products. Reactant molecules with energy equal to or greater than the activation energy can go on to form products. Reactant molecules with energy lower than the activation energy will not go on to form products. In addition, the lower the activation energy the faster the rate of reaction. Conversely the higher the activation energy the slower the rate of reaction. This explains why although petrol is very flammable you can safely fill up a car's tank at the petrol station because the activation energy needed for the combustion of petrol is high. It also explains why there are 'No smoking' signs on display at petrol stations – a flame near petrol would supply the activation energy needed for combustion to occur.

GO! Activity 3.2.5

1. The potential energy diagrams for two reactions are shown below.

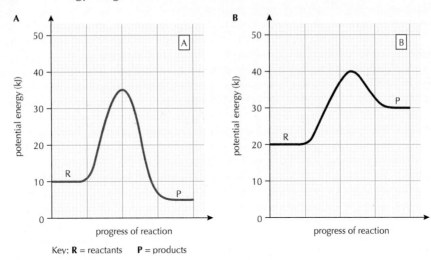

Key: **R** = reactants   **P** = products

Figure 3.2.22

(a) Identify which reaction is exothermic and explain your choice.

(b) For each reaction calculate (i) the activation energy, E_a

(ii) the enthalpy change, ΔH.

(c) Which reaction is likely to be the faster? Explain your choice.

2. Nitrogen monoxide is produced inside a petrol engine when the mixture of petrol and air is sparked.

$$\tfrac{1}{2}N_2(g) + \tfrac{1}{2}O_2(g) \rightarrow NO(g) \; \Delta H = +90 \text{ kJ mol}^{-1}$$

(a) Sketch the shape of the potential energy diagram for the reaction and show clearly the ΔH value.

(b) Explain the role of the spark in the reaction.

3.

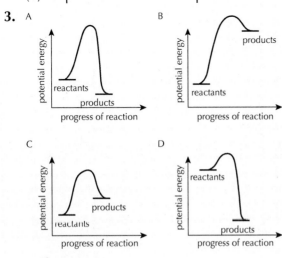

Figure 3.2.23

Which of the potential energy diagrams, A, B, C and D

(a) represent exothermic reactions?

(b) represents the most exothermic reactions?

(c) represents the most endothermic reactions?

(d) shows the largest activation energy?

(e) shows the smallest activation energy?

CHEMISTRY IN CONTEXT: EXTRACTING IRON IN A BLAST FURNACE

Iron is extracted from its ore in a blast furnace. A mixture of iron ore, coke (a source of carbon) and limestone are loaded from the top.

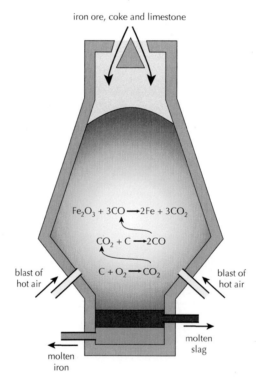

Figure 3.2.24: *Blast furnace*

The three main reactions which take place are:

(1) *Coke reacts with the oxygen of the air being blown (blasted) in to give carbon dioxide. This is an exothermic reaction:*

$$C(s) + O_2(g) \rightarrow CO_2(g) \; \Delta H = -394 \text{ kJ mol}^{-1}$$

The energy released heats up the contents of the blast furnace.

(2) *The carbon dioxide reacts with more coke, producing carbon monoxide. This is an endothermic reaction:*

$$C(s) + CO_2(g) \rightarrow 2CO(g) \quad \Delta H = +173 \text{ kJ mol}^{-1}$$

The energy comes from the surroundings, which lose energy and cool down.

(3) *The iron ore reacts with the carbon monoxide and is reduced to iron. This is an exothermic reaction:*

$$Fe_2O_3(s) + 3CO(g) \rightarrow 2Fe\,(\ell) + 3CO_2(g)$$
$$\Delta H = -23 \text{ kJ mol}^{-1}$$

The enthalpy changes are shown in the potential energy diagrams (not to scale).

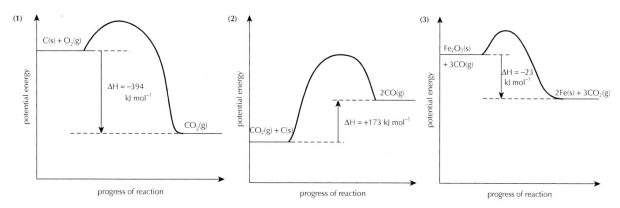

Figure 3.2.25, 1–3: *Potential energy diagrams for the main reactions in the extraction of iron from its ore*

GO! Activity 3.2.6

Reactions (a) and (b) are associated with iron and steel production:

(a) $S(s) + O_2(g) \rightarrow SO_2(g) \quad \Delta H = -297 \text{ kJ mol}^{-1}$

(b) $CaCO_3(s) \rightarrow CaO(s) + CO_2(g) \quad \Delta H = +177 \text{ kJ mol}^{-1}$

    (i)   Sketch potential energy diagrams for both reactions (they do not have to be drawn to scale).

    (ii) Indicate ΔH and E_a on each diagram.

    (iii) For each reaction, state whether it is exothermic or endothermic.

         Explain your choices.

The activated complex

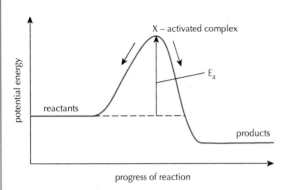

Figure 3.2.26: *The activated complex is formed at the top of the energy barrier*

As a reaction progresses there is a stage reached where an intermediate product is formed known as the activated complex. The top of the potential energy barrier represents the point at which the activated complex has formed.

The activation energy can be defined as the minimum energy needed by colliding particles to form the activated complex. Activated complexes are very unstable and only exist for a short time. Not all activated complexes lose energy by going on to form products – they can break down to reform reactants. This is indicated by the arrows in figure 3.2.26.

The structures of many activated complexes are not known. When two diatomic molecules react, a 'square' activated complex can form – the dotted lines indicate bonds breaking and bonds forming:

GO! Activity 3.2.7

The diagram below represents reactants forming products in a chemical reaction.

Draw a possible structure for the activated complex.

Figure 3.2.27: *A 'square' activated complex can form when two diatomic molecules react*

When bromoethane reacts with a hydroxide ion to produce methanol the activated complex thought to be formed is as shown.

$$HO^- + H-\underset{\underset{H}{|}}{\overset{\overset{H}{|}}{C}}-Br \longrightarrow H-O----\underset{\underset{H\ \ H}{\diagup\diagdown}}{C}----Br \longrightarrow H-O-\underset{\underset{H}{|}}{\overset{\overset{H}{|}}{C}}-H + Br^-$$

activated complex   **methanol**

Catalysts and activation energy

A catalyst is a substance which increases the rate of a particular reaction without being used up in the reaction. Catalysts are essential in many important industrial processes, some of which were covered in the National 5 course – they are summarised in table 3.2.4.

Table 3.2.4: *Catalysts used in some important industrial processes*

Process	Catalyst	Reaction
Haber – making ammonia	iron	$N_2 + 3H_2 \rightarrow 2NH_3$
Ostwald – making nitric acid	platinum	$4NH_3 + 5O_2 \rightarrow 4NO + 6H_2O$
Hydrogenation – making margarine	nickel	Unsaturated oils + $H_2 \rightarrow$ saturated fats

The catalytic converter connected to the exhaust system of cars to remove polluting gases uses a mixture of platinum and rhodium to catalyse the conversion of polluting gases to non-toxic gases. The honeycomb structure provides a very large surface area for the reaction to take place on.

Figure 3.2.28: *Cutaway of a catalytic converter showing the large surface area of the catalyst*

The gases pass over the surface of the metal where at least one of the reactants temporarily attach to the surface of the catalyst. The catalytic oxidation of carbon monoxide to carbon dioxide is shown in figure 3.2.29. The molecules are held close together and their internal covalent bonds weaken, which allows a reaction with lower activation energy to occur. The carbon dioxide molecules then leave the surface. If the bonds are too weak then the reactant molecules will not be held in place. If the bonds formed at the surface of the catalyst are too strong then detaching becomes difficult and products can't leave the surface of the catalyst. This is why tungsten would not be suitable for use in a catalytic converter.

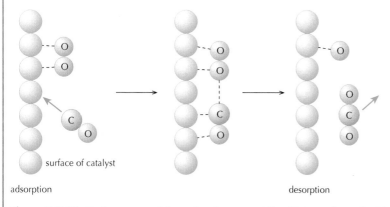

Figure 3.2.29: *Carbon monoxide molecules are oxidised into carbon dioxide on the surface of the catalyst in the catalytic converter*

The catalyst acts as a site for the reaction to occur by a different route to the one which would take place if no catalyst was used. The steps in this alternative pathway each have lower activation energy than the route without the catalyst so more molecules have enough energy to react. This is shown in the potential energy diagram in figure 3.2.30.

Figure 3.2.30: *Potential energy diagram comparing the E_a of the catalysed conversion of carbon monoxide to carbon dioxide with the uncatalysed reaction*

Whenever a catalyst is used its surface area is made as big as possible to provide a large area for collisions between the catalyst and reactant molecules. The catalyst is often referred to as 'finely divided'.

The fact that a catalyst is regenerated at the end of a reaction does not mean the catalyst doesn't take part in the reaction. This can be shown in the reaction between potassium sodium tartrate (Rochelle's salt) and hydrogen peroxide (both colourless) which can be catalysed by adding a solution of pink cobalt(II) ions. The colour of the reaction mixture immediately turns green and the reaction is at its fastest. As the reaction slows the pink colour reappears showing the catalyst is regenerated in its original form. The presence of the green colour shows that the catalyst takes part in the reaction.

Researching chemistry – general laboratory apparatus

You should know how and when to use glassware such as test tubes, boiling tubes and conical flasks. In this experiment, where a fairly strong heat is required and no flammable substances are involved, a bunsen burner with a blue flame or an electric hot plate can be used.

Figure 3.2.31: *Cobalt(II) ions (pink) are acting as a catalyst and take part in the reaction (green) and are regenerated at the end of the reaction (pink)*

🔵 Activity 3.2.8

1. The diagram shows four steps (A to D) which are thought to take place as nitrogen and hydrogen react when passed over an iron catalyst.

Figure 3.2.32

(a) Describe what is happening in each of the stages B to D.

(b) Catalysts generally tend to be in the form of gauzes or small lumps. Explain why this is the case.

2. (i) Sketch a potential energy diagram for an exothermic reaction.

(ii) Add to your sketch a dotted line showing how the potential energy varies when a catalyst is used in the same reaction.

(iii) Mark clearly the enthalpy change and activation energy for both the catalysed and uncatalysed reactions.

CHEMISTRY IN CONTEXT: CATALYSTS AND THE FUTURE

Catalysing hydrogenation

Press release 27 June, 2013: New iron catalyst promises green future for hydrogenation

This was the headline of the press release from the Japanese research institute RIKEN in June 2013. It refers to a new iron nanoparticle catalyst which has been developed to speed up hydrogenation. Hydrogenation is the addition of hydrogen to another compound or element. Hydrogenation is one of the most widely studied chemical reactions, with industrial applications ranging from petrochemistry to pharmaceuticals and food production. The hardening of vegetable oils to make margarine is an example of hydrogenation. Nickel is traditionally used as the catalyst. Most of the applications of hydrogenation use rare metal catalysts such as palladium to speed up chemical reactions. They are highly efficient but are expensive and limited in supply, which has both economic and environmental challenges.

Iron is a far less expensive and more abundant metal. The main problem with using iron as a catalyst in hydrogenation is that in the presence of water and air it rusts and becomes inactive. The new technique produces iron nanoparticles inside a polymer structure which protects the iron surface from rusting but still allows the reactants to reach the surface of the metal and react. The technique is claimed to be safe, cheap and environmentally friendly.

Linker

●	Iron nanoparticle
●	Polystyrene bead
	Polyethylene glycol coating

Figure 3.2.33: *An iron nanoparticle with a polymer coating*

The company has a number of research projects including one aimed at making the Haber process, the production of ammonia, more efficient.

Catalytic clothing

An unusual idea to help reduce air pollution is to coat clothing in a photocatalyst – a catalyst which uses light to break down polluting gases in the air. Titanium oxide has been found to be particularly effective at breaking down pollutants in the air. When the light shines on the photocatalyst, the electrons in the material are rearranged and they become more reactive. The pollutants are then broken down into non-harmful chemicals. The catalyst can be incorporated into clothing when it is washed, for example, via a special fabric conditioner containing a catalyst. It has been calculated that in order to make this effective in a big city like London, for every metre width of pavement 30 people would have to walk past every minute.

Figure 3.2.34: *The dye used in denim jeans is good at absorbing the catalyst which can break down atmospheric pollutants*

KEEP UP TO DATE!
You can keep up to date with information on the development of new catalysts by looking up 'catalytic clothing' or 'new industrial catalysts' on the internet.

Learning checklist

In this chapter you have learned:

- Reaction rates must be controlled in industrial processes; too low then it will not be economically viable; too high and there is a risk of explosion.

- For reactants to form products they must first come into contact with each other (collide).

- The higher the concentration or pressure the more successful collisions and so the faster the reaction.

- The smaller the particle size the bigger the surface area so the higher the chance of collision.

- Before collisions can be successful and lead to products a minimum amount of energy, known as the activation energy (E_a), is required.

- Temperature is a measure of the average kinetic energy of the particles in a substance.

- Increasing the temperature increases the number of particles with energy greater than E_a, which results in more successful collisions and an increase in rate.

- Energy distribution diagrams can be drawn to show how increasing the temperature results in more particles with energy greater than E_a.

- Relative rate of reaction is inversely proportional to time, i.e. rate = 1/t.

- Rate of reaction is directly proportional to the concentration of the reactants.

- Rate of reaction is not directly proportional to temperature – a small increase in temperature results in a large increase in rate.

- Collision geometry has an effect on reaction rate.

- A potential energy diagram can be used to show the energy pathway for a reaction.

- Enthalpy is the name given to stored energy in chemicals and has the symbol H.

- The enthalpy change is the energy difference between products and reactants.

- Change in enthalpy for a reaction is given the symbol ΔH. Δ is the Greek symbol 'delta' and means 'change of'.

- ΔH is measured in kJ and kJ mol^{-1} when one mole of substance is reacted or produced.

- ΔH and E_a can be calculated from a potential energy diagram for exothermic and endothermic reactions.

- ΔH values are negative for exothermic reactions and positive for endothermic reactions.

- E_a is shown as an energy barrier in a potential energy diagram.

- An activated complex is an unstable arrangement of atoms formed at the top of the potential energy barrier.

- E_a can be considered to be the minimum amount of energy needed by colliding particles to form an activated complex.

- Catalysts provide an alternative pathway for reactants to form products – each step has a lower E_a than the uncatalysed reaction.

- A potential energy diagram can be used to show the effect of a catalyst on activation energy.

3 Chemical energy

- When a burning fuel is used to heat a liquid the energy transferred is calculated using the relationship $E_h = c \times m \times \Delta T$.

(National 5 Chemistry: Nature's chemistry: Energy from fuels)

- Enthalpy is the name given to stored energy in chemicals and is given the symbol H.
- The change in enthalpy for a reaction is given the symbol ΔH. Δ is the Greek symbol 'delta' and means 'change of'.
- ΔH is measured in kJ and kJ mol^{-1} when 1 mole of substance is reacted or produced.
- ΔH can be identified in a reaction profile for exothermic and endothermic reactions.
- ΔH values are negative for exothermic reactions and positive for endothermic reactions.

(Higher Chemistry: Chemistry in society: Controlling the rate)

Learning Intentions

In this chapter you will learn about:

- The importance of controlling the amount of heat in industrial processes.
- Measuring heat energy released by experiment.
- Enthalpy of combustion.
- Energy cycles and Hess's law.
- Bond and mean bond enthalpies.

SQA KEY AREA

Controlling the amount of heat

All chemical reactions involve a change in energy, which means a transfer of energy to and from the chemicals in the reaction. This results in energy being either given out to the surroundings (exothermic) or taken in (endothermic) during the reaction. The energy in chemicals is referred to as enthalpy (H) and the change in enthalpy (ΔH) during reactions can be measured. (See 'Reaction pathways', page 249.) For industrial processes chemists have to be able to calculate the amount of heat given out or taken in. Endothermic reactions require heat to be supplied and this is likely to push costs up. If a reaction is exothermic the heat will have to be removed to prevent the temperature getting too high and causing thermal runaway. Thermal runaway refers to a situation where an increase in temperature changes the conditions in a way that causes a further increase in temperature. The reaction

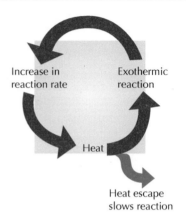

Figure 3.3.1: *Diagrammatic representation of thermal runaway – ensuring heat is removed as it is produced reduces the risk of explosion*

goes out of control, often resulting in an explosion. Most industrial reactions are exothermic and nearly every large scale chemical process has at least one step with the potential for thermal runaway, if the conditions are right. The resulting disastrous thermal explosion can cause severe damage to the plant, the workers and the environment.

Thermal runaway has contributed to industrial chemical accidents, most notably the 1947 Texas City disaster, from overheated ammonium nitrate in a ship's hold, and the disastrous release of a large volume of methyl isocyanate gas from a Union Carbide plant in Bhopal, India in 1984 (see Chapter 3.1, page 196). Thermal runaway is most often caused by failure of the reactor vessel's cooling system. Failure of the mixer can result in localised heating, which initiates thermal runaway.

Modern chemical plants are built with emergency venting and cooling systems to avoid thermal runaway. The heat that is produced is not wasted. It is often used to provide heat where needed in other parts of a process, either supplied to a reaction mixture or used to produce steam to drive pumps needed to compress gases. The Chemistry in context section below details the exothermic and endothermic reactions in the production of ammonia and nitric acid.

> ⚠ **Remember this**
>
> Enthalpy is the name given to stored energy in chemicals and is given the symbol **H**. The change in enthalpy for a reaction is given the symbol **ΔH**. Δ is the Greek symbol 'delta' and means 'change of'. ΔH is measured in kJ.

CHEMISTRY IN CONTEXT: THE PRODUCTION OF AMMONIA AND NITRIC ACID

Nitric acid is produced on an industrial scale by reacting ammonia with oxygen from the air. The ammonia is produced by passing nitrogen and hydrogen over an iron catalyst. Throughout the processes taking place, reactants and products are being heated and cooled. Industrial chemists have to know if reactions are exothermic or endothermic to be able to control the conditions accordingly. At the same time they must ensure that any heat produced is not wasted and is used somewhere in the process to keep the heating costs down.

The hydrogen needed for the production of ammonia is mostly obtained by reacting methane and steam to form synthesis gas, a mixture of carbon monoxide and hydrogen:

$$CH_4(g) + H_2O(g) \rightleftharpoons CO(g) + 3H_2(g) \quad \Delta H = +210 \text{ kJ mol}^{-1}$$

The reaction is reversible and the forward reaction is endothermic so should be favoured by high temperature and low pressure (Le Chatelier's Principle – see page 291). In practice, the reactants are passed over a catalyst of finely divided nickel heated in a furnace above 900°C and under a pressure of around 30 atmospheres.

The synthesis gas produced has to be cooled in heat exchangers. The steam formed from the water used in cooling the gases is used to operate the pumps which drive the compressors and to preheat reactants.

The hydrogen produced is then reacted with nitrogen – the process is summarised in figure 3.3.2:

Figure 3.3.2: Diagram of the Haber process showing where heat is added and removed and steam-driven pumps compress and circulate gases

The ammonia is used in the manufacture of nitric acid (the Ostwald process). The first stage of the process involves the oxidation of ammonia to nitrogen monoxide:

$$4NH_3(g) + 5O_2(g) \rightleftharpoons 4NO(g) + 6H_2O(g) \quad \Delta H = -900 \text{ kJ mol}^{-1}$$

Most plants operate with:

- *moderate pressures (10–13 atm)*
- *an alloy of platinum and rhodium as catalyst*
- *temperatures at around 900°C to ensure the reaction rate is as high as possible.*

The reaction is highly exothermic. The hot product gases are cooled and the heat produced is used to reheat the reaction mixture, keep the catalyst at the required temperature or produce superheated steam. The steam may be used to generate power in a steam pump which can then drive the compressors. Air is added to the nitrogen monoxide and the gases compressed again (7–12 atm typically). The temperature rises to over 100°C and the gases need to be cooled further. The gases need to be compressed and then cooled to help move the following equilibria to the right:

$$2NO(g) + O_2(g) \rightleftharpoons 2NO_2(g) \quad \Delta H = -115 \text{ kJ mol}^{-1}$$

$$2NO_2(g) \rightleftharpoons N_2O_4(g) \qquad \Delta H = -58 \text{ kJ mol}^{-1}$$

The gases are then passed through a tower to meet a stream of water, normally flowing in the opposite direction to the gas. Here, oxidation of the nitrogen monoxide continues and absorption occurs with the formation of nitric acid:

$$3N_2O_4(g) + 2H_2O(\ell) \rightleftharpoons 4HNO_3(aq) + 2NO(g) \quad \Delta H = -103 \text{ kJ mol}^{-1}$$

Figure 3.3.3: *The heat produced in the first stage of the manufacture of nitric acid is used to keep the catalyst at the required temperature*

Measuring heat energy released by experiment

Enthalpy of combustion

At National 5 you will have learned how to calculate the quantity of heat energy released when a substance burns completely in oxygen. This is important when working out, say, how good a fuel a certain substance might be. To make a fair comparison the enthalpy change when burning the same quantity of fuel should be compared. Enthalpy changes given in data books are for 1 mole of a substance burning completely in oxygen at standard temperature (25°C) and pressure (1 atmosphere), all substances being in their standard states. This is known as the **standard enthalpy of combustion** (ΔH_c).

The process of measuring energy changes is known as calorimetry, named after an old unit of heat called the calorie. Anything which is used to measure enthalpy changes is known as a calorimeter. A simple calorimeter used to measure the enthalpy of combustion of ethanol in a school laboratory is shown in figure 3.3.4.

The experiment is carried out as follows:

Step 1: Weigh the spirit burner containing the ethanol and measure the temperature of the water.

Step 2: Heat the metal beaker containing a known mass of water by about 20°C. Blow out the flame and note the highest temperature the water reaches.

Step 3: Reweigh the spirit burner.

The change in temperature (ΔT) can be worked out by subtracting the final temperature from the initial temperature.

The mass of water (**m**), in kg, is known (1 cm³ = 1 g).

The energy needed to raise the temperature of 1 kg (1 litre) of water by 1°C (the specific heat capacity of water, (**c**)) is 4·18 kJ kg⁻¹ °C⁻¹.

Figure 3.3.4: *A simple calorimeter used to determine the enthalpy of combustion of ethanol*

From the experimental results the amount of energy transferred to the water (E_h) in kJ, can be calculated by entering the values into a simple equation which connects them:

$$E_h = c \times m \times \Delta T$$

The mass of ethanol burned is known so the enthalpy of combustion of ethanol, i.e. the energy given out when 1 mole of ethanol is burned completely, can be calculated. This is shown in the worked example.

Researching chemistry – common chemical apparatus

A thermometer reading to the nearest 0·1–0·2°C would be used in this type of experiment to increase the accuracy. This is important as the change in temperature will be used in a calculation so the more accurate the measurements here, the more accurate the final answer will be.

Worked example

0·79 g of ethanol raises the temperature of 200 g of water in the metal can by 21°C. Calculate the enthalpy of combustion (ΔH_c) of ethanol.

Worked answer:

Step 1: Work out the energy transferred to the water (E_h):

$$E_h = c \times m \times \Delta T$$
$$= 4·18 \times 0·2 \times 21·0$$
$$E_h = 17·56 \text{ kJ}$$

Step 2: Calculate the amount of fuel used, in moles:

Mass of 1 mole of ethanol (C_2H_5OH) = 46 g.

Moles (n) of ethanol in 0·79 g = mass (m)/mass of 1 mole (GFM)

= 0·79/46 = 0·017 mol

Step 3: Work out the energy transferred to the water when 1 mole of ethanol burns, i.e. the enthalpy of combustion:

0·017 mole of ethanol releases 17·56 kJ

So, 1 mole of ethanol releases 17·56/0·017 = 1033 kJ

So, the enthalpy of combustion of ethanol = −1033 kJ mol^{-1}.

Note here that there is a − sign before the numerical value because the reaction is exothermic. The units are kJ mol^{-1} because enthalpy of combustion of ethanol is the energy released when 1 mole of ethanol is burned.

> ⚠ **Remember this**
>
> The relationship $E_h = c\, m\, \Delta T$ can be found in the SQA data booklet, along with the value of c. From this relationship:
>
> $$c = \frac{E_h}{m\Delta T}$$
> $$m = \frac{E_h}{c\Delta T}$$

Table 3.3.1 gives the standard enthalpy of combustion of some of fuels. Notice how the experimental value for ethanol is a fair bit lower than the standard value in the table. This is because the experimental value is not obtained under standard conditions and there are considerable heat losses to the surroundings from the flame and the metal can, i.e. not all the heat from the flame and the metal can reaches the water. There is no value in table 3.3.1 for petrol because it is a complex mixture of over 100 compounds. Octane, one of the constituents of petrol, has a standard enthalpy of combustion of −5470 kJ mol^{-1}, which indicates why petrol is such a good fuel.

Table 3.3.1: *Standard enthalpy of combustion of some fuels*

Fuel	Main constituent	Formula and standard state	ΔH_c of main constituent (KJ mol^{-1})
hydrogen	hydrogen	$H_2(g)$	−286
compressed natural gas (CNG)	90% methane	$CH_4(g)$	−890
liquid petroleum gas (LPG)	95% propane	$C_3H_8(g)$	−2219
methanol	methanol	$CH_3OH(\ell)$	−726
ethanol	ethanol	$C_2H_5OH(\ell)$	−1367

GO! **Activity 3.3.1**

1. The table below summarises the results obtained by a group of pupils who carried out experiments to work out the enthalpy of combustion of three alcohols: methanol (CH_3OH), ethanol (C_2H_5OH) and propan-1-ol (C_3H_7OH). The experiment arrangement is shown in figure 3.3.4.

Table 3.3.2:

	Methanol	Ethanol	Propan–1-ol
volume of water used (cm^3)	100	100	100
initial temperature of water (°C)	23·2	22·8	23·1
final temperature of water (°C)	45·6	46·3	47·2
initial mass of alcohol burner (g)	76·84	80·75	77·24
final mass of alcohol burner (g)	76·19	80·29	76·86

   (a) Calculate the enthalpy of combustion for each of the alcohols.

   (b) From the students' results, predict the enthalpy of combustion of butan-1-ol.

   (c) Suggest why the experimental results are less than the data booklet values.

2. 0·41 g of ethanol was burned and the heat produced used to heat 100 g of water. 8·54 kJ of energy was produced.

   Calculate the rise in temperature of the water, assuming all of the energy was transferred to the water.

CHEMISTRY IN CONTEXT: THE ENERGY VALUES OF FOODS

The experimental arrangement used to find the enthalpy of combustion of ethanol (figure 3.3.4) is an example of a very simple bomb calorimeter. Figure 3.3.5 is a diagram of a bomb calorimeter used in industry to find accurate enthalpy of combustion for fuels.

precision thermometer

electrical connections to Fe ignition wire

waterbath stirrer

high pressure oxygen combustion bomb

Parr Model 1341 Oxygen Bomb Calorimeter

Figure 3.3.5: *The bomb calorimeter is used to get accurate values for enthalpy of combustion*

The sample is weighed and placed inside a stainless steel container – the bomb – and filled with oxygen under pressure. The fuel is ignited electrically. The energy produced is transferred to the water and the temperature rise measured. Energy losses to the surroundings are reduced to almost zero. The bomb calorimeter is used to measure the enthalpy of combustion of different foods. Although our bodies don't burn food in the same way as a car engine burns petrol, the outcome is the same – oxygen is used up and heat energy is produced. Our bodies do lose some heat to the surroundings – that's why we wear clothes to reduce the heat loss – but not a lot of energy is lost to the surroundings. Most is used to maintain electrical and chemical functions in our body or is stored. Too much stored energy can lead to being overweight. Food manufacturers now publish the energy content of foods on nutrition labels. Figure 3.3.6 shows a typical nutrition label for a breakfast cereal. Notice that the units of energy are given in both kJ and kcal (kilo calories) – 1 kcal is approximately 4·2 kJ. Most food companies in the UK use both kJ and kcal on their labels.

...in (19% RDA) and adding a handful of fruit will count as one of your 5-a-Day.

Typical values	100g contains	45g serving contains
Energy	1570kJ 375kcal	710kJ 170kcal
Protein	16.5g	4.6g
Carbohydrate	73.8g	33.2g
of which sugars	15.0g	6.8g
Fat	2.0g	0.9g
of which saturates	0.3g	0.1g
Fibre‡‡	8.2g	3.7g
Sodium	0.2g	0.1g
Salt equivalent	0.6g	0.3g

‡‡Fibre has been determined by AOAC anal...
For guideline daily amou...

Figure 3.3.6: *Typical nutrition label for a breakfast cereal with the energy value highlighted*

SQA KEY AREA

Heat energy released during neutralisation

When an acid reacts completely with an alkali the reaction is called neutralisation. The reaction between hydrochloric acid and sodium hydroxide is an example of neutralisation:

hydrochloric acid + sodium hydroxide → water + potassium chloride

$HCl(aq)$ + $NaOH(aq)$ → $H_2O(\ell)$ + $NaCl(aq)$

$H^+(aq) + Cl^-(aq)$ + $Na^+(aq) + OH^-(aq)$ → $H_2O(\ell)$ + $Na^+(aq) + Cl^-(aq)$

The ionic equation shows that $Cl^- + K^+$ are spectator ions. The ions which have taken part in the reaction are the $2H^+$ and the OH^- ions. Water is the only new product. Rewriting the equation without the spectator ions:

$H^+(aq)$ + $OH^-(aq)$ → $H_2O(\ell)$

This is the same for any neutralisation reaction.

The heat energy released during neutralisation can be determined in the laboratory using the simple calorimeter shown in figure 3.3.7.

The experiment is carried out as follows:

Step 1: Measure out accurately a known volume of acid and measure its temperature.

Step 2: Repeat step 1 with an alkali.

thermometer reading to 0.1 °C

expanded polystyrene cup with lid

Figure 3.3.7: *A simple calorimeter used to measure the heat energy released during neutralisation*

Step 3: Mix the acid with the alkali in a polystyrene cup, stir the mixture and record the highest temperature reached.

Step 4: Calculate the change in temperature (ΔT) by subtracting the average temperature of the acid and alkali from the highest temperature recorded.

The enthalpy change can be calculated using $E_h = c \times m \times \Delta T$. In this experiment the mass (m) is the combined volume of acid and alkali. Even although it is not pure water absorbing the heat produced, the specific heat of water (c) is still used, i.e. $4 \cdot 18$ kJ kg^{-1} °C^{-1}.

> **Researching chemistry – common chemical apparatus**
>
> The volumes of acid and alkali are usually measured out in a measuring cylinder. However, to improve the accuracy of the measurement a pipette or burette could be used.

Worked example

In a school laboratory experiment, 50 cm^3 of $1 \cdot 0$ mol^{-1} hydrochloric acid was added to 50 cm^3 of $1 \cdot 0$ mol^{-1} sodium hydroxide. The temperature rise was $6 \cdot 1$°C. Calculate (i) the heat energy released during neutralisation (ii) the enthalpy change when one mole of water is formed.

Worked answer:

(i) Work out the energy transferred to the water (E_h):

$$(m = 50 + 50 = 100 \text{ cm}^3 = 100 \text{ g} = 0 \cdot 1 \text{ kg})$$

$$E_h = c \times m \times \Delta T$$

$$= 4 \cdot 18 \times 0 \cdot 1 \times 6 \cdot 1$$

$$E_h = 2 \cdot 55 \text{ kJ}$$

(ii) Step 1: Calculate the amount of acid (or alkali) used, in moles:

moles (n) = concentration (c) × volume (V)

$$= 1 \cdot 0 \times 0 \cdot 05$$

moles = $0 \cdot 05$ mol

We know that the reaction taking place is:

$$H^+(aq) \quad + \quad OH^-(aq) \quad \rightarrow \quad H_2O(l)$$

From the balanced equation

	1 mol	1 mol	→	1 mol
So,	$0 \cdot 05$ mol	$0 \cdot 05$ mol		$0 \cdot 05$ mol

i.e. $0 \cdot 05$ mol of water formed.

Step 2: Work out the energy transferred when 1 mole of water is formed, i.e. the enthalpy of neutralisation:

When $0 \cdot 05$ moles of water is formed the heat energy released is $2 \cdot 55$ kJ

So, when 1 mole of water is formed it releases the heat energy released is 2·55/0·05 = 51·0 kJ

So, the enthalpy of neutralisation = −51·0 kJ mol^{-1}.

The data booklet value for the enthalpy of neutralisation is −57·2 kJ mol^{-1}. The difference in values is due to heat loss to the surroundings during the laboratory experiment.

Note that the enthalpy of neutralisation is −57·2 kJ mol^{-1} regardless of the acid and alkali used because the same reaction is happening each time, i.e. water is produced.

GO! Activity 3.3.2

1. A group of students mixed 20 cm^3 of 1·0 mol^{-1} hydrochloric acid with 20 cm^3 of 1·0 mol^{-1} potassium hydroxide. The temperature rise was 6·5 °C.

   HCl(aq)   +   KOH(aq)   →   H$_2$O(l)   +   KCl(aq)

   Calculate the enthalpy of neutralisation using their results.

2. A group of students mixed 25 cm^3 of 1·0 mol^{-1} sulfuric acid with 50 cm^3 of 1·0 mol^{-1} sodium hydroxide. The temperature rise was 8·2°C.

   H$_2$SO$_4$(aq)   +   2NaOH(aq)   →   2H$_2$O(l)   +   Na$_2$SO$_4$(aq)

   Calculate the enthalpy of neutralisation using their results.

CHEMISTRY IN CONTEXT: CHEMICAL COLD PACKS

When substances are dissolved in water, heat energy can either be released into the water or lost from the water, depending on the substance being dissolved. Chemical cold packs, which are commonly found in first aid kits to treat sprains and other sports injuries, include chemicals which, when they dissolve in water, cause the temperature of the resulting solution to drop – an endothermic process. The exact contents of the pack are a closely guarded secret by the manufacturers, but a common example is one which usually contains water and a packet of ammonium chloride/ ammonium nitrate. The cold pack is activated by breaking the barrier separating the water and the chemicals, allowing them to mix and form a solution.

The heat energy change that takes place when a substance dissolves can be determined in the laboratory using a simple calorimeter similar to the arrangement shown in figure 3.3.7.

Figure 3.3.8: *Chemical cold packs used to treat sports injuries work because when chemicals in the pack dissolve in water the temperature of the solution formed drops – an endothermic process*

The experiment is carried out as follows:

Step 1: *Measure out accurately a known volume of deionised water and measure its temperature.*

Step 2: *Add an accurately weighed mass of the solute to the water and stir until it has completely dissolved.*

Step 3: *Record the highest/lowest temperature reached.*

Step 4: *Calculate the change in temperature (ΔT) by subtracting the temperature of the water at the start from the highest/lowest temperature recorded.*

The heat energy change can be calculated using
$E_h = c \times m \times \Delta T.$

Note: *see the Researching chemistry section (page 322) for a description of using a balance.*

Worked example

The results obtained from an experiment in which potassium nitrate was dissolved in water are shown below.

Table 3.3.3:

Measurement	Result
mass of potassium nitrate (KNO_3) (g)	2·9
mass of water (g)	50
initial temperature of water (°C)	20·3
final temperature of solution (°C)	17·8

Calculate (i) the energy transferred from the water (E_h) and (ii) the energy transferred from the water when one mole of potassium nitrate dissolves.

Worked answer:

(i) *Work out the energy transferred from the water (E_h):*

$$(m = 50\ g = 0·05\ kg;\ \Delta T = 2·5°C)$$

$$E_h = c \times m \times \Delta T$$

$$= 4·18 \times 0·05 \times 2·5$$

$$E_h = 0·52\ kJ$$

(ii) Step 1: *Calculate the number of moles of potassium nitrate dissolved:*

Gram formula mass of KNO_3:
$39·1 + 14·0 + (3 \times 16) = 101·1\ g$

moles (n) = mass (m)/gram formula mass (GFM)

$$= 2·9/101·1$$

$$= 0·029\ mol$$

Step 2: *Work out the energy produced when 1 mole of potassium nitrate dissolves:*

When 0·029 moles of potassium nitrate dissolves the energy absorbed is 0·52 kJ.

So, when 1 mole of potassium nitrate dissolves the energy absorbed is 0·52/0·029 = 17·93 kJ.

So, the enthalpy of solution of potassium nitrate = +17·93 kJ mol^{-1}.

Notice that there is a + sign before the numerical value to indicate the reaction is endothermic.

Activity 3.3.3

1. Results from an experiment to find the quantity of heat transferred when potassium chloride dissolves are shown below.

   Table 3.3.4:

Measurement	Result
mass of potassium chloride(KCl) (g)	7·5
mass of water (g)	100
initial temperature of water (°C)	20·4
final temperature of solution (°C)	17·2

   Calculate the enthalpy change when 1 mole of potassium chloride is dissolved.

2. Results from an experiment to find the quantity of heat transferred when sodium hydroxide dissolves are shown below:

   Table 3.3.5:

Measurement	Result
mass of sodium hydroxide (NaOH) (g)	0·75
mass of water (g)	50
initial temperature of water (°C)	20·1
final temperature of solution (°C)	24·2

   Calculate the enthalpy change when 1 mole of sodium hydroxide is dissolved.

Energy cycles and Hess's law

Some enthalpies of reaction can be measured experimentally. However, many enthalpies of reaction cannot, so an indirect approach using energy cycles is used.

Using energy cycles to work out enthalpy of reaction relies on **Hess's law** which states that the enthalpy change for a chemical reaction is independent of the route taken from reactants to products, so long as the starting and finishing conditions are the same for each route. This is shown in an energy cycle in figure 3.3.9:

Figure 3.3.9: *An energy cycle illustrating Hess's law:* $\Delta H_1 = \Delta H_2 + \Delta H_3 + \Delta H_4$

The overall enthalpy change for route 2 must be the same as for route 1, i.e.

$$\Delta H_1 = \Delta H_2 + \Delta H_3 + \Delta H_4.$$

We can use this idea to work out the enthalpy of formation of methane:

$$C(s) + 2H_2(g) \quad \rightarrow \quad CH_4(g) \quad \Delta H_f \quad \text{(target equation)}$$

Methane cannot be made directly from its elements carbon and hydrogen, but Hess's law can be used to calculate the enthalpy of formation by an indirect route. By burning carbon, hydrogen and methane we can calculate the enthalpy of combustion for each and then use them to devise an energy cycle to calculate the enthalpy of formation.

The equations for the combustion of carbon, hydrogen and methane are shown below:

$$C(s) + O_2(g) \quad \rightarrow \quad CO_2(g) \qquad \qquad \Delta H_1 = -394 \text{ kJ mol}^{-1}$$

$$H_2(g) + \tfrac{1}{2}O_2(g) \quad \rightarrow \quad H_2O(\ell) \qquad \qquad \Delta H_2 = -286 \text{ kJ mol}^{-1}$$

$$CH_4(g) + 2O_2(g) \quad \rightarrow \quad CO_2(g) + 2H_2O(\ell) \quad \Delta H_3 = -891 \text{ kJ mol}^{-1}$$

The equations can be arranged in the following energy cycle:

Figure 3.3.10: *The energy cycle for working out enthalpy of formation of methane from enthalpies of combustion*

Important notes on the energy cycle:

1. ΔH_2 has to be **multiplied by 2**, i.e. $2\Delta H_2$, because in the target equation 2 moles of hydrogen react.

2. ΔH_3 has to be **reversed**. i.e. $-\Delta H_3$, because in the cycle the carbon dioxide and water combine to form methane and oxygen, the reverse of combustion.

3. Applying Hess's law:

$$\Delta H_f = \Delta H_1 + 2\Delta H_2 - \Delta H_3$$
$$= -394 + (2 \times -286) - (-891)$$
$$\Delta H_f = -75 \text{ kJ mol}^{-1}$$

It is not always necessary to draw out an energy cycle when working out the enthalpy of reaction. By writing out the equation for route 1 (target equation) and the equations for the enthalpy of reaction for each of the steps in route 2, rearranging them as required and then applying Hess's law, the enthalpy of formation can be calculated.

Worked example 1: Calculate the enthalpy of formation of methanol from the enthalpy of combustion of carbon, hydrogen and methanol.

$C(s) + 2H_2(g) + \frac{1}{2}O_2 \rightarrow CH_3OH(\ell) \quad \Delta H_f$ (target equation)

$C(s) + O_2(g) \rightarrow CO_2(g) \quad \Delta H_1 = -394 \text{ kJ mol}^{-1}$

$H_2(g) + \frac{1}{2}O_2(g) \rightarrow H_2O \quad \Delta H_2 = -286 \text{ kJ mol}^{-1}$

$CH_3OH(\ell) + \frac{1}{2}O_2(g) \rightarrow CO_2(g) + 2H_2O(\ell)$
$\Delta H_3 = -727 \text{ kJ mol}^{-1}$

Worked answer:

Target equation: $C(s) + 2H_2(g) + \frac{1}{2}O_2 \rightarrow CH_3OH(\ell) \quad \Delta H_f$

1 mole of carbon needed on the left hand side of the target equation so **leave ΔH_1**.

2 moles of hydrogen needed on left-hand side of target equation so ΔH_2 **must be multiplied by 2**.

1 mole of methanol needed on right-hand side of target equation so ΔH_3 **must be reversed**.

Applying Hess's law: $\Delta H_f = \Delta H_1 + 2\Delta H_2 - \Delta H_3$
$$= -394 + (2 \times -286) - (-727)$$
$$\Delta H_f = -239 \text{ kJ mol}^{-1}$$

Worked example 2: Carbon tetrachloride (CCl_4) is prepared by the reaction of chlorine gas (Cl_2) with methane (CH_4).

$$CH_4(g) + 4Cl_2(g) \rightarrow CCl_4(g) + 4HCl(g)$$

Calculate the enthalpy change, in kJ mol^{-1}, for this reaction using the following enthalpies of formation.

1. $C(s) + 2H_2(g) \rightarrow CH_4(g)$ $\Delta H = -75$ kJ mol^{-1}

2. $C(s) + 2Cl_2(g) \rightarrow CCl_4(g)$ $\Delta H = -98$ kJ mol^{-1}

3. $\frac{1}{2}H_2(g) + \frac{1}{2}Cl_2(g) \rightarrow HCl(g)$ $\Delta H = -92$ kJ mol^{-1}

Worked answer:

Reverse 1

$$CH_4(g) \rightarrow C(s) + 2H_2(g) \quad \Delta H = +75 \text{ kJ mol}^{-1}$$

Leave 2

$$C(s) + 2Cl_2(g) \rightarrow CCl_4(g) \quad \Delta H = -98 \text{ kJ mol}^{-1}$$

Multiply 3 by 4

$$2H_2(g) + 2Cl_2(g) \rightarrow 4HCl(g) \quad \Delta H = -368 \text{ kJ mol}^{-1}$$

Applying Hess's law

$$\Delta H_{reaction} = (+75) + (-98) + (-368)$$

$$\Delta H_{reaction} = -391 \text{ kJ mol}^{-1}$$

GO! Activity 3.3.4

1. The equation for the formation of propane is $3C(s) + 4H_2(g) \rightarrow C_3H_8(g)$.

   Calculate the enthalpy of formation of propane, using the enthalpies of combustion shown below:

$C(s) + O_2(g)$	$\rightarrow CO_2(g)$	$\Delta H_1 = -394$ kJ mol^{-1}
$H_2(g) + \frac{1}{2}O_2(g)$	$\rightarrow H_2O(\ell)$	$\Delta H_2 = -286$ kJ mol^{-1}
$C_3H_8(g) + 5O_2(g)$	$\rightarrow 3CO_2(g) + 4H_2O(\ell)$	$\Delta H_3 = -2220$ kJ mol^{-1}

2. The equation for the formation of ethanol is $2C(s) + 3H_2(g) + \frac{1}{2}O_2 \rightarrow C_2H_5OH(\ell)$.

   Use the enthalpies of combustion of carbon, hydrogen and ethanol (from the SQA data booklet) to calculate the enthalpy of formation of ethanol.

3. The equation for the formation of ethyne is (C_2H_2), is $2C(s) + H_2(g) \rightarrow C_2H_2(g)$.

   Use the enthalpies of combustion of carbon, hydrogen and ethyne (from the SQA data booklet) to calculate the enthalpy of formation of ethyne.

4. The equation for the formation of benzene is (C_6H_6), is $6C(s) + 3H_2(g) \rightarrow C_6H_6(g)$.

    Use the enthalpies of combustion of carbon, hydrogen and benzene (from the SQA data booklet) to calculate the enthalpy of formation of benzene.

5. The equation for the reaction of ethene with hydrogen chloride to produce chloroethane is:

    $$C_2H_4(g) + HCl(g) \rightarrow C_2H_5Cl(g)$$

    Use the enthalpies of formation below to calculate the enthalpy of reaction of ethene with hydrogen chloride.

    Table 3.3.6: *Enthalpies of formation*

	ΔH_f (kJ mol^{-1})
$C_2H_4(g)$	+52
$HCl(g)$	−92
$C_2H_5Cl(g)$	−109

6. The equation for the enthalpy of combustion of carbon disulfide, CS_2, is $CS_2(\ell) + 3O_2(g) \rightarrow CO_2(g) + 2SO_2(g)$.

    Calculate the enthalpy of combustion for carbon disulfide using the following enthalpies of formation:

$C(s) + O_2(g) \rightarrow CO_2(g)$	$\Delta H_f = -394$ kJ mol^{-1}
$S(s) + O_2(g) \rightarrow SO_2(g)$	$\Delta H_f = -297$ kJ mol^{-1}
$C(s) + 2S(s) \rightarrow CS_2(\ell)$	$\Delta H_f = +88$ kJ mol^{-1}

Bond and mean bond enthalpies

When fuel molecules react with oxygen energy is released. During the reaction, bonds within the reacting molecules are broken and new bonds are made when products are formed. **Bond enthalpy** is the energy required to break a bond between two atoms in a gaseous molecule. More precisely, it is the energy required to break 1 mole of bonds between the atoms in a mole of diatomic molecules, at standard temperature and pressure (25°C and 1 atmosphere). For diatomic molecules such as hydrogen (H_2) and hydrogen chloride (HCl) there is only one possible bond energy for each, as the H–H bond and H–Cl bond can only exist in these molecules. This is not the case for the likes of the C–C bond which can exist in alkanes, cycloalkanes, alcohols, etc. The C–C bond will have slightly different bond enthalpy depending on the type of molecule it exists in. The bond enthalpies quoted in these cases is the **mean bond enthalpy**, which is an average value.

Table 3.3.7 and Table 3.3.8: *Selected bond and mean bond enthalpies*

Bond Enthalpies		Mean Bond Enthalpies	
Bond	**Enthalpy (kJ mol⁻¹)**	**Bond Mean**	**Enthalpy (kJ mol⁻¹)**
$H-H$	432	$Si-Si$	222
$O=O$	497	$C-C$	346
$N\equiv N$	941	$C=C$	602
$F-F$	155	$C\equiv C$	835
$Cl-Cl$	243	$H-O$	458
$Br-Br$	194	$H-N$	387
$I-I$	149	$C-H$	414
$H-F$	569	$C-O$	358
$H-Cl$	428	$C=O$	798
$H-Br$	362	$C-F$	486
$H-I$	295	$C-Cl$	326
		$C-Br$	285
		$C-I$	213

> **Hint**
>
> Bond enthalpies and mean bond enthalpies can be found in the SQA data booklet. The values may be different from those quoted in tables 3.3.6 and 3.3.7 because they are from different sources.

Bond breaking is an endothermic process because energy has to be put in to overcome the force of attraction between the atoms. Bond making is an exothermic process – if energy needs to be put in to break a bond then the same amount of energy should be given out when the same bond forms. Take hydrogen as an example:

Bond breaking: H–H(g) → H(g) + H(g) $\Delta H = +432$ kJ mol⁻¹

Bond making: H(g) + H(g) → H–H(g) $\Delta H = -432$ kJ mol⁻¹

Bond enthalpies and mean bond enthalpies can be used to estimate the enthalpy changes for different gas phase reactions. The enthalpy of reaction is the difference between the energy needed to break bonds and the energy released when bonds are made. When a fuel burns, the energy produced when bonds are made is greater than the energy needed to break bonds between reactant molecules. For example, when hydrogen burns in oxygen:

Bond breaking   Bond making

H–H(g) + ½O = O(g)   →   H–O–H

432   +   ½(497)   2(–458)

$\Delta H = 432 + 248{\cdot}5 + (-916) = -235{\cdot}5$ kJ mol⁻¹

This can be shown diagrammatically:

Figure 3.3.11: *Diagrammatic representation of bond breaking and bond making when hydrogen burns*

Worked example

Use bond enthalpies and mean bond enthalpies in table 3.3.7 and table 3.3.8 to calculate the energy released when 1 mole of methane burns completely in oxygen.

Worked answer:

Step 1: Write down the equation for the reaction:

$$CH_4(g) + 2O_2(g) \rightarrow CO_2(g) + 2H_2O(g)$$

Step 2: Draw out full structural formulae to show all the bonds:

$$\begin{array}{c} H \\ | \\ H-C-H \\ | \\ H \end{array} + 2\,O=O \longrightarrow O=C=O + 2\,H-O-H$$

Step 3: List all the bonds breaking and bonds being made and the bond enthalpies:

Bond breaking	Bond making
$4 \times (C-H) + 2 \times (O=O)$	$2 \times (C=O) + 4 \times (O-H)$
$4 \times (+414) + 2 \times (+497)$	$2 \times (-798) + 4 \times (-458)$
$+2650$	-3428

$\Delta H = 2650 - 3428 = -778$ **kJ mol^{-1}**

The standard enthalpy of combustion for methane is −891 kJ mol⁻¹. This is different to the value obtained using bond enthalpies. This is mainly due to the fact that the standard state of water is liquid but when dealing with bond energies all the molecules must be in the gaseous state, and energy is given out when water changes from gas to liquid (condenses).

The standard enthalpy of combustion of methanol is less than that of methane even although they have the same number of carbon and hydrogen atoms. This is because of the way the atoms are bonded – methanol already has one O–H bond. When methane burns all four O–H bonds must be made, which gives a more exothermic reaction.

Octane, one of the compounds in petrol, has 18 C–H bonds and seven C–C bonds. Methane has just four C–H bonds. Although it takes more energy to break all the bonds in a mole of octane compared to methane, far more energy is released when new bonds are formed. The standard enthalpy of combustion of octane is −5470 kJ mol⁻¹ compared to methane, which is −891 kJ mol⁻¹.

GO! Activity 3.3.5

1. Table 3.3.7 and table 3.3.8 lists bond enthalpies and mean bond enthalpies. Explain the difference between the two.

2. Methanol is used as a fuel in some types of motor racing. Use the bond enthalpies listed in tables 3.3.7 and 3.3.8 to estimate the energy released when 1 mole of methanol is burned.

$$CH_3OH(g) + \tfrac{3}{2}O_2(g) \rightarrow CO_2(g) + 2H_2O(g)$$

3. Use the bond enthalpies listed in tables 3.3.7 and 3.3.8 to estimate the enthalpy change for the following reactions:

   (a) $C_2H_4 + H_2 \rightarrow C_2H_6$

   (b) $C_2H_2 + 2H_2 \rightarrow C_2H_6$ (the structural formula for C_2H_2 is $H - C \equiv C - H$)

   (c) $H_2 + F_2 \rightarrow 2HF$

CHEMISTRY IN CONTEXT: ENERGY DENSITY – CHOOSING THE RIGHT FUEL

It is important that we get the maximum energy we can from any fuel we use. Most forms of transport have to carry the fuel with them, e.g. petrol or diesel in a car. We can work out the amount of energy released by 1 kg of fuel. This is known as the energy density of the fuel. Energy density can be calculated from the enthalpy of combustion and the gram formula mass (gfm) of a compound:

Octane (C_8H_{18}) is one of the constituents of petrol. Calculate the energy density of octane, given the enthalpy of combustion is -5470 kJ mol^{-1}.

Worked example

Worked answer:

Gfm for octane: $C_8H_{18} = (8 \times 12) + (18 \times 1) = 114$ g.

114 g (1 mol) of octane releases -5470 kJ mol^{-1} of energy.

1000 g (1 kg) of octane releases $(1000/114) \times 5470$

$$= 47982 \text{ kJ kg}^{-1}.$$

Petrol is a complex mixture of hydrocarbons which includes octane and has an energy density of 46 000 kJ kg^{-1}, which indicates it is a very concentrated energy form.

Table 3.3.9 shows values for some fuels – petrol is not included as it is a mixture not an individual compound.

Table 3.3.9: *Energy density values for three fuels*

Fuel	Formula	ΔHc (kJ mol^{-1})	Mass of 1 mole (g)	Energy density (kJ kg^{-1})
hydrogen	H_2	-286	2	143000
methane	CH_4	-891	16	27800
methanol	CH_3OH	-727	32	22700

The table indicates that hydrogen has a very high energy density so should be an excellent fuel. Liquified hydrogen was used as the fuel for the rockets which launched the space shuttles.

Figure 3.3.12: *The rocket which carried the space shuttle used liquid hydrogen as a fuel*

Figure 3.3.13: *The Toyota Mirai uses a hydrogen fuel cell*

KEEP UP TO DATE!
Hyundai, Honda and Toyota all have hydrogen fuel cell cars on the market. You can keep up to date with the production of hydrogen fuel cell vehicles by looking up 'fuel cell vehicles' on the internet.

Figure 3.3.14: *The smaller hydrogen atoms are trapped between the larger metal atoms in a metal hydride lattice*

One of the major disadvantages of using hydrogen in cars is the difficulty in storing it. Liquefying hydrogen would mean cooling it to −253°C, which costs more than four times what it costs to produce the equivalent amount of petrol. A number of companies have developed hydrogen fuel cells for use in motor vehicles. In 2018 there were over 5000 Toyota Mirai fuel cell cars worldwide, mainly in the USA and Japan. The cost of these cars is still out of the reach of most people but it is expected that this will drop in time. An experimental 'Hydroflex' train which uses a hydrogen fuel cell began tests in the UK in 2019. The attraction of using hydrogen as a fuel is that, if hydrogen is prepared without using fossil fuels, it would not contribute to carbon dioxide emissions – water would be the only chemical product.

A number of methods of storing hydrogen are being investigated. Storing the hydrogen as a metal hydride is one of them. There are a number of metals being tested, one of them being palladium. The hydrogen is absorbed in substantial quantities into the crystal structure of the metal and can be released when needed.

> **GO!** Activity 3.3.6
>
> Calculate the energy density for propane (C_3H_8) given $\Delta H_c = -2220$ (kJ mol^{-1}).

Learning checklist

In this chapter you have learned:

- Enthalpy is a measure of the chemical energy of a substance.

- In industry, endothermic reactions require heat to be supplied, which incurs costs.

- In industry, the heat produced during exothermic reactions often needs to be removed to avoid the temperature rising too far.

- The enthalpy change associated with a reaction can be determined from the quantity of heat energy released.

- The enthalpy of combustion is the enthalpy change when 1 mole of a substance burns completely in oxygen.

- Enthalpy of combustion is always exothermic.
- The quantity of heat energy released during a reaction can be determined experimentally and calculated using $E_h = c \times m \times \Delta T$, where m = mass of water (kg); c = specific heat capacity of water (4·18 kJ kg^{-1} °C^{-1}); ΔT = change in temperature (°C).
- Enthalpy of reaction is measured in kJ mol^{-1}.
- The quantities c, m and ΔT can be calculated from $E_h = c \times m \times \Delta T$.
- How to use Hess's law to calculate enthalpy changes.
- For a diatomic molecule, XY, the molar bond enthalpy is the energy required to break 1 mole of XY bonds.
- The mean molar bond enthalpy is the average bond enthalpy for bonds which exist in different molecular environments.
- The difference between the energy needed to break bonds in gaseous reactants and the energy released when new bonds are made gives an estimate of the enthalpy change for the reaction.

4 Equilibria

You should already know

- The rate of a chemical reaction can be increased by increasing the concentration, decreasing the particle size and raising the temperature of reactants and by adding a catalyst.
- Rate of reaction is directly proportional to the concentration of the reactants.
- A small increase in temperature results in a large increase in rate.
- Reaction profiles can be drawn to show how the potential energy changes as a reaction progresses.

(Higher Chemistry: Chemistry in society: Controlling the rate)

- Ammonia is made industrially by the Haber process.
- The reaction of nitrogen with hydrogen to make ammonia is reversible and the ammonia breaks down if the temperature is too high.
- The Haber process needs a temperature of 450°C, pressure of 200 atmospheres and an iron catalyst.

(National 5 Chemistry: Chemistry in society: Fertilisers)

Learning intentions

In this chapter you will learn about:
- Reversible reactions and dynamic equilibrium.
- How changing concentration, pressure and temperature affects the equilibrium position.
- How to predict how changing conditions will affect the equilibrium position.
- The effect of catalysts on equilibrium.
- Improving yield in industrial reactions which involve equilibria.

Reversible reactions and equilibrium

Many of the reactions we have looked at so far, like neutralisation and combustion, appear to be irreversible and for practical purposes they are.

Burning magnesium in oxygen can be considered as a reaction which goes to completion:

$$2Mg(s) + O_2(g) \rightarrow 2MgO(s)$$

The single arrow in the equation tells us the reaction is irreversible and goes to completion.

However, many reactions can be reversed. A reversible reaction is one which can take place in both directions, i.e. the products can reform reactants.

A reversible reaction you are likely to have seen in the laboratory is the colour change which happens when blue cobalt chloride paper turns pink when water is dropped on it. The paper changes back to blue when the paper is warmed and the water is evaporated off. The reactions taking place are:

$$CoCl_2 \quad + \quad 6H_2O \qquad \rightarrow \qquad CoCl_2.6H_2O$$

cobalt chloride   hydrated cobalt chloride

(blue)   (pink)

heat

$$CoCl_2.6H_2O \qquad \rightarrow \qquad CoCl_2 \quad + \quad 6H_2O$$

hydrated cobalt chloride   cobalt chloride

(pink)   (blue)

The equations can be written using a double arrow symbol to show it is reversible:

$$CoCl_2 \quad + \quad 6H_2O \quad \rightleftharpoons \quad CoCl_2.6H_2O$$

Figure 3.4.1: *Blue cobalt chloride paper turns pink when water is added. The paper turns blue again when the reaction is reversed by warming the paper.*

We can represent any general reversible reaction as:

$$A + B \rightleftharpoons C + D$$

If we start with reactants A and B and allow them to react then, initially, the rate of the forward reaction (left to right) is high because the concentrations of A and B are high. The rate of the backward reaction (right to left) is zero initially because the concentrations of C and D are zero. As the reaction progresses the concentrations of A and B decrease while the concentrations of C and D increase. This means the rate of the forward reaction falls and the rate of the backward reaction increases. This continues until the two rates are equal – a state of balance is formed. This is known as chemical **equilibrium**. At this point the concentration of reactants and products are unchanging. It is important to understand that although the concentrations are unchanging they are very seldom the same. The changes in concentration of reactants and products and rate of the forward and backward reactions with time are shown in figures 3.4.2 and 3.4.3.

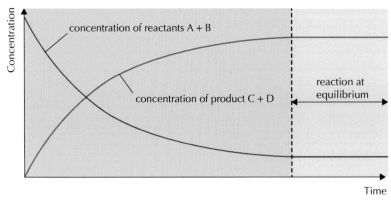

Figure 3.4.2: *Graph showing change in* **concentration** *over time for the forward and backward reactions in a reversible reaction which reaches equilibrium*

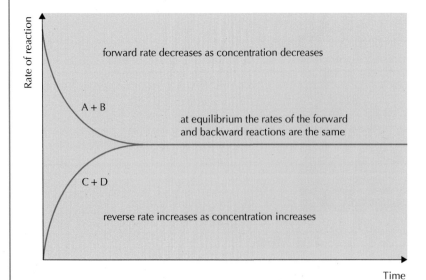

Figure 3.4.3: *Graph showing change in* **rate** *over time for the forward and backward reactions in a reversible reaction which reaches equilibrium*

Although at equilibrium the concentration of the reactants and products are unchanging it does not mean that the reaction has stopped. Reactant molecules still react to form products and product molecules reform reactants at the same rate – the process is said to be **dynamic**. Because reactions are still taking place the equilibrium is described as **dynamic equilibrium**.

An equilibrium can only be established in a **closed system**, that is, where no reactants or products can escape. Take, for example, heating calcium carbonate (limestone) in a closed container. The following equilibrium is set up:

$$CaCO_3(s) \rightleftharpoons CaO(s) + CO_2(g)$$

If some of the carbon dioxide is allowed to escape the rate of the reverse reaction becomes slower because the concentration of carbon dioxide is reducing. This results in more products being formed. If the lid is taken off the container and all of the carbon dioxide is allowed to escape then we have an **open system** and an equilibrium cannot be formed, so all of the calcium carbonate forms products. This is what happens in a blast furnace during the extraction of iron from iron ore. Limestone is added to produce calcium oxide, which removes impurities such as silicon dioxide. Because it is an open system there is no equilibrium formed and all of the calcium carbonate decomposes – the reaction is irreversible.

$$CaCO_3(s) \rightarrow CaO(s) + CO_2(g)$$

GO! Activity 3.4.1

1. Blue cobalt chloride paper can be used to test for the presence of water.

    (a) Describe what you would see happening to the paper if water was present.

    (b) The blue colour of the paper can easily be restored. Suggest how this could be done.

    (c) Explain why the changes in (a) and b) take place.

    (d) Write an equation to show what is happening in (a) and (b).

    (e) The cobalt chloride paper has to be stored away from the air to maintain its blue colour. Suggest why this is the case.

2. The graph shows how the rate of the forward and backward reactions in a reversible reaction change over time.

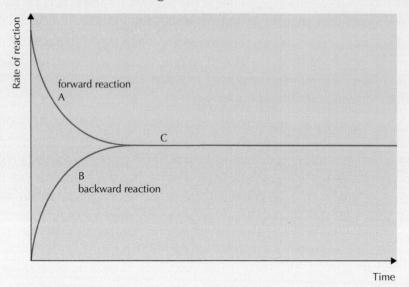

Figure 3.4.4

Explain what is happening at points A, B and C on the graph.

3. The diagram shows the equilibrium which is formed between carbon dioxide gas and carbon dioxide in solution in a bottle of soda (fizzy) water.

pressure
of CO_2 (g)
constant

concentration
of CO_2 (aq)
constant

Figure 3.4.5

(a) This situation is described as a 'closed system'. Explain what is meant by a 'closed system'.

(b) What could be done to change the closed system into an open system?

(c) Explain what would happen to the equilibrium in the bottle in an open system.

(d) Explain why the soda water eventually goes flat in an open system.

CHEMISTRY IN CONTEXT: THE WORK OF MAX ERNST BODENSTEIN (1871–1942)

Max Ernst Bodenstein was a German chemist who investigated the reversible reaction between hydrogen and iodine:

$$H2(g) \quad + \quad I2(g) \quad \rightleftharpoons \quad 2HI(g)$$

Hydrogen and iodine mixtures were sealed in glass containers and kept at the same temperature. The same procedure was carried out with a container of hydrogen iodide. The flasks were cooled at certain time intervals to stop the reactions in the containers and the contents of the flasks analysed. The results of the experiments are shown in figure 3.4.7.

Figure 3.4.6: *Max Ernst Bodenstein*

Figure 3.4.7: *Graph of the experimental results for the reaction* $H_2(g) + I_2(g) \rightleftharpoons 2HI(g)$ *at 448°C*

The blue line shows the number of moles of hydrogen iodide present in the flask which started off with 0·5 mol H_2 and 0·5 mol I_2, measured at certain time intervals. If the reaction went to completion there would be 1 mol HI in the container and zero mol H_2 and I_2. However this was not the case – only 0·78 mol HI was present after 84 minutes. The red line shows that by starting with 1 mol HI, at the same temperature, 0·78 mol HI was also present after 84 minutes. It didn't matter how long after 84 minutes samples of both flasks were analysed, the amount of all three chemicals present was the same. At 84 minutes the reaction had reached its equilibrium position, regardless of whether the container started off with reactants only or products only.

The position of equilibrium

It is important to realise that at equilibrium it is very unusual to have equal concentrations of reactants and products. In some reactions equilibrium isn't reached until the forward reaction is nearly complete – we say the equilibrium lies to the right. The concentration of the products is greater than the concentration of the reactants. This is shown as a graph in figure 3.4.8 for the general reaction $A + B \rightleftharpoons C + D$.

The graph shows at equilibrium the concentrations of products C and D are much greater than A and B so the equilibrium lies to the right. In other reactions equilibrium can be reached early in the reaction – we say the equilibrium lies to the left. This is shown as a graph in figure 3.4.9. The concentrations of C and D are much less than A and B so the equilibrium lies to the left.

In his experiments with hydrogen and iodine reacting to form hydrogen iodide (see page 289) Max Bodenstein showed that for a reversible reaction under the same conditions the same equilibrium position is reached regardless of whether we start from reactants or products. This can also be illustrated by setting up the experiment shown in figure 3.4.10. Iodine is soluble in both trichloroethane ($C_2H_3Cl_3$) and aqueous potassium iodide solution (KI(aq)). X and Z represent the two starting positions. If the test tubes are shaken both X and Z quickly reach the same equilibrium position shown in Y.

Figure 3.4.8: *The graph shows the concentrations of reactants (A & B) and products (C & D) in an equilibrium which lies to the right*

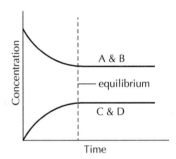

Figure 3.4.9: *The graph shows the concentrations of reactants (A & B) and products (C & D) in an equilibrium which lies to the left*

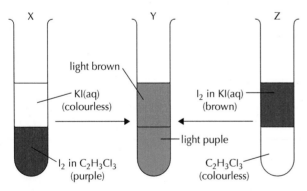

Figure 3.4.10: *The equilibrium position attained in a reversible reaction is the same whether you start with reactants or products*

🔵 GO! Activity 3.4.2

In a reversible reaction, the concentration of reactants and products were measured during the reaction. The results are shown in the following graph.

Figure 3.4.11: *Graph of concentration against time for a reversible reaction*

(a) Explain whether the equilibrium lies towards the reactants or products side.

(b) At which point on the graph is equilibrium reached?

Changing the position of equilibrium

Many industrial reactions involve reactions which are reversible. This creates challenges for industrial chemists who want to make as much product as possible as cheaply as possible. They have to be able to change the reaction conditions so that the maximum amount of product is formed. Equilibrium is reached when the rate of the forward and backward reactions become equal so we can look at the factors which affect the rate of a reaction to see how they affect the equilibrium position.

The French chemist Henri Le Chatelier observed many reversible reactions and formulated the following principle:

'The position of the equilibrium of a system changes to minimise the effect of any imposed change in condition.'

The conditions referred to are: concentration, pressure and temperature.

Concentration

The reaction between iron(III) ions (Fe^{3+}) and thiocyanate ions (CNS^-) can be used to show the effect on an equilibrium when the concentration of reactants or products are changed:

$$Fe^{3+}(aq) \ + \ CNS^-(aq) \ \rightleftharpoons \ [FeCNS]^{2+}(aq)$$

pale yellow   colourless   red

The two reactants are mixed and a deep red solution forms – this indicates the equilibrium lies towards the right. The equilibrium mixture contains $Fe^{3+}(aq)$, $CNS^-(aq)$ and $[FeCNS]^{2+}(aq)$ ions. The solution is diluted with water until it is an orange colour and poured into four separate test tubes. Test tube A is kept as a control – nothing else is added to it. The other three solutions (B, C and D) each have chemicals added to them which causes a colour change in each test tube, as shown in figure 3.4.12:

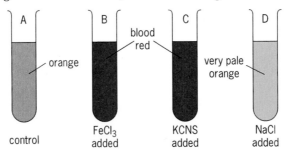

Figure 3.4.12: *Changing the concentration of reactants and products changes the position of equilibrium*

Observations:

Test tube B: $Fe^{3+}(aq)$ ions are added, i.e. the concentration of one of the reactants is increased. The equilibrium shifts to the right, forming more product. This is indicated by the blood red colour forming as more $[FeCNS]^{2+}(aq)$ ions are made. The chloride ions are spectator ions.

Test tube C: $CNS^-(aq)$ ions are added, i.e. the concentration of one of the reactants is increased. The equilibrium shifts to the right, forming more product. This is indicated by the blood red colour forming as more $[FeCNS]^{2+}(aq)$ ions are made. The potassium ions are spectator ions.

Test tube D: Adding NaCl removes $Fe^{3+}(aq)$ ions – the Cl^- ions form a complex with $Fe^{3+}(aq)$ ions. This results in the concentration of $Fe^{3+}(aq)$ ions decreasing so the equilibrium shifts left forming more reactants. This is indicated by the orange solution becoming paler as the red $[FeCNS]^{2+}(aq)$ ions form $Fe^{3+}(aq)$ (pale yellow) and $CNS^-(aq)$ (colourless) ions.

General rules:

- Increasing the concentration of reactants shifts the equilibrium position right, for the forward reaction, i.e. more product is formed.

- Reducing the concentration of reactants shifts the equilibrium position left, for the forward reaction, i.e. product reforms reactants.

- Removing product shifts the equilibrium position right, i.e. more product is formed.

Esters are produced on a large scale in industry and are used as solvents and flavourings. They are formed when a carboxylic acid is reacted with an alcohol. The reaction is reversible and an equilibrium exists:

$$\text{carboxylic acid} \ + \ \text{alcohol} \ \rightleftharpoons \ \text{ester} \ + \ \text{water}$$

In order to maximise the amount of product formed the equilibrium has to shift right. This can be achieved by adding more reactant – in industry this will be whichever is cheaper. Removing water as the reaction proceeds causes the equilibrium to shift to the right so more ester is produced.

GO! Activity 3.4.3

1. Bromine dissolves in water to form the equilibrium shown in the following equation:

$$Br_2(\ell) + H_2O(\ell) \ \rightleftharpoons \ Br^-(aq) + BrO^-(aq) + 2H^+(aq)$$

   (a) Explain the effect on the equilibrium if dilute hydrochloric acid (source of $H^+(aq)$ ions) is added.

   (b) Explain the effect on the equilibrium if dilute sodium hydroxide (source of $OH^-(aq)$ ions) is added.

2. When chlorine gas is passed over iodine a reaction occurs which results in an equilibrium forming between liquid iodine monochloride ($ICl(\ell)$), chlorine gas ($Cl_2(g)$) and solid iodine trichloride ($ICl_3(s)$).

$$ICl(\ell) \ + \ Cl_2(g) \ \rightleftharpoons \ ICl_3(s)$$
   brown liquid   yellow crystals

   (a) Describe what you would see if the concentration of chlorine was increased.

   (b) Explain your answer to (a).

   (c) Describe what you would see happening if the chlorine was then removed.

   (d) Explain your answer to (c).

3. The hypochlorite ion, $ClO^-(aq)$, acts as a bleach. It is formed in a reversible reaction between chlorine and water and the following equilibrium is set up:

$$Cl_2(g) + H_2O(\ell) \ \rightleftharpoons \ ClO^-(aq) + 2H^+(aq) + Cl^-(aq)$$

   What effect would adding each of the following have on the bleaching action?
   (a) Nitric acid ($H^+(aq)$ ions).

   (b) Sodium chloride.

   (c) Sodium hydroxide ($OH^-(aq)$ ions).

   (d) Explain each of the answers you gave in (a)–(c).

Pressure

A change in pressure only affects reactions which involve at least one gas reactant or product. Changing the pressure has the same effect as changing concentration of a solution.

Gas pressure is caused by the gas molecules moving around and hitting the walls of the container. If the size of the container is decreased this has the effect of increasing the number of collisions with the walls of the container and so increases the pressure. We can study the effect of changing the pressure using nitrogen dioxide (NO_2), a brown gas. Nitrogen dioxide actually exists in equilibrium with dinitrogen tetroxide (N_2O_4), which is colourless. If the gas mixture is placed in a glass syringe (figure 3.4.13) the effect of increasing and decreasing the pressure can be seen by noting the colour change in the gas. If the mixture gets darker then more NO_2 is present. If the mixture gets lighter then more N_2O_4 is present.

$$N_2O_4 \rightleftharpoons 2NO_2$$
colourless   brown

Figure 3.4.13: *A gas syringe with an* $N_2O_4 \rightleftharpoons 2NO_2$ *equilibrium mixture*

Observations:

When the gas is put under pressure the gas mixture eventually goes a lighter brown. This indicates that more N_2O_4 (colourless) is formed, so the equilibrium must be shifting left. This happens because there are fewer moles of gas molecules on the left of the equation. Fewer molecules means less pressure as there are fewer molecules hitting the walls of the container.

When the pressure is decreased the gas mixture eventually goes a darker brown. This indicates that more NO_2 (brown) is formed, so the equilibrium must be shifting right. This happens because there are more moles of gas molecules on the right of the equation. More gas molecules means more pressure as there are more molecules hitting the walls of the container.

If an equilibrium has the same number of moles of gas on each side of the equation then changing the pressure will have no effect on the position of the equilibrium. However, increasing pressure will increase the rate of the forward and backward reactions so equilibrium will be reached quicker. Changing pressure has no effect on equilibria where no gases are present.

Similar experiments give the same results. The effect of changing pressure on an equilibrium involving gases is equivalent to changes in concentration on an equilibrium involving solutions.

General rules:

- Increasing pressure causes an equilibrium to move in the direction where there are fewer moles of gas molecules.

- Decreasing the pressure causes an equilibrium to move in the direction where there are more moles of gas molecules.

- If an equilibrium has the same number of moles of gas on each side of the equation then changing the pressure will have no effect on the position of the equilibrium.

In the industrial preparation of methanol a mixture of carbon monoxide and hydrogen gas (synthesis gas) is passed over a catalyst under high pressure. The balanced equation shows clearly why high pressure results in more methanol:

$$CO(g) + 2H_2(g) \rightleftharpoons CH_3OH(g)$$
$$\text{3 moles of gas} \qquad\qquad \text{1 mole of gas}$$

There are 3 moles of gas on the left-hand side of the equation and 1 mole on the right so increasing the pressure forces the equilibrium to the right, the side with fewer gas molecules. In practice the methanol is liquefied as it forms, which forces the equilibrium right, resulting in almost 100% conversion.

GO! Activity 3.4.4

Predict the effect that increasing the pressure would have on the position of the following equilibria:

(a) $N_2(g) + 3H_2(g) \rightleftharpoons 2NH_3(g)$

(b) $CH_4(g) + H_2O(g) \rightleftharpoons CO(g) + 3H_2(g)$

(c) $H_2(g) + I_2(g) \rightleftharpoons 2HI(g)$

(d) $2SO_2(g) + O_2(g) \rightleftharpoons 2SO_3(g)$

(e) Explain each of the answers you gave in (a)–(d).

Temperature

The effect of temperature on an equilibrium depends on whether a reaction is exothermic or endothermic. If, say, the forward reaction is exothermic then the backward reaction will be endothermic. The effect of changing temperature can be shown using the nitrogen dioxide (NO_2), dinitrogen tetroxide (N_2O_4) equilibrium:

$$N_2O_4 \rightleftharpoons 2NO_2 \quad \Delta H = positive$$
$$\text{colourless} \qquad \text{brown}$$

For an equation written this way the ΔH value is for the forward reaction, which in this case is endothermic (positive). The enthalpy change for the backward reaction must therefore be exothermic (negative).

Three test tubes of the gas mixture are prepared so that they all have the same brown colour at room temperature. One is kept at room temperature (B), another (C) is placed in a beaker of hot water to raise the temperature and the third (A) is placed in a freezing ice/salt mixture to lower the temperature.

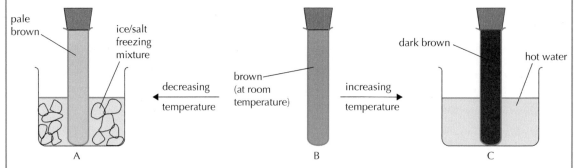

Figure 3.4.14: *The intensity of the brown colour seen in the $N_2O_4 \rightleftharpoons 2NO_2$ equilibrium changes depending on the temperature*

Observations:

Test tube C: The colour gradually darkens compared to (B) indicating that more NO_2 (brown) is formed. The equilibrium is moving right, the direction of the endothermic reaction.

Test tube A: The colour gradually lightens compared to (B), indicating that more (N_2O_4) (colourless) is formed. The equilibrium is moving left, the direction of the exothermic reaction.

General rule:

- For a system in equilibrium, a rise in temperature favours the endothermic reaction. A decrease in temperature favours the exothermic reaction.

In the industrial manufacture of methanol the mixture of carbon monoxide and hydrogen gas (synthesis gas) used can be produced from methane in an endothermic reaction:

$$CH_4(g) + H_2O(g) \rightleftharpoons CO(g) + 3H_2(g) \quad \Delta H = +206 \text{ kJ mol}^{-1}$$

An increase in temperature favours the forward reaction (endothermic) so it is carried out at around 800°C. Even in reactions which are exothermic the temperature used can be fairly high in order that the equilibrium position can be reached quickly.

GO! Activity 3.4.5

1. Under certain conditions the following equilibrium can be established:

    $$2CH_4(g) \;\rightleftharpoons\; 3H_2(g) \;+\; C_2H_2(g) \quad \Delta H \;=\; +377 \text{ kJ mol}^{-1}$$
    $$\text{ethyne}$$

    Explain what effect increasing the temperature would have on the yield of ethyne.

2. The manufacture of sulfuric acid involves the following equilibrium:

    $$2SO_2(g) \;+\; O_2(g) \;\rightleftharpoons\; 2SO_3(g) \quad \Delta H \;=\; -196 \text{ kJ mol}^{-1}$$

    (a) What effect would raising the temperature have on the equilibrium position?

    (b) What effect does raising the temperature have on the rate at which the equilibrium position is reached?

Catalysts

A catalyst speeds up a reaction because it gives a different route to products which overall has a lower activation energy (E_a) than the reaction would have without a catalyst. This is shown in figure 3.4.15.

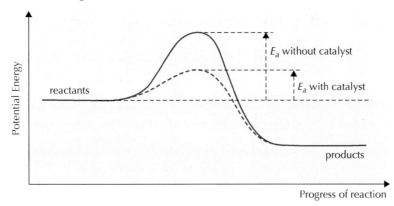

Figure 3.4.15: *Potential energy diagram showing E_a for an uncatalysed and catalysed reversible reaction*

A close look at figure 3.4.15 shows that not only does a catalyst lower the energy of activation for the forward reaction but also for the backward reaction. This means that in a reversible reaction the rate of the backward reaction will also be speeded up. This means that the catalyst does not affect the equilibrium position – it does however allow the equilibrium position to be reached more quickly. Catalysts also allow reactions to be carried out at lower temperatures which make the reactions more economical. Catalysts are an essential in the economical production of chemicals on an industrial scale, many of which are produced by routes that involve reactions which are reversible.

SQA KEY AREA

Summary of the effects of changing conditions on equilibrium

Changing the conditions of a system in equilibrium follows Le Chatelier's principle – if a system at equilibrium is subjected to a change, the system will adjust to oppose the effect of the change.

A summary of the effects of changing conditions of a system in equilibrium is shown in table 3.4.1.

Table 3.4.1: *The effects of changing conditions of a system in equilibrium*

Change	System change applied to	Effect on equilibrium position
increasing concentration	reactants products	shift to right shift to left
decreasing concentration	reactants products	shift to left shift to right
increasing pressure	more moles of gas product than reactant	shift to left
	more moles of gas reactant than product	shift to right
increasing temperature	if ΔH_f is positive (endothermic)	shift to right
	if ΔH_f is negative (exothermic)	shift to left
addition of catalyst	any	no effect

SQA KEY AREA

Equilibria in industry – the Haber process

The Haber process is the industrial manufacture of ammonia from nitrogen and hydrogen:

$$N_2(g) + 3H_2(g) \rightleftharpoons 2NH_3(g) \quad \Delta H = -92 \text{ kJ mol}^{-1}$$

This is a reversible reaction which in a closed system would form a dynamic equilibrium and so the equilibrium position can be changed by changing certain conditions.

1. **Pressure** – There are four moles of gases on the left-hand side and two moles on the right hand side. Increasing the pressure would cause the equilibrium to shift to the right because there are fewer moles of gas on the right, i.e. more ammonia would be formed.

2. **Temperature** – The forward reaction is endothermic so a drop in temperature would theoretically cause the equilibrium to shift to the right.

In industry, however, the conditions used are not always the theoretical conditions, mainly for economic reasons. In choosing the right temperature manufacturers must consider the percentage yield and rate of reaction. Temperature has a major effect on the rate of reaction. If the temperature is too low, which would in theory result in more ammonia being formed, the rate at which ammonia is formed would not be fast enough. Manufacturers use a combination of a moderate temperature and a catalyst to ensure the rate of production of ammonia is high.

High pressure improves the yield and rate of formation, but the higher the pressure the more it costs to build and run the plant. The higher the pressure the thicker the pipes need to be and the more energy is needed to maintain a high pressure.

Figure 3.4.16: *Graph showing the effect of temperature on the percentage of ammonia in the equilibrium mixture*

Figure 3.4.17: *Graph showing the effect of pressure on the percentage of ammonia in the equilibrium mixture*

Most manufacturers use:

- A relatively high pressure of between 100–200 atmospheres.

- A moderate temperature of around 400°C.

- A finely divided iron catalyst.

The operating conditions are not a closed system. The ammonia is continually removed so equilibrium is not reached and the reactants are recycled and continuously passed over the catalyst, which improves the yield of ammonia, up to 98%. Researchers continue to look for alternative catalysts which will work at lower temperature and pressure which will cut costs. In the USA scientists are working on alternative sources of hydrogen. The current source of hydrogen is mainly natural gas, a finite resource. Researchers are using electricity produced from wind power to electrolyse water and produce hydrogen.

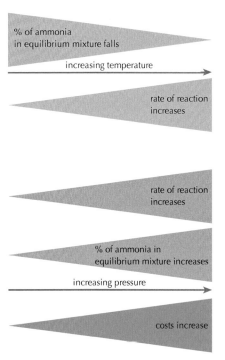

Figure 3.4.18: *Summary of the effects of changing conditions on the production of ammonia in the Haber process*

Activity 3.4.6

1. The Haber process is the industrial manufacture of ammonia from nitrogen and hydrogen:

$$N_2(g) \quad + \quad 3H_2(g) \quad \rightleftharpoons \quad 2NH_3(g) \qquad \Delta H_f = -92 \text{ kJ mol}^{-1}$$

(a) (i)   What effect would raising the pressure have on the yield of ammonia?

(ii) Explain why a pressure of 400 atmospheres is not used in industry.

(b) (i)   What effect would raising the temperature have on the yield of ammonia?

(ii) Explain why a moderately high temperature is used in industry.

(c)   Explain why a catalyst is used in the Haber process even although it has no effect on the yield of ammonia.

2. Figure 3.4.16 shows how the yield of ammonia changes with temperature.

(a) What happens to the yield of ammonia as the temperature increases?

(b) Explain why this happens to the yield.

3. Figure 3.4.17 shows how the yield of ammonia changes with pressure.

(a) What happens to the yield of ammonia as the pressure increases?

(b) Explain why this happens to the yield.

(c) What would the percentage yield be if the reaction was carried out at 150 atmospheres and 400°C?

Learning checklist

In this chapter you have learned:

- Many reactions are reversible.

- Reversible reactions attain a state of dynamic equilibrium when the rates of the forward and backward reactions are equal.

- Dynamic equilibrium will only be attained in a closed system where no products can escape or reactants be added.

- At equilibrium the concentration of reactants and products remain constant, but rarely equal.

- Increasing the concentrations of reactants shifts the equilibrium to the right (products).

- Increasing the pressure shifts the equilibrium in the direction, which results in a decrease in the number of moles of gas reactant or product.

- Increasing the temperature shifts the equilibrium in the direction of the endothermic reaction (ΔH = positive).

- Catalysts do not shift the equilibrium position but allow equilibrium to be reached quicker.

- In industry reaction conditions are changed so that product yield is maximised at the lowest cost.

- In industrial reactions a balance has to be reached between shifting the equilibrium position towards products and reaching the equilibrium position as quickly as possible.

5 Chemical analysis

SQA KEY AREA

Chromatography

Chromatography is the term used to describe a set of techniques which can be used to separate, identify and, in some instances, obtain individual substances from complex mixtures. There are many different chromatographic methods including paper, thin layer, gas and gas-liquid chromatography. However the principles for each method are the same.

Chromatography uses differences in size and polarities of the molecules of substances to separate them.

In Nature's chemistry Chapter 4, *Proteins*, the work of Frederick Sanger in identifying the amino acids in insulin was highlighted. Sanger used chromatography to separate the amino acids. Chromatography was first developed by a Russian chemist, Mikhail Tswett, who used the process to separate plant pigments.

Figure 3.5.1: *High performance liquid chromatography columns*

How does chromatography work?

All chromatographic techniques work on the same principle. There is a **mobile phase**, a liquid or gas, which carries the substances over or through **a stationary phase**, a solid or a liquid absorbed onto a solid.

In Tswett's original work the mobile phase was the petroleum ether/ethanol mixture that he used as solvent for the plant pigments. Powdered limestone acted as the stationary phase. Running the solvent mixture through the column containing the powdered limestone separated the plant extract into its separate pigments.

> ### 🔍 Hint
>
> SQA do not require you to know details of any specific chromatographic method or experiment.

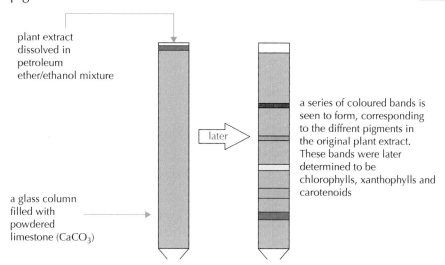

plant extract dissolved in petroleum ether/ethanol mixture

later

a series of coloured bands is seen to form, corresponding to the diffrent pigments in the original plant extract. These bands were later determined to be chlorophylls, xanthophylls and carotenoids

a glass column filled with powdered limestone ($CaCO_3$)

Figure 3.5.2: *Plant extract can be separated into its various pigments by chromatography*

Two methods commonly used in the laboratory are **paper chromatography and thin layer chromatography (TLC)**. The methods are similar and principles the same.

In thin layer chromatography, a thin layer of silica gel or alumina can be applied to a glass slide and the chromatogram run in much the same way as with paper chromatography, using suitable solvent.

As the solvent begins to soak up the paper or TLC plate, it dissolves the compounds that have been spotted on the chromatogram. The compounds will then move up the chromatogram as the solvent continues to move upwards.

Figure 3.5.3: *A thin layer chromatography plate*

When the chromatogram is being run molecules continually change from being in the mobile phase, i.e. dissolved in the solvent and moving, to being stopped due to intermolecular attractions to the molecules of the stationary phase.

The speed at which the compounds move will therefore depend on two factors:

- how attracted they are to the stationary phase
- their solubility in the solvent.

Both the factors depend on intermolecular forces.

Attraction to the stationary phase

Silica and alumina used in TLC, are covalent network substances. However, on the surfaces the oxygen atoms are bonded to hydrogens. The surfaces of silica and alumina are covered in highly polar hydroxyl groups.

Because the coatings used on TLC plates have polar hydroxyl groups it means that molecules that can form strong intermolecular bonds to the surfaces will be carried up the chromatography plate more slowly.

The **more polar** the compounds in the substance **the slower it will be carried** up the chromatogram.

For carbon compounds the expected order of movement due to increasing polarity would be:

Figure 3.5.4: *Silica and alumina have polar –OH groups on their surface*

Move most quickly		Saturated hydrocarbons	Least polar
		Unsaturated hydrocarbons	
		Esters	
		Ketones	
		Aldehydes	
Move most slowly	↓	Alcohols	Most polar

Although the cellulose in paper also has hydroxyl groups on the surface, polar water molecules attach themselves to the cellulose and act as the stationary phase in paper chromatography.

Solubility in the solvent

Solvents vary from being completely non-polar, such as hexane, to extremely polar, such as ethanol and ethanoic acid. Solvent mixtures, made by mixing different solvents in varying proportions, are also used in paper and thin layer chromatography.

Polar substances are more soluble in polar solvents and non-polar substances in non-polar solvents. In paper and thin layer chromatography solvents are chosen to give the best separation of the different compounds. The choice of solvent to be used will therefore depend on the substances to be separated.

R$_f$ values

Using chromatography to separate coloured inks gives a very visual result.

However, not all chromatograms are as easily interpreted. When amino acids are separated the spots need to be developed using a spray that turns them a lilac or yellow colour.

Since many of the spots are similar another method needs to be used to identify them.

R$_f$ values (retention or retardation factors) are a measure of how far a substance travels compared to the solvent front, the distance travelled by the solvent. The R$_f$ value is constant for a substance if other conditions such as paper and solvent used remain the same.

Different compounds will have different R$_f$ values.

For molecules with similar polarity the larger the molecule the smaller the R$_f$ value, i.e. the slower it will move up the plate or paper.

A polar molecule will have a higher R$_f$ value in polar solvents than it will have if a non-polar solvent is used.

Gas chromatography and gas-liquid chromatography

Gas chromatography, GC, and gas-liquid chromatography, GLC, are techniques that have been developed to separate mixtures of gases and volatile liquids. These techniques can be used to separate very small quantities. An unreactive carrier gas is used to carry the mixture through the chromatograph, i.e. acts as the mobile phase. The stationary phase is a fine powdered solid material or a viscous liquid that is adsorbed onto a finely powdered material. The chromatography column is normally made by placing the material being used for the stationary phase in a long tube that is wound into a coil to save space. The temperature of the coiled column, which can be 5–10 metres long and have a bore of between 2 and 10 mm, is controlled by an oven.

Figure 3.5.5: *As the solvent moves up the paper the colours in the ink separate out*

Figure 3.5.6: *A paper chromatogram*

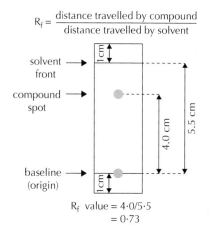

$$R_f = \frac{\text{distance travelled by compound}}{\text{distance travelled by solvent}}$$

R$_f$ value = 4·0/5·5 = 0·73

Figure 3.5.7: *Calculate R$_f$ value*

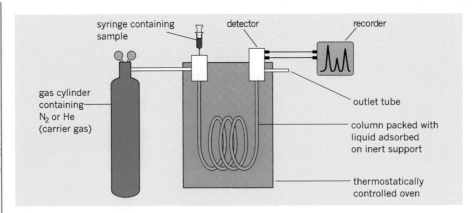

Figure 3.5.8: *The main features of a gas-liquid chromotography apparatus*

The sample to be separated is injected into the column. The molecules of the mixture move in the carrier gas. They can attach to the finely powdered solid or dissolve into the viscous liquid and become stationary for part of the time. Less volatile components of the mixture form stronger intermolecular forces to the stationary phase. Volatile components are carried more quickly than non-volatile components through the chromatography column.

The resulting chromatogram is displayed as a graph. Each peak on the chromatogram represents an individual substance from the mixture.

The time taken for a substance to be carried through a gas chromatograph is known as the **retention time**.

Gas chromatography can also be used quantitatively since the area of the graph under each peak is directly related to the amount of the particular component present. Since GLC is very sensitive and able to detect minute amounts of substances it has become a standard method of detecting banned substances in sport and for determining blood alcohol levels for drivers who may be suspected of driving under the influence of alcohol.

Figure 3.5.9: *A gas-liquid chromotogram of additives in a soft drink*

CHEMISTRY IN CONTEXT: CURIOSITY MARS ROVER

Curiosity, the Mars Rover, landed on the red planet in August 2012. It is designed to investigate the chemical and isotopic composition of the Martian atmosphere and any volatile compounds from powdered solid surface samples. On 24 September 2019, in an area known as Glen Etive, the rover was able to carry out wet chemistry experiments on a drilled sample of Martian rock for the first time. Scientists had been waiting to find just the right place to carry out this type of experiment.

Curiosity contains a portable laboratory, SAM – Sample Analysis at Mars, that is being used to carry out analysis of samples and is conducting a sensitive search for carbon compounds.

One of the instruments in SAM is a gas chromatograph.

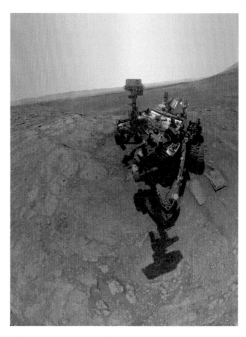

Figure 3.5.10: *A selfie taken by* Curiosity *in Glen Etive*

Figure 3.5.11: *The suite of instruments on* Curiosity *that are used to identify components of the Martian atmosphere and identify volatile compounds in Martian rock*

The Gas Chromatograph has six complementary chromatographic columns. The chromatograph assembly sorts, measures and identifies gases. The mixtures of gases are pushed through long, narrow tubes (wound into coils) with a stream of helium gas. It sorts the gas molecules by weight: they emerge from the tube in order from lightest (out first) to heaviest (out last). The gases are then passed from the gas chromatograph into the Mass Spectrometer to try to identify if key elements (carbon, oxygen, nitrogen, phosporus and sulfur) are present, or into the Tunable Laser Spectrometer which analyses the gases to see if water vapour and methane are present. Results from the analysis of the samples taken from Glen Etive will not be known for several months. A new Mars Rover is due to be launched in July 2020. Keep up to date with its progress by visiting https://mars.nasa.gov/news.

CHEMISTRY IN CONTEXT: RESTORING WORKS OF ART

When an art gallery or a museum wants to restore a painting they must first analyse the paint from the original painting to determine the pigments and the binding medium used by the artist.

Until the Renaissance, which began in the 14th century, artists used egg yolks (tempera) as a binding medium. In the 1400s Italian and Flemish painters began to use oils such as linseed oil to dissolve their pigments.

Gas chromatography can be used to determine the oils used, allowing restorers to match the original paint when restoring the painting.

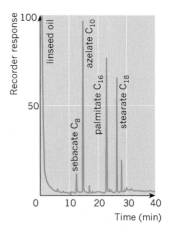

Figure 3.5.12: *Gas chromatogram of the oils in a paint sample from a picture painted in 1500*

Figure 3.5.13: *An artist restoring an original work of art*

Activity 3.5.1

The unique flavour of different brands of whisky arises from a complex blend of trace impurities. The relative amounts of these substances vary from whisky to whisky and can be used to identify particular brands of whisky.

Figure 3.5.14 shows a gas chromatogram for a particular whisky.

Peak list
1. ethanal
2. methanol
3. ethanol
4. propanone
5. propan-2-ol
6. propan-1-ol
7. ethyl ethanoate
8. butan-2-ol
9. ethanoic acid
10. 2-methylbutan-1-ol
11. 3-methylbutan-1-ol

Figure 3.5.14: *Flavour compounds in a whisky*

The chromatogram can be used to show how size of molecules and polarities of molecules affect the retention time for the compounds.

1. Choosing suitable examples explain how (a) size and (b) polarity affects the retention time for compounds.

2. Suggest how the compounds responsible for peaks 1, 9 and 7 may have formed.

Volumetric analysis

Volumetric analysis is a technique which uses titration to determine the concentration of a compound. In order to do this the concentration of the substance being used to react with the compound needs to be known accurately.

A solution of accurately known concentration is referred to as a **standard solution**.

> **Researching chemistry – general practical techniques**
>
> Accurate use of a top pan balance and use of correct **volumetric flasks** are essential when preparing standard solutions. Details of their use can be found in 'Researching chemistry'.

Suppose you were asked to prepare 250 cm^3 of a standard solution of sodium carbonate (GFM = 106 g) that was approximately 0·10 mol l^{-1} and used 2·76 g sodium carbonate to prepare the solution.

The accurate concentration of the solution is calculated as follows:

concentration = $\dfrac{\text{number of moles}}{\text{volume(l)}}$ (moles(n) = m/GFM)

$= \dfrac{2·76/106}{0·25}$

Accurate concentration = 0·104 mol l^{-1}

Titration calculations

Acid/base

In National 5, titration calculations involving acid/base neutralisations were described using equation balancing numbers.

$$\frac{(\text{volume} \times \text{concentration})_{\text{base}}}{\text{balancing no.}_{\text{base}}} = \frac{(\text{volume} \times \text{concentration})_{\text{acid}}}{\text{balancing no.}_{\text{acid}}}$$

Worked example 1:

24·8 cm³ of 0·104 mol sodium carbonate solution was required to neutralise 20·0 cm³ of dilute hydrochloric acid solution. Find the concentration of the hydrochloric acid.

$$Na_2CO_3(aq) + \mathbf{2}HCl(aq) \rightarrow 2NaCl(aq) + CO_2(g) + H_2O(\ell)$$

The balancing number for hydrochloric acid is 2 and for sodium carbonate acid is 1.

$$\frac{(\text{volume} \times \text{concentration})_{\text{acid}}}{\text{balancing no.}_{\text{acid}}} = \frac{(\text{volume} \times \text{concentration})_{\text{base}}}{\text{balancing no.}_{\text{base}}}$$

$$\frac{20 \cdot 0 \times \text{conc}}{2} = \frac{24 \cdot 8 \times 0 \cdot 104}{1}$$

(Note: You don't have to change volumes to litres.)

$$10 \times \text{conc} = 2 \cdot 58$$
$$\text{conc} = 0 \cdot 258 \text{ mol } l^{-1}$$

In acid/base titrations, a suitable indicator is used. Indicators show a colour change at the endpoint, e.g. phenolphthalein, is an indicator that is colourless in acid and neutral solutions but is pink in alkaline solutions.

pH = 7 and below   pH = 10

Figure 3.5.15: *Phenolphthalein changes from colourless (acid/neutral) to pink (alkali)*

Titre volumes within 0·2 cm³ are considered concordant and can be used to work out the average volume.

Worked example 2:

Citric acid ($C_6H_8O_7 \cdot H_2O$) is used to give chewing gum and other sweets a sharp refreshing flavour. The citric acid content of a chewing gum can be determined by titration using phenolphthalein as the indicator.

Chemists working for the chewing gum manufacturer carried out the following experiment to work out the mass of citric acid in 1 g of the gum:

A sample of the chewing gum was rolled out to give a very thin strip which was then cut into small pieces. 1 g was weighed out and then stirred in 100 cm³ water for about 30 minutes to dissolve the citric acid. A few drops of phenolphthalein was added and the solution titrated with 0·010 mol l⁻¹ sodium hydroxide solution. The average titre was found to be 27·7 cm³.

Citric acid and sodium hydroxide react in the ratio 1:3.

Worked answer:

Step 1: calculate the moles of sodium hydroxide reacting and so the moles of citric acid reacting:

$$mol_{NaOH} = c \times v$$
$$= 0·010 \times 0·0277$$
$$mol_{NaOH} = 0·000277 \text{ mol}$$

So,

$$mol_{citric\ acid} = \frac{0·000277}{3}$$
$$mol_{citric\ acid} = 0·0000923 \text{ mol}$$

Step 2: calculate the mass of citric acid from the number of moles:

Gram formula mass of citric acid ($C_6H_8O_7 \cdot H_2O$) = 210 g.

$$mass = mol \times gfm$$
$$= 0·0000923 \times 210$$
$$mass = 0·0194 \text{ g}$$

🟢 GO! Activity 3.5.2

A group of students repeated the experiment carried out in worked example 2 and found that 29·2 cm³ of 0·01 mol l⁻¹ sodium hydroxide was needed to react completely with the citric acid in the 1·0 g sample.

(a) Calculate the mass of citric acid in the sample.

(b) Suggest what the students should do to improve the accuracy of their result.

(c) Calculate the percentage of citric acid in the 1·0 g sample.

Redox

If a substance is able to be oxidised or reduced its concentration can be determined using a redox titration. This is similar to an acid/base titration but uses **oxidising** and **reducing agents**.

Worked example

The concentration of a hydrogen peroxide solution was checked by titrating 25 cm³ samples of the solution with acidified potassium permanganate solution concentration, 0·101 mol l⁻¹. The average titre was 15·8 cm³.

Oxidation $H_2O_2(\ell) \rightarrow 2H^+(aq) + O_2(g) + 2e^-$

Reduction $MnO_4^-(aq) + 8H^+(aq) + 5e^- \rightarrow Mn^{2+}(aq) + 4H_2O(\ell)$

Redox $2MnO_4^-(aq) + 6H^+(aq) + 5H_2O_2(\ell) \rightarrow 2Mn^{2+}(aq) + 8H_2O(\ell) + 5O_2(g)$

In this reaction the hydrogen peroxide is the reducing agent (it is being oxidised, i.e. it is donating electrons to the permanganate). The balancing number for $H_2O_2(\ell)$ is 5.

The acidified permanganate solution is the oxidising agent (it is being reduced, i.e. it is accepting electrons from the peroxide). The balancing number for $MnO_4^-(aq)$ is 2.

Note: the balancing numbers can also be found by considering the factors that the oxidation and reduction equations would be multiplied by in order to balance electrons lost and gained when forming the redox equation.

Oxidation $\quad H_2O_2(\ell) \rightarrow 2H^+(aq) + O_2(g) + 2e^- \times \mathbf{5}$

Reduction $\quad MnO_4^-(aq) + 8H^+(aq) + 5e^- \rightarrow$ $Mn^{2+}(aq) + 4H_2O(\ell) \times \mathbf{2}$

> ### 🔍 Hint
> It's not just the concentration of a reactant that can be determined given a balanced equation. The volume of a solution can also be calculated given the volume of the other reactant and the concentration of both solutions.

The information in the example can be summarised in a table to make it easier to handle:

	Reducing agent $H_2O_2(\ell)$	Oxidising agent $MnO_4^-(aq)$
volume	25·0 cm³	15·8 cm³
concentration	c (to be calculated)	0·101 mol l⁻¹
Balancing no.	5	2

$$\frac{(\text{volume} \times \text{concentration})_{\text{reducing agent}}}{\text{balancing no.}_{\text{oxidising agent}}} = \frac{(\text{volume} \times \text{concentration})_{\text{oxidising agent}}}{\text{balancing no.}_{\text{reducing agent}}}$$

$$\frac{25 \cdot 0 \times \text{conc } H_2O_2}{5} = \frac{15 \cdot 8 \times 0 \cdot 101}{2}$$

$5 \times \text{conc } H_2O_2 = 0 \cdot 7979$

$\text{conc } H_2O_2 = \dfrac{0 \cdot 7979}{5}$

$\text{conc } H_2O_2 = \mathbf{0 \cdot 16 \text{ mol } l^{-1}}$

Self indicators

In the worked example, potassium permanganate acts as its own indicator. The point where the reaction has just reached completion is known as the *endpoint*. In a titration where permanganate is being added, the permanganate initially reacts and loses its colour. The endpoint is indicated when a permanent pink colour is observed in the conical flask.

Figure 3.5.16: *Acidified potassium permanganate will act as its own indicator in redox titrations*

GO! Activity 3.5.3

A solution for killing garden moss contains iron(II) sulfate. A student titrated a 25·0 cm³ sample of the solution with a 0·200 mol l⁻¹ acidified potassium permanganate solution. It was found that 21·0 cm³ of the permanganate solution was needed to react fully react with the Fe²⁺(aq) in the solution of moss killer.

(i) How would the student know that the potassium permanganate had reacted fully with the Fe²⁺(aq) in the sample?

(ii) Write the equations for the oxidation and reduction reactions taking place.

(iii) Combine the equations into a redox equation.

(iv) Calculate the concentration of Fe²⁺(aq) in the sample.

(v) Calculate the mass of iron(II) sulfate in 1 litre of solution.

Learning checklist

In this chapter you have learned:

- There is a range of chromatography techniques used to separate the components present in a mixture. ◯ ◯ ◯

- Size and polarity of molecules are important factors in separating substances by chromatography. ◯ ◯ ◯

- Depending on the type of chromatography used, the identity of a component can be indicated either by the distance it has travelled or the time it has taken to travel through the apparatus. ◯ ◯ ◯

- Volumetric analysis is a quantitative analysis technique. ◯ ◯ ◯

- A standard solution is a solution of accurately known concentration. ◯ ◯ ◯

- Volumetric analysis uses an accurately known concentration of one substance to find the concentration of another.

- Volumetric analysis includes the use of acid/base titrations and redox titrations.

- The endpoint of a titration is the point where the reaction has just reached completion.

- Titre volumes within $0 \cdot 2$ cm^3 are considered concordant.

- An indicator is a substance that changes colour at the endpoint of a reaction.

- In redox titrations using acidified potassium permanganate, an indicator is not needed as purple permanganate solution turns colourless when reduced.

4

Researching chemistry

Researching chemistry

SQA KEY AREA

Understanding our chemical world

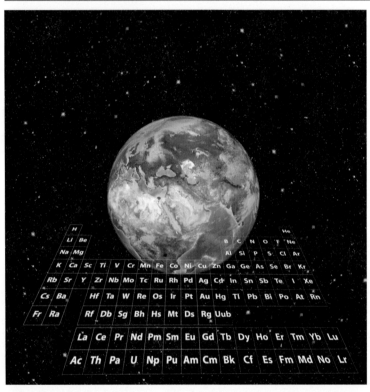

Figure 4.1: *Throughout the world, teams of research chemists are making new discoveries and developing new materials and medicines*

Throughout history people have sought to understand their world better and the sciences have been at the forefront of that drive. That quest for greater understanding continues with many thousands of scientists around the world researching new materials and new technologies that will sustain human development in years to come. Today, many teams of chemists are involved in areas such as the development of new materials with properties to meet technological demands or the development of new drugs with which to combat disease. Research skills are fundamental to these developments.

The purpose of the Researching Chemistry chapter is to help you develop the skills of scientific inquiry – skills that are necessary to allow you to carry out chemical research. These skills will help you undertake the assignment that is part of the course assessment required by SQA.

Skills of scientific inquiry include:

- **researching current literature** to help understand the underlying chemistry of a topic
- **carrying out practical investigative work** associated with the topic
- **communicating your findings** clearly to others.

Researching underlying chemistry on the internet

No longer do we need to rely only on books for information. The internet has become the number one go-to resource when seeking information on any subject. The world wide web has created a vast bank of instantly available information on every topic you can think of.

Figure 4.2: *The internet*

Following some simple rules will help ensure that the information you find when surfing the internet for information is relevant and reliable.

- Bookmark sites that you might want to return to for information.
- Check the URL suffix. Generally, government and academic sites give **reliable** information. Commercial sites and non-profit organisation sites may well give factually correct information but may be written for a particular purpose.
  - .ac.uk   UK academic institution
  - .edu   US academic institution
  - .gov.uk   UK/Scottish government
  - .org.uk   UK non-profit organisation
  - .co.uk   UK company or individual
  - .com   multinational company
- Evaluate the information.

It is important to consider whether or not the information you find is relevant and reliable. Is it supported by information on other websites? Does the information appear biased in any way?

Wikipedia is often a good starting place for information. It is effectively an online encyclopedia that relies on users to update and correct information that is posted. Because of this it might not always be 100% accurate or the material may show bias.

Sometimes, due to contrasting evidence and opinions expressed on websites and in news articles it can be difficult to come to firm judgements in relation to an issue. In these cases it is better to be balanced in what you write, i.e. give both points of view or state the evidence for and against.

The internet is a valuable resource when seeking to understand the underlying chemistry of a topic, as Activity 1 illustrates.

GO! Activity 1

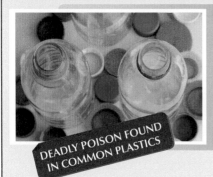

DEADLY POISON FOUND IN COMMON PLASTICS

Bisphenol A, BPA, is a chemical intermediate in the production of polycarbonate plastics. There is concern about using polycarbonate plastics to make food containers since this can lead to exposure to BPA.

Figure 4.3: *Polycarbonate plastic bottles*

Research

Research information about the use of bisphenol A by searching the internet using the term 'bisphenol A' or by using phrases such as 'uses of polycarbonate plastics' or 'risks of using polycarbonate plastics'. As you gather information you may refine your search using more specific terms such as 'polycarbonate baby bottles'.

Search for 'bisphenol A' at www.bbc.co.uk or www.scientificamerican.com. You could also use a search engine such as Google to identify sites that give information about the use of bisphenol A.

Consider the information in terms of relevance to the use of polycarbonate plastics for food containers and the concerns regarding exposure to bisphenol A.

State whether you feel the information presented by each site you visit is reliable. Is it balanced or does it show bias? If you find information that appears to show bias, consider the reasons there might be for this.

Present a short report about the use of polycarbonate plastics for food containers. Remember, when writing a report the sources of information need to be acknowledged in order that someone reading your report can check the information.

Common chemical apparatus and general practical techniques

In order to carry out the practical investigative work you will need to be familiar with basic chemical apparatus and techniques used in chemistry.

Apparatus

You should be familiar with, and know when and how to use, the pieces of apparatus listed in table 1.

You should also be familiar with the following techniques.

Techniques

Filtration

Filtration is used to separate a solid residue from a liquid or solution.

Table 1: *Common laboratory apparatus*

Beaker
Burette
Condenser
Conical flask
Delivery tubes
Distillation flask
Dropper
Evaporating basin
Filter paper
Funnel
Measuring cylinder
Pipette and safety filler
Test tube/boiling tube
Thermometer
Volumetric flask

Filtration

Figure 4.4: *A simple filtration set-up. The process can be quite slow*

Distillation

Distillation is a process that is used to boil off a liquid component of a mixture. This liquid component is known as the distillate. In chemistry laboratories water used to prepare stock solutions is either passed through a deioniser or distilled in order to remove impurities.

Distillation

Figure 4.5: *A simple laboratory distillation set-up*

Figure 4.6a: *Step 1: place a creased weighing paper on the balance pan and push the tare button to zero the balance*

Figure 4.6b: *Step 2: carefully add substance to the paper. Record mass*

Figure 4.7: *Very accurate balances have glass housings to prevent draughts affecting readings*

Figure 4.8: *Transferring a weighed sample to a beaker using a loop of paper to pick up the weighing bottle*

Distillation is also used to separate mixtures of liquids. In this instance the process is known as fractional distillation. The liquid fractions are collected over a temperature range. For this reason, in the set-up of the apparatus, it is important that the bulb of the thermometer is at the same level as the outlet arm of the distillation flask or the stillhead if quickfit apparatus is used. (This is the piece of apparatus that connects a quickfit flask to a quickfit condenser.) When Liebig condensers are used, the water inlet is at the bottom so that the flowing water completely surrounds the inner tube.

> ### GO! Activity 2
> Use the internet to find out how distillation is used in desalination and in making whisky.

The use of a balance

A balance allows you to accurately weigh the mass of a substance. Typical school balances will measure masses, in grams, correct to one or two decimal places. More accurate balances used for analytical work will measure to four decimal places.

The accuracy and associated errors can be as much to do with technique as with the balance.

In most instances it is sufficient to use a top-pan balance and use the 'tare' facility when weighing out chemicals. The tare button will re-set the balance to zero allowing the mass being weighed to be read directly from the display.

For some work greater care needs to be taken.

Very accurate top-pan balances are often housed in a glass casing. This prevents any draughts from affecting the balance reading.

The way in which a solid is weighed out can also be important.

To minimise errors a technique described as 'weighing by difference' is used. A few grams of the substance to be weighed out are placed into a weighing bottle, the mass recorded and the approximate amount required is tapped out into a small beaker.

The weighing bottle is picked up with a loop of paper or tongs, to prevent transferring oils from our hands to the weighing bottle.

The weighing bottle with the remaining substance is reweighed. The mass transferred is given by the difference in the two recorded masses.

Preparing a standard solution

In Chemistry in society, Chapter 5, *Chemical analysis*, the use of volumetric analysis to determine concentrations was described. A standard solution is a solution whose concentration is known accurately.

Preparing standard solutions requires the use of glassware that gives accurate indications of volume. Beakers give only rough indications of volume and while measuring cylinders can be used to prepare solutions with an approximate concentration or for rough dilutions, standard solutions need to be prepared using standard or volumetric flasks. A volumetric flask has a narrow neck with a graduation mark on the neck. The neck is narrow to make measurement of the volume as accurate as possible.

Suppose you wish to prepare 500 cm^3 of a standard 0·10 mol l^{-1} sodium carbonate solution. The following steps show how you should carry out the procedure.

Step 1: Calculate the mass of sodium carbonate required.

$$\text{No of moles} = \text{volume(l)} \times \text{concentration (mol l}^{-1})$$
$$= 0·5 \times 0·1$$
$$= 0·05 \text{ mol}$$
$$\text{Mass required} = 0·05 \times 106 \text{ g}$$
$$= \underline{5·3 \text{ g}}$$

Step 2: Weigh out approximately 5·3 g accurately (it doesn't need to be exactly 5·3 g but you do need to know exactly how much you have weighed out). See 'The use of a balance' on page 322.

Step 3: Dissolve the sodium carbonate in a small amount of deionised water and transfer the solution to a 500 cm^3 volumetric flask. Rinse the beaker and stirring rod with deionised water and transfer the rinsings to the flask.

(This can be done more than once.)

Step 4: Make the flask up to the mark with deionised water, adding the last few drops with a dropper. (The flask is filled to the correct level when the bottom of the meniscus just touches the graduation mark on the neck of the flask.)

Step 5: Stopper the flask and invert it several times to ensure thorough mixing of the solution.

Step 6: Calculate the accurate concentration and label the flask accordingly.

If 5·41 grams of sodium carbonate had been transferred.

$$\text{Concentration} = \frac{\text{Number of moles}}{\text{Volume(l)}}$$
$$= \frac{5{\cdot}41/106}{0{\cdot}5}$$
$$= 0{\cdot}102\,\text{mol}\,l^{-1}$$

Titration

In Chemistry in society, Chapter 5, *Chemical analysis*, the use of volumetric analysis to determine concentrations is described.

To carry out the procedure accurately it is important to know how to use pipettes and burettes properly and how to carry out the titration.

Filling a pipette

Figure 4.9: *Using a safety filler to draw liquid up into the pipette*

Figure 4.10: *The graduation mark on the stem of the pipette indicates when the pipette contains the exact volume*

A pipette is used to deliver a precise volume of liquid. A safety filler should always be used to fill a pipette (Figure 9). The pipette should be rinsed with water and then a small volume of the liquid to be pipetted. The liquid is drawn up into the pipette to above the graduation mark on the stem of the pipette. The pipette is then removed from the liquid and the liquid released slowly until the bottom of the meniscus just touches the graduation mark.

The liquid can then be transferred to a conical flask.
(Although the word 'liquid' is used here, the method applies to a solution.)

Using a burette

A burette allows you to know the volume of liquid added during a titration accurately. The burette should be rinsed with the liquid to be used and then clamped vertically in a burette stand.

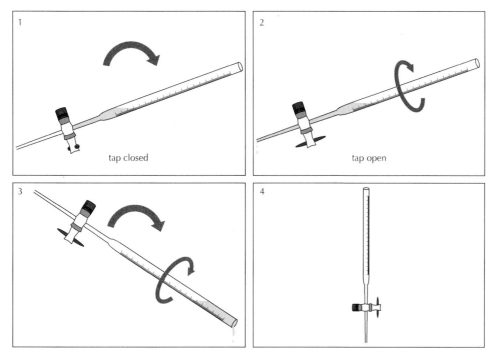

Figure 4.11: *The correct method for rinsing a burette*

A filter funnel can be used when filling a burette but this must be removed before taking the initial burette reading and carrying out the titration. The burette is filled to above the scale and then the tap opened to allow the liquid or solution to run down onto the scale. You must be careful to ensure that no air bubbles are trapped in the jet of the burette. Bubbles can be removed by quickly opening and closing the stopcock of the burette several times. The bottom of the meniscus is used to read the initial volume from the scale. It is important that your eye level is the same as the liquid level.

A piece of filter paper placed behind the burette will help you see the level of the bottom of the meniscus more clearly. For very highly coloured liquids such as potassium permanganate a light placed behind the burette can also be of help or the top of the meniscus can be read.

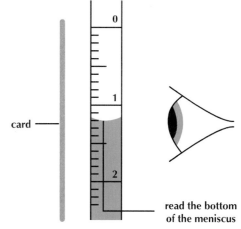

Figure 4.12: *When reading a burette, your eye should be level with the liquid. The reading here is 1·2 cm³*

Figure 4.13: *Carrying out the titration correctly*

Carrying out the titration

The correct procedure for carrying out a titration is to swirl the titration flask at the same time as adding the liquid from the burette. The stopcock of the burette is operated using the left hand and the flask swirled with the right hand. This can be difficult and requires practice. A white tile is used to help identify the permanent colour change that indicates the endpoint of the titration.

As the endpoint is approached the liquid from the burette is added dropwise. If the drop lands on the side of the flask it can be washed in using de-ionised water from a wash bottle.

Titrations are repeated until concordant titres (within 0·2 cm³ of each other) are achieved. The volume from the first titration carried out is usually ignored.

Methods for the collection of a gas

The method used to collect a gas depends on the properties of the gas. If the gas is insoluble in water then it can be collected by the displacement of water.

If a gas is soluble in water or the volume of gas needs to be measured, then a gas syringe can be used.

Both methods are shown in figure 4.14

Figure 4.14: *Collecting gases*

If a dry sample of gas is required then the gas can be passed through a tube containing a suitable drying agent before collection in a gas syringe.

gas in ⟶

drying agent must touch
top and bottom of tube.

Figure 4.15: *Passing a gas through a drying agent*

Safe methods for heating

There are three common methods used in school chemistry laboratories for heating substances:

- using a Bunsen burner
- using a water bath
- using a heating mantle.

Heating using a Bunsen burner

Although using a Bunsen burner will heat something rapidly, care needs to be taken, particularly if flammable liquids are involved. It is often better to use a water bath or heating mantle when heating flammable liquids.
It is also important that any activity involving heating using a Bunsen is never left unattended.

Figure 4.16: *A Bunsen burner is used to heat a solution rapidly*

Figure 4.17: *Using a water bath to warm a solution*

Figure 4.18: *A heating mantle*

Heating using a water bath

The use of water baths is fairly restricted. A major limitation is that they can only be used when it is not required to heat liquids above 100°C.

A simple water bath can be set up by heating a beaker of water. This can be used when carrying out reactions, such as chemical tests, that will take place fairly quickly on low boiling point ammable liquids such as ethanol. When used in this way the water should be heated and the Bunsen burner extinguished before adding the test tube containing the reaction mixture.

For experiments where the reaction mixture requires to be kept at a constant temperature for an extended period, e.g. measuring reaction rates at different temperatures, an electric water bath would be used.

Heating using a heating mantle

A heating mantle uses an electric current to provide heat. The container is not in direct contact with the heated wires, increasing safety. The temperature can be varied using a control.

Determining enthalpy changes using *Eh*

When determining enthalpy changes for chemical reactions the relationship $E_h = cm\Delta T$ is used, where ΔT is the change in temperature for the reaction. It is important to record temperatures as accurately as possible and to minimise heat transfer between the system and its surroundings. Thermometers that are graduated in 0·1 or 0·2°C divisions are suitable for recording temperatures.

Worked example

If the enthalpy change for the reaction of 25 cm³ 1 mol l⁻¹ hydrochloric acid with 25 cm³ of 1mol l⁻¹ sodium hydroxide solution was being determined, the experiment would be carried out in a polystyrene cup or other insulated system to prevent heat transfer to the surroundings.

The initial temperature of the system would be found by averaging the temperatures T_1 and T_2 of the two separate solutions. Note that this can only be done if the volumes being used are the same.

The solutions would then be mixed and the highest temperature reached (T_3) recorded.

$$\text{Initial temperature} = \frac{T_1 + T_2}{2}$$

$$\text{Final temperature} = T_3$$

$$\Delta T = \text{Final temperature} - \text{Initial temperature}$$

Make the Link

Using $Eh = cm\Delta T$ to calculate energy changes during reactions is covered in *Chemistry in society: Chemical energy.*

For combustion reactions it is important to transfer as much energy to the water as possible.

For this reason a copper beaker is used since copper is an excellent heat conductor. A draught shield prevents disturbance of the flame and minimises heat loss due to air movement and convection.

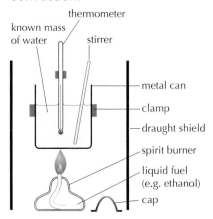

Figure 4.19: *A simple calorimeter used to determine the enthalpy of combustion of ethanol*

The mass of fuel burned is found by weighing the burner and cap at the beginning and end of the experiment. The burner is capped when not being used to prevent evaporation of the fuel from the wick. This increases the accuracy of the mass being used to heat the metal beaker and water.

Reporting experimental work

Drawing diagrams

One of the most effective ways of communicating experimental information is to use a well-drawn and labelled diagram.

In chemistry experimental set-ups are often represented by two-dimensional cross-sectional diagrams known as line diagrams.

Worked example

The diagram below clearly shows a simple experimental set-up that is used to prepare esters in the laboratory.

Figure 4.20: *A simple set-up to prepare esters*

More examples of line (sectional) diagrams can be found on page 321.

Processing experimental results

Processing experimental results includes:

- Tabulating data using appropriate headings and units of measurement
- Representing the data as a scatter graph
- Sketching lines of best fit to represent trends
- Calculating average mean values
- Identifying rogue points
- Commenting on the reproducibility of results where measurements have been repeated.

Worked example

If a student was asked to investigate the effect of concentration on the rate of reaction of magnesium with dilute hydrochloric acid they would probably carry out the investigation by dropping identical pieces of magnesium strip into different concentrations of dilute acid and timing how long it took for the magnesium to react completely.

They would be likely to record their results in a table.

Concentration of acid (mol l⁻¹)	Time (s)
0·2	242
0·5	93
1·0	45
2·0	22

The student would then need to process the results using the relationship

Relative rate = 1/t

Concentration of acid (mol l⁻¹)	Time (s)	Relative rate 1/t (s⁻¹)
0·2	242	0·004
0·5	93	0·011
1·0	45	0·022
2.0	22	0.045

> **🔎 Hint**
>
> The headings for the table must include units if these are appropriate.

Drawing a scattergraph of the results gives a more visual indication of any trend.

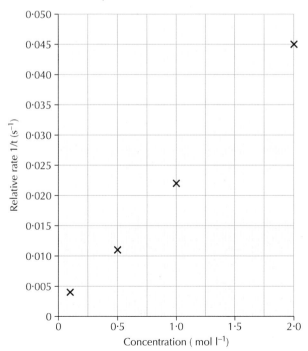

Figure 4.21: *A scattergraph*

> **🔎 Hint**
>
> Axes need to be correctly scaled and labelled. A correct label will include the units. A line of best fit can be added to the graph to show the trend for the results.

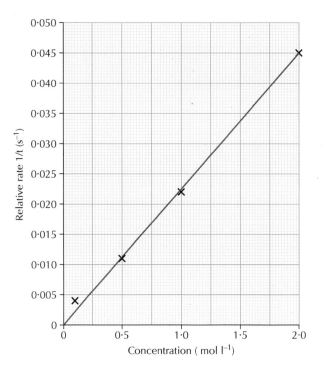

Figure 4.22: *A scattergraph showing the line of best fit*

Identifying and eliminating rogue values and points

When graphing results it is fairly easy to identify a rogue point as it will probably lie well off the line of best fit.

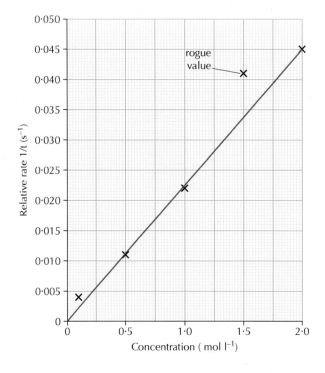

Figure 4.23: *A scattergraph showing a rogue value*

When carrying out investigations it is important to repeat experiments to ensure that results are reproducible. This means the results will be in close agreement.

When carrying out titrations concordant titres are examples of reproducible results.

If groups of students were carrying out the same titration and each group logged its results in a table, it would be clear that Group 3 had produced a rogue result.

Table 2: *Group results for titration*

Group	Titre (cm³)
1	24·6
2	24·8
3	19·8
4	24·7

This could be due to something as simple as an error in the method they used. For instance they may have used a 20 cm³ pipette while the other groups used 25 cm³ pipettes.

Any rogue result would be omitted from the calculation of an average (mean) value.

For the results in table 2, the average value would therefore be $(24·6 + 24·8 + 24·7) / 3 = 24·7$ cm³.

Uncertainty

The measurements we make are not always exact. If we are measuring temperature with a thermometer that has 1°C scale divisions then a recorded reading of 29°C could actually represent a temperature in the range 28·5°C to 29·5°C. The temperature could be shown as $29·0 \pm 0·5$°C. This represents the range of figures that could represent the true value. $\pm 0·5$°C represents the uncertainty in the reading that has been recorded.

In chemistry the size of the uncertainty is normally plus or minus half of the smallest scale division of the measuring instrument.

GO! Activity 3

1. In the lab, nitrogen dioxide gas can be prepared by heating copper(II) nitrate.

    $$Cu(NO_3)_2(s) \longrightarrow CuO(s) + 2NO_2(g) + \tfrac{1}{2}O_2(g)$$

    Nitrogen dioxide has a boiling point of 22°C.

    Complete the diagram to show how nitrogen dioxide can be separated and collected.

    copper(II) nitrate

    oxygen gas

    Figure 4.24

2. When magnesium is reacted with dilute hydrochloric acid the hydrogen produced in the reaction can be contaminated with small quantities of hydrogen chloride vapour.

    This vapour is very soluble in water.

    Complete the diagram to show how the hydrogen chloride can be removed before the hydrogen is collected.

    hydrochloric acid

    gas syringe to collect hydrogen

    hydrochloric acid + magnesium

    Figure 4.25

Your chemistry assignment

Your course assessment in Higher Chemistry has two components: a question paper and an assignment.

The purpose of the Researching Chemistry chapter is to equip you with the skills to research chemistry. These skills will allow you to carry out the chemistry assignment.

Your assignment will be to carry out both literature research and practical work relating to a key area of the course and to communicate your findings in a report. Carrying out the research activities of the assignment will allow you to meet the requirements of the course assessment criteria. Your report write-up will be marked by SQA and will contribute to the mark that your overall course award will be based upon.

Structure of the assignment

In order to carry out your assignment you may be provided with a briefing document that will contain a number of **focus questions**.

From this you will be able to research the underlying chemistry relating to the question and plan the practical investigation of an aspect of the chemistry relating to the topic.

It would be advisable to keep a log of the information you gather, the activities you carry out and the results you obtain throughout the course of your assignment. These will be required when you complete your report write-up of the investigation.

You are given a briefing document relating to a healthy diet and choose to look at the focus question,

'Why is vitamin C an important part of a healthy diet?'

Step 1:   Researching the underlying chemistry

Look up 'vitamin C in our diet' or 'health benefits of vitamin C' on the internet.

Bookmark sites that give information you may want to come back to. You should have a minimum of two sites.

Example

 Hint

You don't have to restrict your search to using the internet. Textbooks and journals may be more readily available in the laboratory and give you lots of useful information.

Select your sites and note down the main points you want to take from the sites.

Your initial search however may be lacking in chemistry and you may have to search using other chemical terms, e.g. instead of 'vitamin C' try using 'ascorbic acid'. Note that, although you may find interesting general/historical/biological information relating to your topic that you might choose to include in your report it is only the chemistry you descibe that will be awarded marks.

When answering your focus question consider whether your answer relates directly to the question.

For instance an answer relating to 'The benefits of vitamin C in our diet' might include:

- The structural formula for ascorbic acid and some of its properties.
- Why it is necessary in the diet, e.g. the body can't make it.
- The chemistry of the body that vitamin C is involved in
    - antioxidant function
        - what are antioxidants?
        - free radicals
        - why vitamin C can be oxidised related to its structure
        - what forms when vitamin C is oxidised
    - role in formation of the protein, collagen
        - protein structure
        - structure of amino acid proline, hydroxyproline
        - health issues related to vitamin C
        - sources of vitamin C
        - recommended dietary allowances.

🔵 Activity 4

Although you may be able to collaborate with others in carrying out some of the research activities, answering the focus question is done as an individual student activity. It is important therefore that you make your own notes that will allow you to answer the focus question.

Using information from the internet relating to the bullet points above, prepare an answer to the focus question, 'Why is vitamin C an important part of a healthy diet?'

You may wish to give your answer to another student for their comment.

Step 2: Carrying out a practical investigation relating to vitamin C in our diet

This could include

- determining the vitamin C content of various fruits or drinks
- investigating the effect of cooking on the vitamin C content of vegetables.

First decide on a method. Remember you can work as a group on the practical aspects of your investigation, i.e. you can discuss an appropriate method with other students. If determining the vitamin C content of fruits and fruit juices, different members of the group could use different juices and share results.

Activity 5

Suppose you wanted to compare the vitamin C content of commercially produced orange juices with freshly squeezed juice.

Since vitamin C can be oxidised, a redox titration would seem an appropriate method to use to make a comparison.

Both iodine and acidified potassium permanganate could be used to oxidise vitamin C.

What are the things to consider when planning your Practical investigation?

1. Which oxidising agent to use? Suggest why using iodine would be better than using potassium permanganate?

2. You have decided to titrate 25 cm³ portions of orange juice with iodine solution. The label on the commercially produced orange juice states that it contains 30 mg of vitamin C per 100 cm³ of juice.

   (a) What would be the advantage of determining the vitamin C content of the commercially produced juice first?

   (b) Deciding the concentration of iodine solution you should use in the titration.

$$C_6H_8O_6(aq) \ + \ I_2(aq) \ \longrightarrow \ C_6H_6O_6(aq) \ + \ 2H^+(aq) \ + \ 2I^-(aq)$$

   The equation shows that 1 mol vitamin C reacts with 1 mol iodine.

   Ideally choose a concentration of iodine solution that will mean that at least two titrations can be carried out using a filled burette.

   If the concentration of iodine used is such that only a small volume is needed to react with the vitamin C then the error will be large and results will be less reliable. If a large volume of lower concentration iodine solution is used then the burette may need to be refilled between titrations.

   To decide the best concentration to use you need to first work out moles of vitamin C in the 25cm³ of orange juice and then the volume of iodine solutions of different concentrations that would be needed to completely react with the vitamin C.

   (i) Calculate the number of moles of vitamin C in 25 cm³ of the orange juice.

   (ii) Calculate the volume of iodine solution with the following concentrations which would be needed to react with the vitamin C in 25 cm³ of orange juice and explain why using 0·002 mol l⁻¹ would seem to be the best option:

   0·01 mol l⁻¹; 0·002 mol l⁻¹; 0·001mol l⁻¹

   (c) The only available iodine solution is a stock solution, concentration 0.10 mol l⁻¹. Describe how you would prepare a 0·002 mol l⁻¹ solution from this stock solution.

 Hint

You only need to work out the volume (v = mol/c) for one concentration. You then use proportion to work out the others. You will need 5 times as much 0·002 mol l⁻¹ solution as 0·01 mol l⁻¹ solution and ten times as much 0·001mol l⁻¹ solution.

Your assignment report write-up

The report write-up for your assignment is part of the external assessment for the course. As such the report will be written up under closely supervised conditions. It is important that you keep a clear record of the sources of information of underlying chemistry and the details and results of the experiments you carried out in the investigation. Your report is then submitted to SQA for marking. Detailed information regarding requirements for each aspect of the assignment will be given by your teacher/lecturer. The 20 marks for the assignment are allocated as follows:

Table 3: *Marking criteria for Higher Chemistry assignment*

Skills, knowledge and understanding		Marks Available
1. Aim		1 mark
2. Underlying Chemistry		3 marks
3. Data collection and handling	a. Brief summary of approach, including safety	1 mark
	b. Sufficient raw data	1 mark
	c. Correct table(s) and correct units for calculated values	1 mark
	d. Values calculated using a chemical relationship	1 mark
	e. Data relevant to the experiment from an internet/ literature source	1 mark
	f. Citation and reference	1 mark
4. Graphical presentation	a. An appropriate graph format	1 mark
	b. Axis/axes with suitable scale(s)	1 mark
	c. Axes with suitable labels and units	1 mark
	d. Accurately plotted points and, where appropriate, line of best fit	1 mark
5. Analysis		1 mark
6. Conclusion		1 mark
7. Evaluation of the investigation		3 marks
8. Structure: A clear and concise report with an informative title		1 mark
Total		**20 marks**

A major part of your report will involve selecting information to include in the report, and then processing, presenting and analysing the information.

Where appropriate you will be expected to:

- identify and eliminate rogue points from results
- calculate averages
- draw scatter plots of results
- draw graphs showing lines of best fit.

When evaluating your investigation, marks are awarded for an appreciation of:

- validity of sources quoted
- reliability of data/information included
- robustness of findings
- reliability and accuracy/reproducibility of experimental procedures used.

Learning checklist

In this chapter you have learned:

- Skills of scientific inquiry including:
  - researching current literature
  - carrying out practical investigative work
  - communicating findings clearly

- You should have knowledge of the correct use of:

Beaker	Filter paper
Burette	Funnel
Condenser	Measuring cylinder
Conical flask	Pipette and safety filler
Delivery tubes	Test tube/boiling tube
Distillation flask	Thermometer
Dropper	Volumetric flask
Evaporating basin	

- You should have knowledge of common laboratory techniques including:
  - filtration
  - distillation
  - use of a balance
  - titration
  - methods for the collection of a gas: over water, using a gas syringe
  - safe methods for heating: Bunsen burners, water baths or heating mantles
  - determining enthalpy changes using Eh

- Assessment requirements for the Higher Chemistry assignment.

Exam-style questions

The Higher Chemistry question papers

The Higher exam consists of two papers. Paper 1 contains multiple choice questions and has 25 marks allocated. Paper 2 contains restricted (short) and extended response questions and has 95 marks allocated. The majority of the marks are awarded for demonstrating and applying knowledge and understanding of the content of the course. The other marks are awarded for applying scientific inquiry skills. Marks are distributed approximately proportionally across the areas which make up the course.

Multiple choice questions

Select the correct response to each question. There is only one correct answer for each question.

Area 1: Chemical changes and structure

1. Which of the following does **not** contain covalent bonds?

    A   Hydrogen gas
    B   Helium gas
    C   Nitrogen gas
    D   Solid sulfur

2. Which of the following elements has the greatest attraction for bonding electrons?

    A   Lithium
    B   Chlorine
    C   Sodium
    D   Bromine

3. Which of the following statements is true?

    A   The potassium ion is larger than the potassium atom
    B   The chloride ion is smaller than the chlorine atom
    C   The sodium atom is larger than the sodium ion
    D   The oxygen atom is larger than the oxide ion

4. Which of the following elements would require the most energy to convert one mole of gaseous atoms into gaseous ions each carrying two positive charges?
    (You may wish to use the data booklet.)

    A   Scandium
    B   Titanium
    C   Vanadium
    D   Chromium

5. Which of the following is **not** an example of a van der Waals' force?

    A   Covalent bonding
    B   Hydrogen bonding
    C   London dispersion forces
    D   Permanent dipole–permanent dipole interactions

6. Which type of bonding is **never** found in elements?

    A   Metallic
    B   London dispersion forces
    C   Polar covalent
    D   Non-polar covalent

7. In which of the following molecules will the chlorine atom carry a partial positive charge ($\delta+$)?

    A   Cl–Br
    B   Cl–Cl
    C   Cl–F
    D   Cl–I

8. Coniceine is a deadly poison extracted from the plant hemlock.

    coniceine

    Which of the following would be the best solvent for coniceine?

    A   Propanoic acid
    B   Propan-l-ol
    C   Heptane
    D   Water

9. The shapes of some common molecules are shown below and each contains at least one polar bond.

   Which molecule is non-polar?

   A $H-Cl$

   B $\underset{H}{}O\underset{H}{}$

   C $O=C=O$

   D
   $$\underset{\underset{Cl}{Cl\diagdown \quad \diagup Cl}}{\overset{\overset{H}{|}}{C}}$$

10. Which of the following elements is the strongest reducing agent?

    A Fluorine   B Hydrogen
    C Potassium   D Magnesium

11. During a redox process in acid solution, iodate ions, $IO_3^-(aq)$, are converted into iodine, $I_2(aq)$.

    $$IO_3^-(aq) \rightarrow I_2(aq)$$

    The numbers of $H^+(aq)$ and $H_2O(\ell)$ required to balance the ion-electron equation for the formation of 1 mol of $I_2(aq)$ are, respectively

    A 3 and 6   B 6 and 3
    C 6 and 12   D 12 and 6

12. One of the reactions taking place within a carbon monoxide sensor is

    $$2CO + 2H_2O \rightarrow 2CO_2 + 4H^+ + 4e^-$$

    This reaction is an example of

    A reduction
    B redox
    C oxidation
    D hydration

Area 2: Nature's chemistry

1. An ester has the following shortened structural formula:

$CH_3CH_2CH_2COOCH_2CH_3$

The name of this ester is

A propyl propanoate

B ethyl butanoate

C butyl ethanoate

D ethyl propanoate

2. An ester has the structural formula:

$$CH_3-CH_2-\overset{\overset{\displaystyle O}{\|}}{C}-O-\underset{\underset{\displaystyle CH_3}{|}}{\overset{\overset{\displaystyle CH_3}{|}}{C}}-H$$

On hydrolysis, the ester would produce

A ethanoic acid and propan-1-ol

B ethanoic acid and propan-2-ol

C propanoic acid and propan-1-ol

D propanoic acid and propan-2-ol

3. Oils are generally

A solid at room temperature and contain a high proportion of unsaturated molecules

B solid at room temperature and contain a high proportion of saturated molecules

C liquid at room temperature and contain a high proportion of unsaturated molecules

D liquid at room temperature and contain a high proportion of saturated molecules

4. The arrangement of amino acids in part of a protein molecule is Z–X–W–V–Y where the letters V, W, X, Y and Z represent amino acids.

On partial hydrolysis of the molecule, which of the following sets of dipeptides is possible?

A V–Y, Z–X, W–Y, X–W

B Z–X, V–Y, W–V, X–W

C Z–X, X–V, W–V, V–Y

D X–W, X–Z, Z–W, Y–V

5. The following molecules are found in herbicides.
Which of the following contains an amide link?

A

B

C

D

6. Some amino acids are called α-amino acids because the amino group is on the carbon atom next to the acid group.
Which of the following is an α-amino acid?

A $CH_3-CH-COOH$
           |
         CH_2-NH_2

B $CH_2-CH-COOH$
         | |
        SH NH_2

C

D

7. Which of the following organic compounds is an isomer of hexanal?

A   2-methylbutanal
B   3-methylpentan-2-one
C   2,2-dimethylbutan-1-ol
D   3-ethylpentanal

8. Which process is used to convert ethanal to ethanoic acid?

A   Hydrogenation   B   Condensation
C   Hydration   D   Oxidation

9. A compound with molecular formula $C_6H_{12}O_2$ could be

A   Hexanal   B   Hexan-2-ol
C   Hexan-2-one   D   Hexanoic acid

10. Which of the following is an isomer of hexan-2-ol?

A
$$CH_3—CH_2—CH_2—CH_2—\overset{\overset{\displaystyle CH_3}{|}}{CH}—OH$$

B
$$CH_3—\overset{\overset{\displaystyle CH_3}{|}}{\underset{\underset{\displaystyle OH}{|}}{CH}}—CH_2—CH_2—CH_2—CH_3$$

C
$$H_2C\overset{\displaystyle CH_2—CH_2}{\underset{\displaystyle CH_2—CH_2}{\big<}}CH—OH$$

D
$$CH_3—\overset{\overset{\displaystyle CH_3}{|}}{C}—\overset{\overset{\displaystyle CH_3}{}}{\underset{\underset{\displaystyle CH_3OH}{|}}{CH}}—CH_3$$

11. Which of the following structural formulae represents a tertiary alcohol?

A
$$CH_3—\overset{\overset{\displaystyle CH_3}{|}}{\underset{\underset{\displaystyle CH_3}{|}}{C}}—CH_2—OH$$

B
$$CH_3—\overset{\overset{\displaystyle CH_3}{|}}{\underset{\underset{\displaystyle OH}{|}}{C}}—CH_2—CH_3$$

C
$$CH_3—CH_2—CH_2—\overset{\overset{\displaystyle H}{|}}{\underset{\underset{\displaystyle OH}{|}}{C}}—CH_3$$

D
$$CH_3—CH_2—\overset{\overset{\displaystyle H}{|}}{\underset{\underset{\displaystyle OH}{|}}{C}}—CH_2—CH_3$$

12. Which of the following could **not** be a possible source of a fatty acid?

A   Soaps   B   Edible oils

C   Emulsifiers   D   Essential oils

13. Limonene is one of the terpene molecules responsible for the flavour of lemons.

How many isoprene units are used in the production of one limonene molecule?

A   1   B   2

C   3   D   4

14. Myrcene is a simple terpene. Terpenes contain at least one isoprene unit.

Which of the following shows a correctly highlighted isoprene unit?

A

B

C

D

15. Caryophyllene is a natural product which can be extracted from clove oil using a solvent.

caryophyllene

Which of the following would be the best solvent for extracting caryophyllene?

A   Hexane   B   Hexanal

C   Hexan-2-ol   D   Hexan-3-one

16. 4-Hydroxy-6-methyl-2-pyrone is a cyclic ester responsible for the smell of chocolate.

The number 2 identifies the position of the carbonyl group in the pyrone ring counting from the oxygen atom within the ring.

What is the structure of 4-hydroxy-6-methyl-2-pyrone?

A

B

C

D

17. Which line in the table shows correct functional groups for aldehydes and ketones and fats and oils?

	Aldehydes and ketones	Fats and oils
A	carbonyl	hydroxyl
B	carboxyl	hydroxyl
C	carboxyl	ester link
D	carbonyl	ester link

18. A step in the synthesis of nicotinic acid (vitamin B$_3$) is shown.

nicotinyl alcohol   nicotinic acid

The type of reaction taking place in this step is

A   hydration

B   oxidation

C   reduction

D   condensation

19. Benzaldehyde and vanillin are examples of flavour molecules.

benzaldehyde   vanillin

Vanillin is soluble in water and is fairly volatile.

Which line in the table correctly compares benzaldehyde to vanillin?

	Solubility in water	Relative volatility
A	greater than vanillin	greater than vanillin
B	greater than vanillin	less than vanillin
C	less than vanillin	less than vanillin
D	less than vanillin	greater than vanillin

20. A compound with the following structure is used in perfumes to help provide a sweet, fruity fragrance.

This compound could be classified as

A   an aldehyde

B   a carboxylic acid

C   an ester

D   a ketone

21. Which of the following diagrams and explanations best describes a step in the cleansing action of soap?

	Diagram	Explanation
A	water	Hydrophobic head dissolves in water. Hydrophilic tail dissolves in oil droplet.
B	water	Hydrophilic head dissolves in water. Hydrophobic tail dissolves in oil droplet.
C	water	Hydrophobic head dissolves in oil droplet. Hydrophilic tail dissolves in water.
D	water	Hydrophilic head dissolves in oil droplet. Hydrophobic tail dissolves in water.

22. Humulene is a terpene which contributes to the aroma of beer.

$$\begin{array}{c}
\text{CH}_2 \quad \text{CH}_3 \\
\text{HC} \diagdown \text{C} \diagup \\
\| \qquad \diagdown \\
\text{H}_3\text{C} \diagdown \text{CH} \qquad \text{CH} \\
\text{C} \qquad \qquad | \\
\text{H}_3\text{C} | \qquad \text{CH}_2 \\
\text{CH}_2 - \text{CH} \quad \text{CH}_2 \\
\text{C} \\
| \\
\text{CH}_3
\end{array}$$

humulene

How many isoprene units were used to form a humulene molecule?

A   2

B   3

C   4

D   5

Area 3: Chemistry in society

1. Calcium carbonate reacts with nitric acid as follows.

$$CaCO_3(s) + 2HNO_3(aq) \rightarrow Ca(NO_3)_2(aq) + H_2O(\ell) + CO_2(g)$$

0·05 mol of calcium carbonate was added to a solution containing 0·08 mol of nitric acid.

Which of the following statements is true?

A   0·05 mol of carbon dioxide is produced

B   0·08 mol of calcium nitrate is produced

C   Calcium carbonate is in excess by 0·01 mol

D   Nitric acid is in excess by 0·03 mol

2. A student obtained a certain volume of carbon dioxide by the reaction of 20 cm³ of 2 mol l⁻¹ hydrochloric acid with excess sodium carbonate.

$$2HCl(aq) + Na_2CO_3(aq) \rightarrow 2NaCl(aq) + CO_2(g)$$

Which solution of sulfuric acid would give the same final volume of carbon dioxide when added to excess sodium carbonate?

$$H_2SO_4(aq) + Na_2CO_3(aq) \rightarrow Na_2SO_4(aq) + CO_2(g)$$

A   10 cm³ of 2 mol l⁻¹ sulfuric acid

B   20 cm³ of 2 mol l⁻¹ sulfuric acid

C   10 cm³ of 4 mol l⁻¹ sulfuric acid

D   20 cm³ of 4 mol l⁻¹ sulfuric acid

3. A mixture of sodium bromide and sodium sulfate is known to contain 5 moles of sodium and 2 moles of bromide ions.

How many moles of sulfate ions are present?

A 1·5

B 2·0

C 2·5

D 3·0

4. $2C_2H_2(g) + 5O_2(g) \rightarrow 4CO_2(g) + 2H_2O(\ell)$
ethyne

What volume of gas would be produced by the complete combustion of 100 cm³ of ethyne gas?

All volumes were measured at atmospheric pressure and room temperature.

A 200 cm³

B 300 cm³

C 400 cm³

D 800 cm³

5. In which of the following will **both** changes result in an increase in the rate of a chemical reaction?

A A decrease in activation energy and an increase in the frequency of collisions

B An increase in activation energy and a decrease in particle size

C An increase in temperature and an increase in the particle size

D An increase in concentration and a decrease in the surface area of the reactant particles

6. The enthalpy change for the forward reaction can be represented by

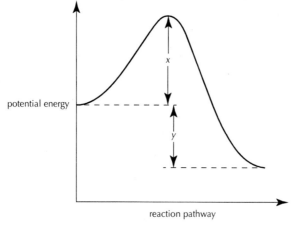

A x

B y

C $x + y$

D $x - y$

7. When copper carbonate is reacted with excess acid, carbon dioxide is produced. The curves shown below were obtained under different conditions.

The change from P to Q could be brought about by

A   increasing the concentration of the acid

B   decreasing the mass of copper carbonate

C   decreasing the particle size of the copper carbonate

D   adding a catalyst

8. Which of the following is **not** a correct statement about the effect of a catalyst? The catalyst

A   provides energy so that more molecules have successful collisions

B   lowers the energy which molecules need for successful collisions

C   provides an alternative route to the products

D   forms bonds with reacting molecules

9. In a reversible reaction, equilibrium is reached when

A   molecules of reactants cease to change into molecules of products

B   the concentrations of reactants and products are equal

C   the concentrations of reactants and products are constant

D   the activation energy of the forward reaction is equal to that of the reverse reaction

10. Ethanol is manufactured by reacting ethane with steam.

$$C_2H_4(g) + H_2O(g) \rightleftharpoons C_2H_5OH(g) \qquad \Delta H = -46 \text{ kJ mol}^{-1}$$

Which set of conditions would give the best yield of ethanol at equilibrium?

A   High temperature, low pressure

B   High temperature, high pressure

C   Low temperature, high pressure

D   Low temperature, low pressure

11. A few drops of concentrated sulfuric acid were added to a mixture of 0·1 mol of methanol and 0·2 mol of ethanoic acid. Even after a considerable time, the reaction mixture was found to contain some of each reactant.

Which of the following is the best explanation for the incomplete reaction?

A   The temperature was too low

B   An equilibrium mixture was formed

C   Insufficient methanol was used

D   Insufficient ethanoic acid was used

12. $2SO_2(g) + O_2(g) \rightleftharpoons 2SO_3(g)$

The equation represents a mixture at equilibrium.

Which line in the table is true for the mixture after a further 2 hours of reaction?

	Rate of forward reaction	Rate of back reaction
A	decreases	decreases
B	increases	increases
C	unchanged	decreases
D	unchanged	unchanged

13. Aluminium reacts with oxygen to form aluminium oxide.

$$2Al(s) + 1\tfrac{1}{2}O_2(g) \rightarrow Al_2O_3(s) \quad \Delta H = -1670 \text{ kJ mol}^{-1}$$

What is the enthalpy of combustion of aluminium in kJ mol^{-1}?

A   −835   B   −1113

C   −1670   D   +1670

14. In the presence of bright light, hydrogen and chlorine react explosively. One step in the reaction is shown below.

$$H_2(g) + Cl(g) \rightarrow HCl(g) + H(g)$$

The enthalpy change for this step can be represented as

A (H-H bond enthalpy) + (Cl-Cl bond enthalpy)

B (H-H bond enthalpy) − (Cl-Cl bond enthalpy)

C (H-H bond enthalpy) + (H-Cl bond enthalpy)

D (H-H bond enthalpy) − (H-Cl bond enthalpy)

15. Consider the reaction pathways shown below.

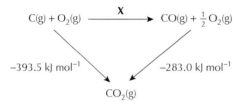

$$C(g) + O_2(g) \xrightarrow{\quad X \quad} CO(g) + \tfrac{1}{2}O_2(g)$$

−393.5 kJ mol⁻¹   −283.0 kJ mol⁻¹

$$CO_2(g)$$

According to Hess's law, the enthalpy change for reaction **X** is

A −676·5 kJ mol⁻¹

B −110·5 kJ mol⁻¹

C +110·5 kJ mol⁻¹

D +676·5 kJ mol⁻¹

16. 45 cm³ of a solution could be most accurately measured out using a

A 50 cm³ beaker

B 50 cm³ burette

C 50 cm³ pipette

D 50 cm³ measuring cylinder

17. An organic chemist is attempting to synthesise a fragrance compound by the following chemical reaction.

compound **X** + compound **Y** → fragrance compound

After one hour, a sample is removed and compared with pure samples of compounds **X** and **Y** using thin-layer chromatography.

Which of the following chromatograms shows that the reaction has produced a pure sample of the fragrance compound?

Area 4: Researching chemistry

1. Aluminium carbonate can be produced by the following reaction.

$$2AlCl_3(aq) + 3K_2CO_3(aq) \rightarrow Al_2(CO_3)_3(s) + 6KCl(aq)$$

The most suitable method for obtaining a sample of the aluminium carbonate is

A   collection over water

B   distillation

C   evaporation

D   filtration

2. The alcohol content of wine was analysed by four students. Each student carried out the experiment three times.

	Experiment 1 (%)	Experiment 2 (%)	Experiment 3 (%)
Student A	10·0	9·0	8·0
Student B	6·4	6·6	6·8
Student C	6·5	6·6	6·6
Student D	9·0	8·5	9·6

The most reproducible results were obtained by

A   Student A

B   Student B

C   Student C

D   Student D

3. Sulfur dioxide gas is more dense than air and is very soluble in water.

Which of the following diagrams shows the most appropriate apparatus for collecting and measuring the volume of sulfur dioxide given off in a reaction?

4. A chemist analysed a mixture of four dyes A, B, C and D using gas-liquid chromatography.

When a polar column was used the following chromatogram was obtained.

concentration

increasing retention time

Which of the following compounds was present in greatest concentration?

Dye	Structure
A	
B	
C	
D	

5. The correct method of filling a 20 cm³ pipette is to draw the liquid into the pipette

    A   doing it slowly at the end, until the top of the meniscus touches the mark
    B   doing it slowly at the end, until the bottom of the meniscus touches the mark
    C   to above the mark and then release liquid from the pipette until the top of the meniscus touches the mark
    D   to above the mark and then release liquid from the pipette until the bottom of the meniscus touches the mark

6. A 0·10 mol 1⁻¹ solution could be prepared most accurately from a 1·0 mol 1⁻¹ solution using

    A   a 1 cm³ dropping pipette and a 10 cm³ measuring cylinder
    B   a 10 cm³ measuring cylinder and a 100 cm³ volumetric flask
    C   a 25 cm³ pipette and a 250 cm³ volumetric flask
    D   a 50 cm³ burette and a 500 cm³ measuring cylinder

Restricted and extended response questions

The questions in paper 2 are a mixture of short answer questions and longer questions which often need detailed explanations. They are often cross-area questions – this means they can test key content from more than one area in the same question.

[Paper 2 will also contain open questions – a detailed explanation and examples of open questions are given at the end of this section.]

1. Attempts have been made to make foods healthier by using alternatives to traditional cooking ingredients.
    (a) An alternative to common salt contains potassium ions and chloride ions.
        (i) Write an ion-electron equation for the first ionisation energy of potassium.
        (ii) **Explain clearly** why the first ionisation energy of potassium is smaller than that of chlorine.

    (b) A calorie-free replacement for fat can be made by reacting fatty acids with the hydroxyl groups on a molecule of sucrose. A structural formula for sucrose is shown.

    How many fatty acid molecules can react with one molecule of sucrose?

2. The structures below show molecules that contain chlorine atoms.

trichloromethane   tetrachloromethane

(a) The compounds shown above are not very soluble in water. Trichloromethane is around ten times more soluble in water than tetrachloromethane.

Explain clearly why trichloromethane is more soluble in water than tetrachloromethane.

Your answer should include the names of the intermolecular forces involved.

(b) Chloromethane can be produced by the reaction of methane with chlorine.

$$CH_4(g) + Cl_2(g) \rightarrow CH_3Cl(g) + HCl(g)$$

Using bond enthalpies from the data booklet, calculate the enthalpy change, in kJ mol^{-1}, for this reaction.

3. Ibuprofen is one of the best selling painkillers in the UK.

(a) Ibuprofen tablets should not be taken by people who suffer from acid indigestion. Name the functional group present in ibuprofen that makes this drug unsuitable for these patients.

(b) From the 1990s, ibuprofen has been synthesised by a 3-step process.
The equation below shows the final step of the synthesis.

ibuprofen

(i) What is the atom economy of this step?

(ii) The diagram below represents the changing potential energy during this reaction carried out without the palladium catalyst.

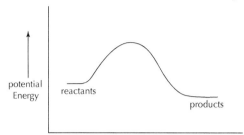

Add a line to the diagram showing the changing potential energy when the catalyst is used.

(c) Small children can find it difficult to swallow tablets or pills so ibuprofen is supplied as an 'infant formula' emulsion.

(i) The emulsifier used is polysorbate 80. Its structure is shown below.

$$CH_2-O-\overset{\overset{\displaystyle O}{\|}}{C}-(CH_2)_6-CH\!=\!CH-(CH_2)_7-CH_3$$

$$HO-CH_2-CH_2-O-CH$$

$$CH$$

$$O\diagdown CH-O-CH_2-CH_2-OH$$

$$H_2C-CH-O-CH_2-CH_2-OH$$

Explain why this molecule acts as an emulsifier.

(ii) The emulsion contains 2 g of ibuprofen in every 100 cm³ of emulsion. The recommended dose for treating a six-month-old baby is 0·050 g. Calculate the volume, in cm³, of 'infant formula' needed to treat a six-month-old baby.

4. Genetically modified bacteria can produce 2-methylpropan-1-ol by fermentation.

(a) Draw a structural formula for 2-methylpropan-1-ol.

(b) 2-methylpropan-1-ol may be used as an alternative to ethanol as a fuel.

(i) Ethanol releases 29·7 kJ of energy for every gram of fuel burned. Using the information from the table below, show by calculation that 2-methylpropan-1-ol releases more energy than the same mass of ethanol when burned.

	2-methylpropan-1-ol
Mass of one mole/g	74
Enthalpy of combustion/kJ mol⁻¹	−2669

(ii)   Problems can be caused by water dissolved in alcohols that are to be used as fuels.

2-methylpropan-1-ol absorbs less water from the atmosphere than ethanol. Water is absorbed because alcohols can form hydrogen bonds with water molecules.

The box below shows a molecule of ethanol. Draw a molecule of water and use a dotted line to show where a hydrogen bond exists between the two molecules.

$$
\begin{array}{ccc}
 & & \text{H} \\
 & & \diagup \\
\text{H} & \text{O} & \\
| & | & \\
\text{H--C--C--H} & \\
| & | & \\
\text{H} & \text{H} &
\end{array}
$$

5.   Fluorine is an extremely reactive element. Its compounds are found in a range of products.

(a)   Iodine can be extracted from iodide salts by reacting them with acidified permanganate solution.

$$10I^-(aq) + 2MnO_4^-(aq) + 16H^+(aq) \rightarrow 5I_2(aq) + 2Mn^{2+}(aq) + 8H_2O(\ell)$$

Why can fluorine not be produced from fluoride salts using acidified permanganate?

(b)   Fluorine reacts with methane via a free radical chain reaction.
Some steps in the chain reaction are shown in the table below.

Reaction step	Name of step
$F_2 \rightarrow 2F\bullet$	
$F\bullet + CH_4 \rightarrow HF + \bullet CH_3$ $\bullet CH_3 + F_2 \rightarrow CH_3F + F\bullet$	propagation
$\bullet CH_3 + F\bullet \rightarrow CH_3F$	termination
	termination

Copy the table and complete it by:

(i)   inserting the missing name for the first step;

(ii)   showing another possible termination reaction in the final row of the table.

6. Suncreams contain antioxidants.

(a) The antioxidant, compound **A**, can prevent damage to skin by reacting with free radicals such as $NO_2^{\cdot}$.

Compound A

Why can compound **A** be described as a free radical scavenger in the reaction shown above?

(b) Another antioxidant used in skincare products is vitamin C, $C_6H_8O_6$.
Complete the ion-electron equation for the oxidation of vitamin C.

$$C_6H_8O_6(aq) \rightarrow C_6H_6O_6(aq)$$

7. Methanamide, $HCONH_2$, is widely used in industry to make nitrogen compounds.
It is also used as a solvent as it can dissolve ionic compounds.

(a) Why is methanamide a suitable solvent for ionic compounds?

(b) In industry, methanamide is produced by the reaction of an ester with ammonia.

$HCOOCH_3$	+	NH_3	→	$HCONH_2$	+	CH_3OH
mass of one mole = 60·0 g		mass of one mole = 17·0 g		mass of one mole = 45·0 g		mass of one mole = 32·0 g

   (i) Name the ester used in the industrial manufacture of methanamide.

   (ii) Calculate the atom economy for the production of methanamide.

(c) In the lab, methanamide can be prepared by the reaction of methanoic acid with ammonia.

HCOOH	+	NH_3	→	$HCONH_2$	+	H_2O
mass of one mole = 46·0 g		mass of one mole = 17·0 g		mass of one mole = 45·0 g		mass of one mole – 18·0 g

When 1·38 g of methanoic acid was reacted with excess ammonia, 0·945 g of methanamide was produced.
Calculate the percentage yield of methanamide.

8. Hydrogen sulfide is a toxic gas with the smell of rotten eggs.

(a) Hydrogen sulfide gas can be prepared by the reaction of iron(II) sulfide with excess dilute hydrochloric acid:

$$FeS(s) + 2HCl(aq) \rightarrow FeCl_2(aq) + H_2S(g)$$

(i) Hydrogen sulfide gas is very soluble in water.

Draw a diagram to show an assembled apparatus that could be used to measure the volume of H_2S gas produced when a sample of iron(II) sulfide reacts with hydrochloric acid.

Your diagram should be labelled and should show the names of any chemicals used.

(ii) Calculate the mass, in g, of iron(II) sulfide required to produce 79 cm³ of hydrogen sulfide gas.

(Take the molar volume of hydrogen sulfide to be 24 litres mol⁻¹.)

Show your working clearly.

9. Different fuels are used for different purposes.

(a) Ethanol, C_2H_5OH, can be used as a fuel in some camping stoves.

(i) The enthalpy of combustion of ethanol given in the data booklet is −1367 kJ mol⁻¹.

Using this value, calculate the mass of ethanol, in g, required to raise the temperature of 500 g of water from 18°C to 100°C.

Show your working clearly.

(ii) Suggest **two** reasons why less energy is obtained from burning ethanol in the camping stove than is predicted from its enthalpy of combustion.

(b) Petrol is a fuel used in cars.

Energy released when 1·00 g of petrol burned/kJ	48·0
Volume of 1·00 g of petrol/cm³	1·45

A car has a 50·0 litre petrol tank.

Calculate the energy, in kJ, released by the complete combustion of one tank of petrol.

10. Proteins are an important part of a healthy diet because they provide essential amino acids.

  (a) State what is meant by an **essential amino acid**.

  (b) Eggs and fish are good dietary sources of the essential amino acid, methionine.

      The recommended daily allowance of methionine for an adult is 15 mg per kg of body mass.

      Tuna contains 755 mg of methionine per 100 g portion.

      Calculate the mass, in grams, of tuna that would provide the recommended daily allowance of methionine for a 60 kg adult.

  (c) Mixtures of amino acids can be separated using paper chromatography.

      On a chromatogram, the retention factor, R_f, for a substance can be a useful method of identifying the substance.

$$R_f = \frac{\text{distance moved by the substance}}{\text{maximum distance moved by the solvent}}$$

    (i) A solution containing a mixture of four amino acids was applied to a piece of chromatography paper that was then placed in solvent 1.

       Chromatogram 1 is shown below.

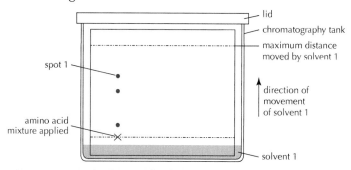

Amino acid	R_f (solvent 1)
alanine	0·51
arganine	0·16
threonine	0·51
tyrosine	0·68

       Identify the amino acid that corresponds to spot 1 on the chromatogram.

(ii) The chromatogram was dried, rotated through 90°, and then placed in solvent 2.

Chromatogram 2 is shown below.

Amino acid	R_f (solvent 1)
alanine	0·21
arganine	0·26
threonine	0·34
tyrosine	0·43

The retention factors for each of the amino acids in solvent 2 are shown in the table above.

Draw a circle around the spot on chromatogram 2 that corresponds to the amino acid alanine.

(iii) Explain why only three spots are present in chromatogram 1 while four spots are present in chromatogram 2.

11. Urea, $(NH_2)_2CO$, is an important industrial chemical that is mainly used in fertilisers. It is made by the Bosch-Meiser process.

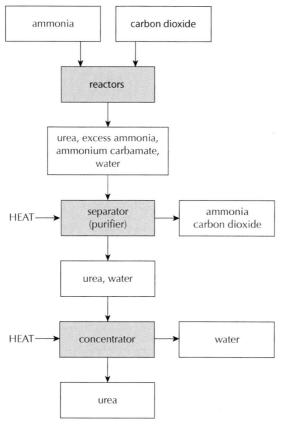

(a) (i) In the reactors, the production of urea involves two reversible reactions.

In the first reaction ammonium carbamate is produced.

$$2NH_3(g) + CO_2(g) \rightleftharpoons H_2NCOONH_4(g)$$

In the second reaction the ammonium carbamate decomposes to form urea.

$$H_2NCOONH_4(g) \rightleftharpoons (NH_2)_2CO(g) + H_2O(g)$$

A chemical plant produces 530 tonnes of urea per day.

Calculate the theoretical mass, in tonnes, of ammonia required to produce 530 tonnes of urea.

(ii) An undesirable side reaction is the production of biuret, a compound that can burn the leaves of plants.

$$2(NH_2)_2CO(aq) \rightleftharpoons NH_2CONHCONH_2(aq) + NH_3(g)$$
$$\text{biuret}$$

State why having an excess of ammonia in the reactors will decrease the amount of biuret produced.

iii) In the separator the ammonium carbamate from the reactors decomposes to form ammonia and carbon dioxide.

$$NH_2COONH_4(aq) \rightleftharpoons 2NH_3(g) + CO_2(g)$$

Explain clearly why a low pressure is used in the separator.

(iv) Look at the flow chart and suggest what could be done to make the Bosch-Meiser process more economical.

(b) Soil bacteria are mainly responsible for releasing nitrogen in urea into the soil so that it can be taken up by plants. The first stage in the process is the hydrolysis of urea using the enzyme urease.

(i) Determine the enthalpy change, in kJ mol⁻¹, for the reaction.

(ii) Acid is a less effective catalyst than urease for this reaction. Add a curve to the potential energy diagram to show the change in potential energy when acid is used as the catalyst.

12. A student analysed a local water supply to determine fluoride and nitrite ion levels.

(a) The concentration of fluoride ions in water was determined by adding a red coloured compound that absorbs light to the water samples. The fluoride ions reacted with the red compound to produce a colourless compound. Higher concentrations of fluoride ions produce less coloured solutions, which absorb less light.

The student initially prepared a standard solution of sodium fluoride with fluoride ion concentration of 100 mg l⁻¹.

(i) State what is meant by the term **standard solution**.

(ii) Describe how the standard solution is prepared from a weighed sample of sodium fluoride.

(iii) Explain why the student should use distilled or deionised water rather than tap water when preparing the standard solution.

(iv) The student prepared a series of standard solutions of fluoride ions and reacted each with a sample of the red compound. The light absorbance of each solution was measured and the results graphed.

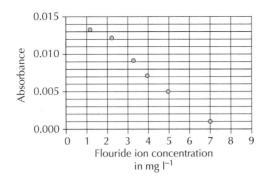

Determine the concentration of fluoride ions in a solution with absorbance 0·012.

(b) The concentration of nitrite ions in the water supply was determined by titrating water samples with acidified permanganate solutions.

(i) An average of 21·6 cm³ of 0·015 mol l⁻¹ acidified permanganate solution was required to react completely with the nitrite ions in a 25·0 cm³ sample of water.

The equation for the reaction taking place is

$$2MnO_4^-(aq) + 5NO_2^-(aq) + 6H^+(aq) \rightarrow 2Mn^{2+}(aq) + 5NO_3^-(aq) + 3H_2O(\ell)$$

Calculate the nitrite ion concentration, in mol l⁻¹, in the water.

Show your working clearly.

(ii) During the reaction the nitrite ion is oxidised to the nitrate ion.

Complete the ion-electron equation for the oxidation of the nitrite ion.

$$NO_2^-(aq) \rightarrow NO_3^-(aq)$$

13. Aspartame is an artificial sweetener which has the structure shown below.

(a) Name the functional group circled.

(b) In the stomach, aspartame is hydrolysed by acid to produce methanol and two amino acids, phenylalanine and aspartic acid.

Two of the products of the hydrolysis of aspartame are shown below.

$$HO-\overset{\overset{O}{||}}{C}-\underset{\underset{\underset{\bigcirc}{CH_2}}{|}}{CH}-NH_2$$

CH_3-OH

methanol   **phenylalanine**

Draw a structural formula for aspartic acid.

14. Chemists have developed cheeses specifically for use in cheeseburgers.

   (a) When ordinary cheddar cheese is grilled the shapes of the protein molecules change and the proteins and fats separate leaving a chewy solid and an oily liquid.

   What name is given to the change in protein structure which occurs when ordinary cheddar is grilled?

   (b) To make cheese for burgers, grated cheddar cheese, soluble milk proteins and some water are mixed and heated to no more than 82°C. As the cheese begins to melt an emulsifying agent is added and the mixture is stirred.

   (i) Why would a water bath be used to heat the mixture?

   (ii) A section of the structure of a soluble milk protein is shown below.

   Draw a structural formula for any **one** of the amino acids formed when this section of protein is hydrolysed.

   (iii) The emulsifier used is trisodium citrate, a salt formed when citric acid is neutralised using sodium hydroxide.

   Complete the equation below showing a structural formula for the trisodium citrate formed.

   $+\ 3NaOH \longrightarrow$ $+\ 3H_2O$

15. (a) In some countries, ethanol is used as a substitute for petrol. This ethanol is produced by fermentation of glucose, using yeast enzymes.

During the fermentation process, glucose is first converted into pyruvate. The pyruvate is then converted to ethanol in a two-step process.

$$CH_3COCOOH \xrightarrow{\text{Step 1}} CH_3CHO \xrightarrow{\text{Step 2}} CH_3CH_2OH$$
$$\text{pyruvate} \qquad\qquad \text{ethanal} \qquad\qquad \text{ethanol}$$
$$\searrow$$
$$CO_2$$

(i) Step 1 is catalysed by an enzyme. Enzymes are proteins that can act as catalysts because they have a specific shape.

Why, when the temperature is raised above a certain value, does the rate of reaction decrease?

(ii) Why can Step 2 be described as a reduction reaction?

(iii) The overall equation for the fermentation of glucose is

$$C_6H_{12}O_6 \rightarrow 2C_2H_5OH + 2CO_2$$

mass of one mole   mass of one mole

= 180 g   = 46 g

Calculate the percentage yield of ethanol if 445 g of ethanol is produced from 1·0 kg of glucose.

Show your working clearly.

(b) The energy density value of a fuel is the energy released when one kilogram of the fuel is burned.

The enthalpy of combustion of ethanol is -1367 kJ mol^{-1}.

Calculate the energy density value, in kJ kg^{-1}, of ethanol.

(c) The quantity of alcohol present after a fermentation reaction is called the % alcohol by volume.

This can be calculated from measurements taken using an instrument called a hydrometer. The hydrometer is floated in the liquid sample, before and after fermentation, to measure its specific gravity.

% alcohol by volume = change in specific gravity of liquid $\times f$

(where f is a conversion factor, which varies as shown in the table)

Change in specific gravity of liquid	f
Up to 6.9	0.125
7.0 – 10.4	0.126
10.5 – 17.2	0.127
17.3 – 26.1	0.128
26.2 – 36.0	0.129
36.1 – 46.5	0.130
46.6 – 57.1	0.131

The hydrometer readings taken for a sample are shown below

Calculate the % alcohol by volume for this sample.

16. A small sample of ammonia can be prepared in the laboratory by heating a mixture of ammonium chloride and calcium hydroxide. The ammonia is dried by passing it through small lumps of calcium oxide and collected by the downward displacement of air.

Complete the diagram to show how ammonia gas can be dried before collection.

17. Some fruit drinks claim to be high in antioxidants such as vitamin C.

(a) Some students carried out an investigation of fruit drinks to determine their vitamin C content. The following steps were followed in each experiment.

Step 1   A 20·0 cm³ sample of fruit drink was transferred to a conical flask by pipette.

Step 2   A burette was filled with a standard iodine solution.

Step 3   The fruit drink sample was titrated with the iodine.

Step 4   Titrations were repeated until concordant results were obtained.

The burette, pipette and conical flask were all rinsed before they were used.

Tick the appropriate boxes below to show which solution should be used to rinse each piece of glassware.

Glassware used	Rinse with water	Rinse with iodine	Rinse with fruit drink
pipette			
burette			
conical flask			

(b) Titrating a whole carton of fruit drink would require large volumes of iodine solution.

Apart from this disadvantages, give another reason for titrating several smaller samples of fruit drink.

18. Proteins are made from monomers called amino acids.

Human hair is composed of long strands of a protein called keratin.

(a) Part of the structure of a keratin molecule is shown.

Circle a peptide link in the structure.

(b) Hair products contain a large variety of different chemicals.

Chemicals called hydantoins are used as preservatives in shampoos to kill any bacteria.

A typical hydantoin is shown.

Name the functional group circled.

(c) Some hair conditioners contain the fatty acid, behenic acid, $CH_3(CH_2)_{19}CH_2COOH$.

Behenic acid is produced by hydrolysing the edible oil, ben oil.

(i) Name the compound, other than fatty acids, which is produced by hydrolysing the edible oil, ben oil.

(ii) When conditioner containing behenic acid is applied to hair, the behenic acid molecules make strong intermolecular hydrogen bonds to the keratin protein molecules.

On the diagram below use a dotted line to show **one** hydrogen bond that could be made between a behenic acid molecule and the keratin.

19. (a) Carbon monoxide gas is produced as a result of the incomplete combustion of fuels.

   The amount of carbon monoxide in the atmosphere is controlled by a series of free radical reactions.

   (i) What is meant by the term *free radical*?

   (ii) Why do free radicals form in the atmosphere?

   (iii) The equation shows one of the steps in the free radical chain reaction which controls the level of carbon monoxide.

   $$CO + HO\bullet \rightarrow CO_2 + H\bullet$$

   What term describes this type of step in the free radical chain reaction?

20. The table shows the boiling points of some alcohols.

alcohol	boiling point/°C
$CH_3CH_2CH_2CH_2OH$	118
$\overset{\displaystyle OH}{\underset{\displaystyle}{CH_3CH_2CHCH_3}}$	98
$\overset{\displaystyle CH_3}{\underset{\displaystyle}{CH_3CHCH_2OH}}$	108
$CH_3CH_2CH_2CH_2CH_2OH$	137
$\overset{\displaystyle OH}{\underset{\displaystyle}{CH_3CH_2CH_2CHCH_3}}$	119

Structure	Boiling point
CH$_3$ | CH$_3$CH$_2$CHCH$_2$OH	128
OH | CH$_3$CH$_2$CCH$_3$ | CH$_3$	101
CH$_3$CH$_2$CH$_2$CH$_2$CH$_2$CH$_2$OH	159
CH$_3$ | CH$_3$CH$_2$CH$_2$CHCH$_2$OH	149
OH | CH$_3$CH$_2$CH$_2$CCH$_3$ | CH$_3$	121

(a) Using information from the table, describe **two** ways in which differences in the structures affect boiling point of **isomeric alcohols**.

(b) Predict a boiling point for hexan-2-ol.

21. Some types of steel contain manganese.

The manganese content of a steel can be determined by converting the manganese into permanganate ions.

The steel is reacted with nitric acid giving manganese ions in solution. These are converted into permanganate ions by reaction with periodate ions.

$$Mn(s) \rightarrow Mn^{2+}(aq) \rightarrow MnO_4^-(aq)$$

During the reaction the periodate ions, $IO_4^-(aq)$, are reduced to iodate ions, $IO_3^-(aq)$.

(a) Complete the ion-electron equation for this reduction reaction:

$$IO_4^-(aq) \qquad\qquad \rightarrow IO_3^-(aq)$$

(b) When light is shone through a permanganate solution some of the light is absorbed.

The concentration of a permanganate solution can be found by measuring the amount of light absorbed and comparing this with the light absorbed by solutions of known concentration.

    (i) To obtain solutions of known concentration a stock solution of accurately known concentration is first prepared.

       Describe how a stock solution of accurately known concentration could be prepared from a weighed sample of potassium permanganate crystals.

(ii) The graph below was plotted using the absorbance of different permanganate solutions.

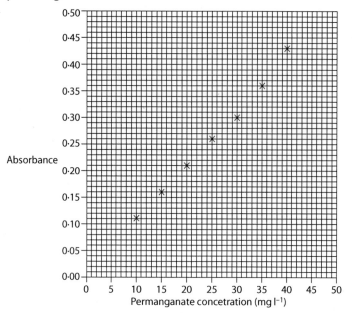

A sample of steel was reacted to give one litre of solution containing permanganate ions. The absorbance of the solution was 0·30.

Use the graph to determine the mass of manganese in the steel sample.

(1 mole of manganese gives 1 mole of permanganate ions.)

22. The combustion reactions of methane and heptane can be studied in different ways.

(a) The combustion of methane produces carbon dioxide and water vapour when carried out at temperatures above 100°C.

$$CH_4(g) + 2O_2(g) \rightarrow CO_2(g) + 2H_2O(g)$$

(i) Using bond enthalpies and mean bond enthalpies from the data booklet, calculate the enthalpy change, in kJ mol⁻¹, for this reaction.

(ii) Explain the difference between bond enthalpy and mean bond enthalpy.

(iii) Calculate the mass, in g, of carbon dioxide produced by the combustion of 200 cm³ of methane in excess oxygen.

Take the volume of 1 mole of methane gas to be 24 litres.

$$CH_4(g) + 2O_2(g) \rightarrow CO_2(g) + 2H_2O(g)$$
$$GFM = 44·0 \text{ g}$$

(b) The enthalpy of combustion of heptane, C_7H_{16}, can be determined using a calorimeter.

The following results were obtained.

Mass of heptane burned (g)	1·1
Mass of 1 mole of heptane (g)	100·0
Volume of water used (cm³)	400
Initial temperature of water (°C)	26
Final temperature of water (°C)	49

(i) State the measurements required to calculate the mass of heptane burned in this experiment.

(ii) Calculate the enthalpy of combustion, in kJ mol⁻¹, for heptane from the experimental results given.

(iii) The theoretical value for the enthalpy of combustion of heptane is significantly higher than the experimental value.

Suggest why the experimental value is different to the theoretical value.

23. Thiols are compounds that contain an –SH functional group. They often have very strong, unpleasant odours.

(a) Ethanethiol is used to add a smell to gaseous fuels in order to give warnings of gas leaks.

$$H-\underset{\underset{H}{|}}{\overset{\overset{H}{|}}{C}}-\underset{\underset{H}{|}}{\overset{\overset{H}{|}}{C}}-S-H$$

ethanethiol

(i) A student used the boiling points of ethanethiol and propan-1-ol to compare the strength of intermolecular forces.

ethanethiol
boiling point = 35°C

propan-1-ol
boiling point = 97°C

(A) State the reason why propan-1-ol was a suitable alcohol to compare with ethanethiol.

(B) Explain why propan-1-ol has a higher boiling point than ethanethiol. Your answer should include the names of the intermolecular forces broken when each liquid boils.

(ii) Name the thiol that contains only one carbon atom.

(iii) The minimum concentration of ethanethiol in air that can be detected by humans is 2.7×10^{-7} mg per cm^3 of air.

Calculate the minimum mass of ethanethiol that needs to be present in a room containing 43 900 litres of air in order for it to be detected.

(b) 2-methyl-2-propanethiol is also used to add a smell to gaseous fuels.

2-methyl-2-propanethiol

(i) Suggest why 2-methyl-2-propanethiol is classified as a tertiary thiol.

(ii) Thiols can be made by the addition of hydrogen sulfide to alkenes. 2-methyl-2-propanethiol can be made by the addition reaction shown.

2-methylpropene
GFM = 56·0

2-methyl-2-propanethiol
GFM = 90·1 g

(A) Draw the structure for the other isomer formed in this addition reaction.

(B) A chemist obtained an 84% yield of 2-methyl-2-propanethiol after starting with 30·5 g of 2-methylpropene.

Calculate the mass, in g, of 2-methyl-2-propanethiol made by the chemist.

Open questions

Paper 2 of the Higher exam contains **open** questions. In open questions there is **no one specific answer**. There are many different ways of answering the question and they could all be correct. Open questions give you the opportunity to let the examiner know how well you **understand** the area the question relates to without expecting a set answer. These questions give you credit for being **creative** and **analytical** in your answers.

Note that open questions are worth a total of **three marks**, which indicates that quite a lot of information is needed in the answer to gain full marks. It doesn't mean that you need three correct points to gain all three marks but the more relevant the information you give, and how well your answer is put together, the more marks you will get. The examiner wants to see that you have a **good understanding**.

You will recognise an open question by the wording '**Using your knowledge of chemistry**, comment on…'

Open questions should not take more than **five minutes** to answer and there will not be more than two open questions in an exam paper.

1. To improve the shelf life of foods, food manufacturers use several methods to remove oxygen from inside the food packaging. In one method, an enzyme is added which catalyses a reaction between oxygen and glucose present in the foods.

   glucose + oxygen + water → gluconic acid + hydrogen peroxide

   Using your knowledge of chemistry, comment on why this method may not be suitable to improve the shelf life of all foods.

2. A TV programme was reproducing a pharmacy from the 19th century and planned to use the original 19th century pharmacy jars that had been kept in a museum. The TV company wanted to know what compounds the jars were likely to contain now.

   Substances used in pharmacies over a hundred years ago included:

   • Essential oils dissolved in ethanol.

   Some molecules included in these essential oils were:

   menthol   eugenol

   • Asprin

   • Ointments that contained animal fats like lard, beef fat or beeswax.

   Using your knowledge of chemistry, comment on what compounds the old pharmacy jars might contain now.

3. The flavour and texture of chocolate comes from a blend of compounds.
   Using your knowledge of chemistry, describe how you could show that there are ionic compounds and covalent compounds present in chocolate.

4. Cooking involves many chemical reactions. Proteins, fats, oils and esters are some examples of compounds found in food. A chemist suggested that cooking food could change compounds from being fat-soluble to water-soluble.

    Use your knowledge of chemistry to comment on the accuracy of this statement.

5. When food is cooked its composition and appearance changes.

    Using your knowledge of chemistry, comment on the changes to food that could occur during the cooking process.

6. Traces of a liquid were discovered in a bottle believed to contain perfume belonging to Queen Hatshepsut, ruler of Egypt over 3500 years ago.

    Perfumes were made by dissolving plant extracts containing pleasant smelling terpenes and esters in an edible oil. A little ethanol and water may also have been added.

    Using your knowledge of chemistry, comment on the possible smell(s) when such a bottle is opened after being stored for thousands of years.

7. Hydrogels are used in disposable nappies. They are fine powders that can absorb up to 500 times their own weight in water.

    A hydrogel is a very long molecule with carboxyl groups at regular intervals along its length. A short section of a hydrogel molecule is shown below.

    Hydrogels are extremely good at soaking up water because the water molecules are strongly attracted to them.

    Using your knowledge of chemistry, comment on how suitable hydrogels would be for absorbing liquids or solutions spilled in a chemistry lab.